Public Goods, Mixed Goods, and Monopolistic Competition

Number Twelve:
Texas A&M University Economics Series

Public Goods, Mixed Goods, and Monopolistic Competition

STEPHEN SHMANSKE

TEXAS A&M UNIVERSITY PRESS
College Station

First Edition

The paper used in this book meets the minimum requirement of the American National Standard for Permanence of Paper for Printed Library Materials, Z39.48–1984.
Binding materials have been chosen for durability. ♾

Library of Congress Cataloging-in-Publication Data

Shmanske, Stephen.
Public goods, mixed goods, and monopolistic competition / by Stephen Shmanske.—1st ed.
p. cm.—(Texas A&M University economics series: no. 12)
Includes bibliographical references and index.
ISBN 0-89096-464-5 (alk. paper)
1. Public goods. 2. Monopolistic competition. I. Title. II. Series
HB846.5.S56 1991
338.3′2—dc20

90-41465
CIP

for
Tina
Elizabeth and Bernard
Gloria and Richard

Contents

Figures and Tables

FIGURES

TABLES

Acknowledgments

I would like to acknowledge my debt to all of those who helped me by reading and commenting on versions of this manuscript. Several people deserve recognition. David Jung and Peggy Stevens made detailed comments on the first draft of Chapter 1. Without their help, I would have started off on the wrong foot in many respects. Their efforts have contributed greatly to a more organized, more readable text. Shyam Kamath read most of the first half of the manuscript. He was most helpful in pointing out arguments that needed tightening and in supplying references to a wide range of topics.

I am especially indebted to Greg Christainsen and Marius Schwartz, each of whom read the entire manuscript. Greg read each chapter as it emerged, making comments on style, adding references, and suggesting extensions. Marius read a more polished version of the entire manuscript but still was able to offer many helpful suggestions regarding the organization of the book and the areas which deserved more or less emphasis.

I have not always followed the advice of these readers. Where I have, the manuscript is undoubtedly the better for it. In those cases where I did not listen, as well as for any errors, I take full responsibility.

I would also like to thank Colin Campbell, whose money and banking course at Dartmouth College got me started in economics; Armen Alchian, whose seminar in microeconomic theory continues to provide perspective and inspiration; Earl Thompson, whose insight and originality influenced the way I think about economics and whose interest in my work and exacting standards guided the early stages of this research; the members of my thesis committee, Earl Thompson, Armen Alchian, Clement Krouse, Robert Geske, and Jack Hirshleifer, whose initial encouragement and direction can never be adequately thanked;

participants in sessions of the Western Economic Association's annual meetings in Seattle (1983) and in San Francisco (1986) whose comments guided my early research in the working-paper stage; participants in workshops at California State University, Hayward, where I presented most of this material; my colleagues in the Economics Department at California State University, Hayward, especially Shyam Kamath and Greg Christainsen, mentioned above, and Charles Baird and Kurt Leube, whose cheerful encouragement kept the process going; and the university itself for various forms of support, including the sabbatical when the writing of the manuscript was initiated.

I would also like to thank my family. My parents have always been my biggest supporters. They, as well as my in-laws, unfailingly bolster my academic efforts. I especially appreciate their exuberance in sharing my satisfaction over the final product.

Above all I would like to thank Tina, who supported my dissertation writing efforts, my teaching and research, and my work on this manuscript. Despite the time spent working on her own degree, she was there throughout. Tina encouraged me through the long months of writing, shared my anxiety waiting to hear from the publisher, and shared in the joys whenever good news about the status of this manuscript would arrive. Whether it was receiving a favorable review, completing a chapter, working out a nettlesome argument, or simply overcoming a temporary case of writer's block, Tina's companionship doubled my joy and redoubled my efforts to continue. It has all been worthwhile.

Public Goods, Mixed Goods, and Monopolistic Competition

CHAPTER ONE

Introduction

A useful definition of a public good is that its consumption by one individual does not reduce the possibility for other individuals to consume it. Paul Samuelson set the agenda for a generation of research on this nonrival consumption characteristic in his classic 1954 article, "The Pure Theory of Public Expenditure."[1] Samuelson's formulation yielded the by now familiar marginal conditions that must be satisfied for Pareto optimality, namely, equality of each individual's marginal rate of substitution with marginal cost for every private good and equality of the sum of the individual's marginal rates of substitution with marginal cost for every public good. Samuelson went on to claim that although perfectly competitive markets could bring about the optimal solution for private goods, no such market mechanism existed for public goods. The title of his paper sums up his conclusions nicely, that is, the existence of public goods makes for a "pure theory of public expenditure."

Samuelson's arguments that the introduction of public goods causes a market failure (in the form of an underproduction of public goods) that can be corrected by the public sector has become conventional wisdom. While there are a few authors who treat private sector production of public goods as possible, if perhaps not optimal, their models are usually dismissed as curious special cases.[2] Unfortunately, this dismissal has caused economists to miss the practically universal relevance of these models. Consequently, the conventional view is that the private sector provision possibility does not mitigate the necessity for public sector involvement most of the time. As just one example of the view that the private provision models are not generally applicable, consider the work of Brito and Oakland, who claim: "The emphasis upon competitive provision in the literature is somewhat surprising in view of the paucity of excludable public goods which are or could be provided within such a framework."[3]

This book argues that there is no good reason to disregard the private sector in public goods provision nor even to consider it as a special case. Correctly understood, public goods are not anomalies or special cases; in fact, they are all around us. And, in many cases, the public goods aspects of consumption are supplied quite profitably in decentralized, competitive markets. Private sector equilibrium may or may not correspond to a technical Pareto optimum, but if the market does fail in this sense, the reasons for the failure will equally hamper public sector provision. Put another way, there is not systematic overproduction or underproduction of public goods by the market. Therefore, there is no systematic tax or subsidy policy that the public sector can apply to nudge private equilibrium toward the optimum. In attempting to determine on a case-by-case basis whether the market undersupplies or oversupplies the public good, the public authority will fail for the same reasons that the private sector firm does.

These policy-motivated conclusions are reached through a reexamination and extension of received public goods theory. Therefore, in addition to the practical importance of the conclusions, the analysis in this book is of theoretical importance as well. Since Samuelson's seminal article, literally hundreds of articles have been written extending, highlighting, criticizing, or otherwise commenting on the issues raised in the original. Indeed, Samuelson himself contributed several more times to ongoing debates in the literature on public goods.[4] The unfortunate consequence is a literature so vast and varied that the mention of public goods brings to mind a dozen different issues, each of which brings along its own idiosyncratic model and relies on its own set of special assumptions.

For example, consider the issues of exclusion costs, demand revelation incentives, congestion, voluntary provision, competitive provision, and price discrimination, as well as the models of externalities, joint supply, clubs, local public goods, crowded public goods, and mixed goods. What each of these issues and models have in common is some sort of summation of marginal rates of substitution, some evidence of jointness brought about by nonrival consumption. What differentiates the models are assumptions about the institutional setting, the nature of exclusion, the existence of congestion, and so on. This book argues for a reexamination of the special assumptions which characterize these different theoretical paradigms. The book aims to suggest a paradigmatic synthesis of public goods thinking and to follow up on the extensions that the synthesis allows.

The synthesis is general enough to encompass all of the received literature, although admittedly, much of the time as degenerate special cases. The benefits of a general synthesis are the obvious ones, not the least of which is to warn against attempting to draw parallels from simplified, special-case frameworks to make general conclusions about public goods. Concretely stated, if one thinks of the lighthouse, or of national defense, or of any other narrowly construed example of a public good and attempts to argue by analogy to the general public goods case, one is asking for trouble.

The provision of a synthesis of public goods thinking is probably insufficient cause for a book-length treatment. The more exciting aspects of this book come from the extension. In particular, the book will show how the extension of received goods public theory brings one first to a model of product quality determination and then to a setting akin to monopolistic competition. Traditionally, both these models have been examined using private sector/private goods frameworks, but, as we shall see, they can be addressed fruitfully from a public goods perspective. Actually, the connection between product quality and public goods was hinted at by Richard Auster in an appendix to a 1977 paper and independently discovered and analyzed more completely by myself.[5] Peter K. Else has extended my work in the direction of multiple dimensions of quality for a monopoly producer.[6] The relatively more difficult extension to multiple producers and monopolistic competition does not yield to article-length treatment and, therefore, provides the impetus for this book.

All the ingredients are here. In nonrival consumption we have a workable definition of public goods and the associated marginal conditions that describe optimal production. From here we go to a splintered literature, full of special cases based on different assumptions, yielding no consensus concerning the comparison of the theoretical optimum with the market equilibrium. And an important policy question hangs in the balance. In light of this background, this book argues that by examining the special assumptions which underlie the multitude of theoretical paradigms, it is possible to develop a general model of public goods provision. This general model not only highlights specific assumptions in the literature in order to make existing theory more understandable, but also allows us to pursue several interesting extensions which show how relevant and important public goods analysis really is. In particular, the general model shows how issues of product quality determination and monopolistic competition, which are traditionally examined using private sector/private goods frameworks, can be illuminated from a public goods perspective. Finally, by allowing us to extend the applicability of public goods analysis to many new areas, the model allows us to reassess whether, in fact, public goods do lead to a "pure theory of public expenditure."

Beginnings: Terminology, Exclusion, and Perspectives

Lest we start off in different directions, it is important to make explicit the definitions of the terms that we shall encounter. This is largely the task of chapters 2, 3, and 4. Most of the definitions are covered in Chapter 3. Although all the definitions could be covered in one lengthy chapter, there are two issues which are important enough to warrant short chapters of their own. These issues are exclusion, which, although mentioned below, is covered extensively in Chapter 2, and the public goods/mixed goods/private goods spectrum, which is covered in Chapter 4.

Notwithstanding the terminology to be addressed in the next three chapters, there are a few things that must be clarified at the outset. Three items, to receive a brief treatment immediately, are: (1) the term, *public goods;* (2) the nature of excludability; and (3) the issue of private versus public provision.

With respect to public goods, note that Samuelson did not, in fact, use this term in his 1954 paper. He used instead *collective consumption good,* as the contrast to private good. Others have shortened this to *collective good,* while still others prefer *joint good* or *public good.* I have been unable to discern an agreed-upon distinction among these terms. Therefore, I treat them interchangeably. What is more important than trying to force a consistent terminology on such a vast literature is the careful outlining and defining of what one means by a public good or a collective good. I suspect that no matter which phrase—joint good, public good, or collective good—is used in the title, authors will still have to spend time in the introduction explaining what they understand by such terminology.

As I have mentioned above, the defining characteristic of a public good upon which I focus is the nonrival consumption aspect. Indeed, it is this aspect which leads to the apparent differences in the optimal marginal equalities between public goods and private goods. Conspicuous so far by its absence, however, is discussion of the excludability or nonexcludability of public goods. This brings us to the second item that must be addressed immediately, the nature of exclusion.

Many economists associate two defining attributes with public goods: the nonrival consumption aspect and the inability to exclude nonpayers from consumption of the good. Others, an early notable example being John G. Head,[7] argue that the two issues of nonrivalry and nonexcludability should be kept separate. I choose to follow the latter course. In Chapter 2, I explain in depth why I think it important to keep these two issues separate. For now I will simply note that there is no logical connection between nonrivalry and nonexcludability. Readers who are comfortable with a definition of public goods that combines both the issues of nonrival consumption and nonexcludability usually define a subset of public goods called "excludable" public goods to deal with goods that only evidence the nonrival consumption characteristic. From this viewpoint my book addresses the private provision of excludable public goods. The only problem I have with this terminology is that it may tempt some to think of nonexcludable public goods as somehow being the normal case while excludable public goods are a minor and curious anomaly. This book will show that excludable public goods are an immensely important category and that considerably more interest should attach to the excludable case.

We have now briefly treated the meaning of the term *public good* and introduced the issue of exclusion. One more preliminary must be disposed of before proceeding to the overview of the remainder of the book. This preliminary involves the perspective one brings to the study of public goods.

There are many different branches that can be traced in the public goods literature. There are, however, two main trunks. One deals with private sector provision and the other, with public sector provision. The issues that are studied in the two different trunks and the background that is required to study those issues differ sharply. There is relatively little overlap between the two trunks. There have been a few treatments of the large question, Should public goods be produced in the private sector or the public sector?[8] This question is, after all, the basic policy question that needs to be answered. However, to properly address this question one first need to know how the public sector will go about allocating resources to public goods provision and, alternatively, what the characteristics of a private market equilibrium with public goods will look like. Since these are by no means settled questions, most research has been in one or the other of these trunks and has tried to determine the properties of public goods supply in the relevant sector. This book develops the analysis in terms of the private sector provision trunk.

The public sector provision models, which are not the subject of this book, are most closely tied to the fields of Public Finance and Public Choice. Taking as given that some public agency is responsible for the allocative decisions (and, possibly, the distributive decisions as well), we can say that the many branches of this trunk cover pseudo-market mechanisms, political exchange, or other algorithms that might be employed to decide production and tax share questions. The issues of political decisionmaking,[9] demand revelation mechanisms,[10] distortionary tax effects,[11] user charges,[12] local public finance,[13] and the relationship between allocative efficiency and distributive effects[14] all receive ample coverage in the literature. I label this trunk of public goods analysis the "public finance view of public goods."

The models of private sector provision of public goods are most closely related to the field of industrial organization, especially the theoretical branches of that field. I label this trunk the "industrial organization view of public goods." The analysis in this book is located at the center of this trunk. The issues in industrial organization concern pricing practices, reaction conjectures, incentive compatibility, monopoly, competition, market structure, and equilibrium. Many branches emanate from this trunk. The distinguishing characteristics of each branch involve differing assumptions concerning the nature of exclusion, the possibility of resale, market structure, and the conjectural variation. A review of the received literature in this area, and the problems confronted therein, is the topic of chapters 5 and 6. This will set the stage for the general model developed in the rest of the book.

Note that the feature distinguishing the two trunks is not the excludable/nonexcludable issue. There are excludable and nonexcludable public goods in each trunk. In the private provision trunk the former are sometimes even labeled as such,[15] while the latter are the subject of the voluntary provision models.[16] In the public provision trunk the former could be financed partially or completely by user charges, while the latter can only be supplied free of charge and financed out of general taxes.

Overview

Having dispensed with the necessary preliminaries, I turn to a discussion of the genesis of my thoughts on the topic of public goods. This is one way of ensuring that the reader is on the same plane as the writer. We start with the notion of nonrival consumption as the distinguishing feature of public goods. Because of nonrival consumption, if Y units of the public goods are produced, then Y can enter identically into each person's utility function. In terms of cost, this last statement can be translated to mean that the marginal cost of consumption for an additional person is zero. However, the marginal cost of production of the public good is not zero. Apparently, marginal cost means two different things in the public goods setting. This dual meaning is actually the first hint that there are two dimensions of interest in public goods models. We shall return to this point below.

For the moment, let us focus on the marginal consumption cost rather than the marginal production cost. If the marginal cost is truly zero, then all persons should be allowed to consume the public good until they are satiated with it; that is, until their own marginal rates of substitution are also zero. Furthermore, if the marginal consumption cost is truly zero, then a leading question arises. Shouldn't just one unit of the public good, used over and over at zero cost, suffice to yield the maximum utility obtainable from consumption of the public good? Yet this is seemingly not the case in an equilibrium where the summation of (positive) marginal rates of substitution is set equal to (positive) marginal production cost. Then what becomes of the zero marginal cost? To what does it refer? The answers follow from recognition of a hidden assumption implicit in the meaning of nonrival consumption. The hidden assumption is that nonrival consumption applies only to consumption across individuals but not to an individual's own consumption. That is, one person's consumption of the public good does not preclude any other additional person from consuming it, but somehow it does preclude additional consumption by the first individual. This is why people require multiple units of the public good. The zero marginal cost refers only to the extension of the public good to additional consumers, where consumption is nonrival, and not to the consumption of the public good by any one individual.

As mentioned above, the two different marginal costs provide a hint that there are actually two dimensions with which to be concerned: first, the production of the public good; and, second, its availability to the universe of consumers. This second dimension, and its relationship to the first, will be the topic of Chapter 7. Of immediate importance, however, is the realization that one's own consumption need not be rival instead of nonrival. Consider, for example, a song or a melody. My humming a tune does not preclude you from humming it as well. This situation exhibits the property of nonrivalry across consumers. Neither does my humming the tune once preclude me from humming it over and over again. Presumably, I keep on humming it at zero marginal cost until I am satiated and my marginal rate of substitution goes to zero.

Most of the existing models of private sector provision of public goods ignore the possibility of an individual's repeated consumption of the same unit of the public good and implicitly add the assumption that each unit of the public good can be consumed once only. Three possible ways of justifying this assumption come to mind. The first is basically an admission that for the sake of simplicity the restrictive assumption is added. We should be wary of unthoughtful application of such results to more general settings. The second method is actually an attempt to justify the restrictive assumption by constraining an individual's marginal rate of substitution to fall to zero after the first humming of the tune. Such a model would clearly not be generally applicable. The third method is to definitionally treat all the multiple uses of the unit of the public good by one person as being just one unit of consumption. As Chapter 7 shows, this involves a compression of what I call the utilization dimension into what is usually considered the standard public good dimension. This may be the position that most writers on this topic had in mind. Still, it is an unfortunate approach in that many of the interesting pricing, exclusion, and interaction features that are central to the industrial organization approach to public goods occur in this compressed dimension and are virtually assumed away.

The attempt to view all the value obtained from repeatedly humming a melody as compressible into the demand price or marginal rate of substitution for that melody contains the first hint that monopolistic competition models may be, somehow, connected to public goods analysis. A similar assumption often underlies the version of monopolistic competition that has come to be known as spatial competition.[17] In spatial competition, consumers are located in a space and firms will endogenously locate themselves in the same space. Each person's demand price for one unit of a firm's production varies inversely with the distance between the location of the consumer and the location of the firm. The assumption that each person will either consume one unit, when the firm's price is less than the person's demand price, or else no units, is seen as a simplifying assumption to allow concentration on the location decision. If the consumer actually desires multiple units, then the reader must consider the total valuation of the multiple units as the demand price for the single consumption unit. At the same time the reader must view the total payment charged by the firm for multiple units as the price of the single unit. Through these dimensional simplifications, we have compressed the multiple consumption units of the individual into a one-unit, all-or-none consumption problem.

Although it is possible to follow this dimensional simplification, a potential problem can arise. Note, for example, that a person consuming n units will pay less than a person consuming $n + 1$ units if pricing is done on a per unit basis but will pay the same if pricing is done on an all-or-none basis. Therefore, there is an important difference in the firm's pricing decision of whether to treat the consumer's decision as an all-or-none problem or as one with multiple units of consumption. Both public goods analysis and spatial competition use this simplification, and both could benefit from relaxing this type of restriction.[18]

A second hint that monopolistic competition is involved comes into focus when the consumer is allowed to consume each unit of the public good repeatedly. Since the consumer will keep humming a melody until satiated, why will the consumer desire another melody to hum? The second melody (unit of the public good) must somehow be different from the first melody. But, if the second melody is different, why is it measured on the same axis as the first melody? As Earl Thompson pointed out, the separate units of the public good must be "distinct" and "interchangeable."[19] They must be distinct because otherwise, the individual could consume only one unit over and over, consequently having no use for the second. They must be interchangeable to be measured on the same axis. This situation certainly seems reminiscent of the symmetric differentiation or uniformity assumption in traditional monopolistic competition models such as those devised by Edward Chamberlin. The product of each monopolistically competitive firm must be, in one sense, distinct from and, in another sense, interchangeable with all the other firms' products. The distinctness property goes under the name of product differentiation, while the interchangeability property is evidenced when the analyst places different firms in the same monopolistically competitive group. As we shall see, the members of the Chamberlinian group and the separate units on the public good axis have much in common.

Consider one more example of the progression of ideas from a simple public goods model to a monopolistic competition framework. An uncrowded bridge is a public good by virtue of its offering nonrival transportation services. Note that the nonrival nature holds across individuals as well as for multiple crossings by the same consumer. An exclusion device for the uncrowded bridge might involve a tollgate that restricts an individual's utilization of the bridge by charging a toll each time a person crosses. The tolls that are collected in this utilization dimension pay for the actual cost of the bridge itself. Consider, now, the simplifications to this example of: (1) fixing all characteristics of the bridge except the number of crossings; and (2) assuming a monopolist seller of the bridge services. Whether a private sector firm will build the bridge depends on whether the total cost will be less than the total collections. A price equal to marginal cost (which is zero) will certainly not produce enough revenue. A uniform price would have to be equal to or greater than average cost to ensure private sector profitability. A monopoly price might or might not produce enough revenue. Indeed, sometimes a discriminatory or nonlinear pricing scheme in the dimension of an individual's utilization is necessary to cover costs. All three of these latter schemes, however, can lead to underutilization of the bridge. With the above simplifications added, we arrive at a situation of decreasing cost or natural monopoly and a well-known but little emphasized topic in price theory: that of price discrimination as a necessary condition for the solvency of the firm. By fixing all the characteristics of the bridge, we have reduced the public good part of the problem to an all-or-none decision in a private goods framework with zero marginal cost.

But we want to go beyond this topic by letting the amount of the public good vary. The amount of the public good can be thought of as the quality, for example, the smoothness of the road surface. Alternatively, the quality could be thought of as inversely related to the time it takes to cross the bridge, which may depend on the number of lanes. We are now in a model of product quality determination by a monopolist who prices in the utilization dimension. The quality dimension is a nonrival consumption dimension, since all people consume the same amount; therefore, it is a public good. Meanwhile, the number of crossings by each individual can be different, and this dimension is analogous to the regular quantity dimension for private goods. Public goods models have been linked to joint supply models[20] and models of positive externalities.[21] In light of this example, however, better analogies are available. Analysis of the number of crossings is analogous to a private goods model with decreasing cost, while a study of the public good dimension of the bridge is analogous to a model of product quality determination by a monopolist. Analysis of this problem is the topic of Chapter 7.

Further benefits, notably the connection to monopolistic competition, come with the relaxation of the single producer, monopoly assumption. Indeed, with no reason to focus on closed market situations, the multiple producer model may be the most important to consider. Again, it is instructive to consider some simplifications to see which other models are just special cases of a general public goods model. In particular, if the quality or public good level of each producer is fixed and if only simple pricing schemes are allowed in the utilization dimension, then we are in a monopolistic competition setting. Each producer's utilization units will be mutually, but not perfectly, substitutable. The decision of each firm would be whether to enter the industry and produce positive amounts of utilization units or to remain out of it. The equilibrium in such a monopolistic competition setting is usually couched in terms of a so-called excess capacity theorem for each firm and in the degree of product differentiation (i.e., the number of firms) that will exist. The difficulty stemming from these results is that they are reached only after the adoption of stringent, specialized, and maybe even internally inconsistent assumptions[22] (a point made clear in chapters 9 and 10).

For example, the excess capacity result requires a downward-sloped demand curve, that is, differentiated goods, some degree of scale economies, simple monopoly pricing, and a zero profit condition. There is nothing wrong with the first two assumptions. Indeed, they are the usual, except for their combination with the zero profit condition. Uncopiable product differentiation alone precludes the existence of free entry necessary for zero profits. The existence of scale economies may also lead to departures from zero profits. The "lumpy" entry, if any, that scale economies implies yields only a "nonpositive profits for an additional entrant" condition which will approach a zero profit condition only as the scale economies disappear. Also, the simple monopoly pricing is only a special case. The price discrimination, multipart pricing, two-part pricing, and other forms of nonlinear pricing that are obviously present in the real world will also negate the excess capacity result. This price discrimination would be considered automatically if the quantity axis in a monopolistic competition setting were analyzed as a part of a generalized public goods framework. Yet for the most part, price discrimination has remained conspicuously absent in monopolistic competition models.[23] Public goods models, then, can be an important analytical tool in the logical extension and completion of price theory in the area of price discrimination.

The perspective afforded by a general public goods model can also help in the analysis of the industry-wide equilibrium in a monopolistic competition setting. The usual results vis-à-vis quality dispersion or degree of differentiation are reached by examining the number of firms in equilibrium. The margin of interest for the welfare economics of these issues is, simply, the number of firms. This number can be calculated in formal models only by coupling a symmetric differentiation condition (which is tantamount to setting, exogenously, the public good level or quality level of each of the firms) with a zero profit condition. The undesirability of the zero profit condition was discussed above. More important, however, is the denial of the ability of firms to change the quality level of their products. It is not only descriptively accurate to allow each firm to vary its degree of quality but helps, too, in sorting out the welfare characteristics of equilibrium. It helps because the equilibrium quality level of each firm is established with reference to its internal profit maximization. Instead of having to derive closed-form solutions of the equilibrium quality (as measured by the number of firms), we can examine the incentives embodied in the equations describing the firm's internal maximization with respect to its endogenous quality choice. As Spence has shown, if we can compare the function that the firm is maximizing with the function that maximizes social welfare, it may be unnecessary to actually compare the closed-form solutions of market equilibrium with closed-form solutions in a Pareto optimal state.[24]

Chapters 9 and 10 show how a general public goods approach can do much to direct the theoretical energy required to address these questions. Indeed, the quality choice dimension is nonrival and is amenable to public goods analysis. The public goods model with multiple competing producers and an explicit utilization dimension in which pricing and, thus, exclusion take place captures the spirit of monopolistic competition models that are motivated by competition among sellers of close substitute goods. Issues of price discrimination, decreasing cost, optimum quality determination, individual utilization, and the reaction conditions among the firms all would take important positions, naturally, in such a model. Unfortunately, monopolistic competition models (springing as they have from the models of perfect competition and simple, one-price monopoly) have focused instead on zero profits, symmetrically differentiated firms, nonreaction of rivals, uniform pricing schemes, and excess capacity.

The general model that is completed in chapters 9 and 10 yields a variety of results. Competition among multiple sellers with endogenous quality and price discrimination is an uncharted area, yet it is in that area where the received competitive production of public goods models have (implicitly) been located. It is no wonder that so many different theorists have reached such different conclusions.

The last chapter is designed to place the results of the analysis in proper perspective. I shall endeavor to present the policy relevance of the general model as well as directions to pursue in future work.

CHAPTER TWO

Public Goods, Private Goods, and Exclusion

In the introductory chapter, I stated that this book will deal mainly with the nonrival consumption aspect of public goods. There is no doubt that many economists are used to a definition of public goods that combines both nonrival consumption and nonexcludability.[1] Therefore, it will behoove us to take the time to separate these two issues in order to examine more closely the connection between them. The goal of this brief chapter is to address the excludability issue and its relationship to public goods, private goods, public provision, and private provision.

It is usually presumed that, if nonpayers cannot be excluded from the benefits of the public good, then no private firm will have an incentive to supply it. Why buy something if you can free-ride and consume it anyway? We therefore tend to conclude that a public good such as national defense must be publicly provided to overcome the free-rider problem. The first characteristic to note about the excludability issue is that is does not necessarily have anything to do with the nonrival aspect of public good consumption. Both public goods and private goods could be characterized by complete, costless exclusion, the impossibility of exclusion at finite cost, or a full range of partial, costly exclusion. For example, a private good, like an automobile, can be stolen. This is an example of a nonpayer not being excluded from consumption of the good. Obviously, this is not the only example, but it serves the purpose of illustrating that nonexcludability can be an issue for goods which are rival in consumption as well as for goods that are nonrival in consumption.

While it may be generally recognized that both private goods and public goods can be characterized by incomplete, or costly, excludability, it is curious that the implications for policy do not seem to be drawn in the same manner for private goods as for public goods. For example, manufacturers put locks on car doors to assist the purchaser of the automobile in excluding nonpayers. Whereas a market failure is claimed to exist because of nonexcludability in the case of national defense, no one suggests that we have a market failure because of resources expended to make the private good an excludable one. At first glance, it may seem that the difference in attitude toward national defense stems from the complete nonexcludability evidenced in that case, whereas for an automobile exclusion is costly but not infinitely costly. However, further inspection indicates that excluding nonpayers from the benefits of national defense is not infinitely costly either. Therefore, the difference between the two cases with respect to the nonexcludability issue seems to be one of degree. At this point, I will not venture to conclude whether this means government should intervene in automobile markets to enhance excludability or whether government should play less of a role in the provision of national defense.

The example about the stealable car served to illustrate that not all nonexcludable (or partially excludable) goods are public goods. We can also show that not all public goods are nonexcludable (or partially excludable). In fact, it is well recognized that public goods may be excludable or nonexcludable.[2] Unfortunately, however, many of the examples used to illustrate public goods, especially the national defense example, also exhibit extremely high exclusion costs. This has allowed the two unusual characteristics of national defense, nonrival consumption and nonexcludability, to become intertwined. There is, however, no necessary connection between the two characteristics in general.

Perhaps the view originally espoused by Samuelson—that public goods lead to a pure theory of public expenditure—is partly the reason why the two conditions of nonexcludability and nonrivalry have been linked. To many economists, each condition, taken individually, leads to a type of market failure. Nonexcludability, for example, has been associated with the free-rider problem. Meanwhile, the nonrival consumption aspect leads to a demand revelation problem.[3] To other economists, however, each of these alleged market failures can be attacked. For example, Brubaker and Christainsen attack the free-rider argument, while Demsetz and Borcherding question whether nonrivalry actually causes a market failure.[4] Taken together, then, the issues of nonexcludability and nonrivalry seem to allow a stronger argument for government intervention to be made. If one criticizes the free-rider argument, then there is always the information or demand revelation problem to fall back on, and vice versa.

Perhaps the definition of public goods should be such that it implies a role for government. That is, maybe we should define a public good as a good having those traits or combinations of traits that lead to market failures that are correctable by government. I believe that this approach would make the analysis much more difficult than it need be. The types of market failure that are talked about because of nonexcludability are of a totally different nature than those owning to the nonrival consumption aspect. To lump both considerations together seems to be a curious way of trying to reach an understanding about the separate influence of each consideration. Indeed, usually the way to address or understand an issue is to pare away the complicating factors so as to highlight or spotlight the issue at hand, rather than to concatenate the separate parts. Even those who define public goods as having both nonexcludability and nonrivalry recognize the need to examine the nonrivalry issue separately by concentrating on "excludable" public goods.

As mentioned in Chapter 1, the distinction between public goods (defined in this book as having only the nonrival consumption aspect) and excludable public goods (defined as a complement to public goods when public goods are understood to have both nonrivalry and nonexcludability) is largely terminological. I concentrate on the distinction as a matter of emphasis. I am amenable to the terminological narrowing of the subject matter of this book to the case of excludable public goods as long as it is understood that excludable public goods are not merely a curious theoretical offshoot. In fact, the nonexcludable case may be even rarer than the excludable case. The remainder of this chapter focuses more closely on exclusion devices and their relevance for both rival and nonrival consumption goods. The further discussion will, I hope, illuminate the general applicability and importance of the nonrival, excludable good case.

Consider again the costly exclusion involved for private goods in the case of the lockable, although possibly still stealable, automobile. After all, it is well known that a lock is only a minor nuisance to a serious car thief. What, then, makes for the common supposition that the car is an excludable private good? The answer lies in the institution of private property rights and the enforcement of those rights, whereby the expectation of sanctions against a captured car thief also works toward exclusive private use of the automobile. It is clear that exclusion is costly for private goods: some of the cost is borne by the manufacturer who installs the lock; some by the user who has to lock and unlock the door; and some by the private property enforcement agency, which may, or may not, be in the public sector. The economics of exclusion would involve the cost-minimizing way of trying to secure that exclusion. And, as just demonstrated, it certainly would not be a topic relevant only for public goods.[5]

What of exclusion for public goods? We may not be able to put locks on lighthouses or on national defense. However, an enforceable property rights scheme can be developed which will require payment for use of the public good. Ronald H. Coase's excellent description of the history of British lighthouses is a case in point.[6] Exclusion, in the case of lighthouses, came not by turning off the lighthouse for refusal to pay. Rather, it came by collecting docking fees from the ships in the harbor. Exclusion, in this case, is evidenced more by making users pay than by prohibiting nonpayers from use. The shippers knew of the fees and could decide whether to consume the lighthouse services by entering a harbor, which would make the shipper liable for the fee. Interestingly, there was even a total fee stipulation that ships had to pay the fee only so many times per year. This allowed the vast majority of ships to use the lighthouses with an effective marginal cost of zero at year's end. Thus, the system had beneficial welfare properties in that there was little economically wasteful exclusion.

Given that both private and public goods can be either excludable or nonexcludable, what leads to the common supposition that private goods are excludable while public goods are not? There are a few possible distinctions between the public goods case and the private goods case that, at first, might seem to make private goods more excludable. The first involves the premise that there seem to be more exclusion mechanisms for private goods than for public goods. The second involves the measurement of consumption of public and private goods. The third revolves around the fact that only excludable private goods will be produced in the private sector while both excludable and nonexcludable public goods will be produced privately. These three possible distinctions will be treated in turn.

Are there actually more exclusion mechanisms for private goods than for public goods? As described above, we can deter the car thief beforehand with locks and afterward by catching and prosecuting car thiefs. For a public good (e.g., a lighthouse) we can only enforce systems of exacting payment after the good has been consumed but cannot prevent the use in the first place. This presumption is probably less true than it seems and, also, probably not very relevant. With respect to the truth of the claim, the above examples do not represent an exhaustive list of exclusion devices, so there may be many more measures or devices that markets could come up with to make public goods excludable. Lighthouses, for example, could be turned on or off through the use of secret codes to which only payers would have access. With respect to relevance, we have already noted that the lock may not be a very effective exclusion device; therefore, the completeness of the exclusion of nonpayers is probably due more to the expectation of *ex post* property right enforcement than to *ex ante* exclusion measures.

The second distinction involves the actual measurement of the consumption of the public or private good. The car thief, presumably, will be awarded his due process while the state or the car owner will have to prove to the court's satisfaction that theft (or consumption by a nonpayer) did occur. A similar arrangement must exist for the case where a ship's captain, who perhaps entered the harbor during daylight, claims to have entered the harbor without using the lighthouse, while the lighthouse owner disputes the claim and demands payment from the sailor. Some jury system or bureaucratic method will have to decide whether the lighthouse services were, in fact, used. A possible distinction arises here in terms of burden of proof. Will the lighthouse owner have to prove that the sailor used the lighthouse or will the sailor have to prove that he did not? I certainly would not relish debating the esoteric point of whether private goods were more or less excludable based on different standards of burden of proof.

This decision of whether a good has actually been consumed becomes very tricky when public goods are universally available for consumption without any identifiable action on the part of the consumer. For example, consider national defense. Presumably, we all consume national defense just on the basis of being alive. We also must pay our taxes or else face confiscation of assets or worse sanctions applicable by the taxing authority. If these are involuntary arrangements, then our exclusion-of-nonpayers institution has the effect of turning free riders who might consume the public good without paying into "forced riders" who must pay the stipulated price regardless of any subjective assessment of the value of the good.[7] Nonexcludability has been conquered, but at a substantial cost in terms of freedom of choice. Presumably, however, these pricing arrangements and the jury or bureaucratic institution that measures consumption could be agreed to, voluntarily, beforehand. If so (and there seems to be substantial incentive in a voluntary exchange economy to do so), then the excludable public good can be as common as the excludable private good. Note also that on this point the distinction between public and private goods with respect to exclusion begins to disappear. The fact that you were never asked if you would like to pay taxes for national defense and the fact that no one ever asked the car thief whether sanctions against car theft were a good idea serve well to further the similarity between exclusion for private goods and for public goods. A possible distinction that still exists in this regard involves the view that the consumption of someone else's car involves an act while the consumption of the collective's national defense does not. Obviously, more work of a philosophical nature could be done on this wrinkle. It is not attempted in this book.

The third distinction between the public goods and the private goods cases concerns the effects that infinite exclusion costs have on the possibility of private production in the alternative settings of private goods and public goods. Actually, it is curious that the issue of excludability is encountered more often with respect to public goods than to private goods because nonexcludability is potentially a much more devastating problem with private goods. If a private good such as an automobile were nonexcludable, it is unlikely that any would ever be produced.[8] Firms would not expend resources to build cars just to place them on the showroom floor so free riders could simply drive them away with no payment whatsoever. No one would pay for an automobile if any nonpayer could claim it at no cost. Nor would anyone be likely to personally build an automobile, for the same reason. Alternatively, regarding nonexcludable public goods: Although firms may not produce them for sale, individuals will produce their own public goods. The voluntary provision of nonexcludable public goods, although not optimal, will not be zero.[9] At the last, each individual will expend resources on the public good to the point where marginal costs equals the individual's marginal rate of substitution. Even though the public good in nonexcludable, the nonrival aspect of its consumption assures individuals of consuming at least their own production. For private goods, with rival consumption and nonexcludability, individuals are not even assured of consuming their own production and, therefore, have no incentive to produce in the first place.

There are two more important issues to note about exclusion that can be mentioned rather briefly. The first involves the fact that all public goods are excludable as an all-or-none choice in the event that the good is not, in fact, produced. This is especially relevant at the margin. One way to reach efficient production at the margin is to require that all persons pay an amount equal to their marginal rate of substitution in order to secure the public good. Presumably, this is what a private sector firm must do in order to produce the marginal unit and not lose money. There will be no free-riding on the marginal unit. Either all who value its consumption must pay for it or it will not be produced and all will be excluded. The problem of exclusion here is not the free-riding of nonpayers but the forced exclusion of willing payers because of the recalcitrance of one or a few. The one or the few, of course, do not have an incentive to withhold their payment or understate their demand because they will, in fact, be excluded from consuming the good if they do so. The existence of gaming, bluffing, or other strategic rent-seeking on the inframarginal units does not alter the fact that, at the margin, exclusion is perfect.[10]

The last brief point is that exclusion can be either complete or partial. A slight use of notation allows this point to be made most clearly. If Y units of a public good are produced, then the ith individual's consumption of it, Y_i, must be less than or equal to Y. Complete exclusion would mean that $Y_i = 0$, while partial exclusion could mean $Y_i < Y$. I say "could mean" because there is another type of partial exclusion that will become central to the analysis of this book. This other type of exclusion involves another dimension of consumption (introduced briefly in Chapter 1), which becomes the focus of Chapter 7. I call this other dimension the utilization dimension.

CHAPTER THREE

Definitions

Economics, like all social sciences, has a reputation that borders on notoriety with respect to the specialized language that has developed to convey ideas. Within the discipline the analysis of public goods has provided far more than its share of this jargon. Some of the language in public goods analysis is consistently used. Economists, who have followed the development of public goods theory, will have no problem with this portion of the language. Therefore, the part of the following discussion that deals with the more familiar language will interest only those who are new to the study of public goods. However, as illustrated in the preceding chapter with respect to the concept of exclusion, some of the language has meanings and interpretations which differ markedly depending on the setting involved. The discussion of some of the terminology, therefore, will be of interest even to seasoned public goods analysts.

This chapter can be taken either as a brief primer on public goods analysis or as a glorified glossary of terms and review of the literature. All the terms, except exclusion and mixed goods, are included in this chapter. The necessarily lengthy treatment of exclusion and the private good/mixed good/public good continua suggest separate chapters for these two issues. Exclusion was discussed above. The many different versions of private good/mixed good/public good continua make up Chapter 4. The remainder of the terms to be defined are included in the present chapter, arranged in alphabetical order.

In light of the theme of this book, that public goods models and monopolistic competition models are related, the discussion of the terms attempts to bring together some of the terminological issues that appear differently in each of the models. For example, consider the following: Separate units of the public good are said to be distinct while separate sellers in a monopolistic competition model are said to sell differentiated goods. Essentially, distinctness in public goods models and differentiation in monopolistic competition are the same thing. Because the two models have developed independently, however, the connection has not been noticed and a different language has developed for each. In the definitions that follow, cases where a duplication of terminology has arisen will be indicated.

Clubs

James Buchanan pioneered the economics of clubs as a middle ground between public goods and private goods.[1] For public goods, nonrival consumption is universal, while for private goods, only one person gets to consume the good. Club goods offer nonrival consumption opportunities to more than one person but to less than the whole population. The welfare economics of clubs is similar to that of public goods. Both have a summation of marginal rates of substitution that is set equal to the marginal cost. A difference arises, however, in that for club goods the summation is taken only over the members of the club.

Two extensions of club theory can be noted briefly. If multiple, competing clubs are possible, then through self-selection consumers might end up in clubs whose members desire the same particular types and amounts of jointly shared goods. Information costs will be lowered and demand revelation problems will be partly overcome in this instance. This would represent just one method that markets could use to produce public goods efficiently. If these multiple clubs are actually communities, then we cross over to models of local public goods.[2]

A second extension goes to the heart of the analysis of clubs. One is led to question why the club good offers nonrival consumption only to a group of finite size. What is it about adding members that detracts from the nonrival nature of the club? The answer comes in the recognition of some capacity constraint or some congestion cost that constrains the club's size. The economics of congested public goods follows directly from this recognition.[3]

Of particular interest in this book's analysis is that the models of clubs explicitly recognize two margins of interest. The first dimension is the one that gives impetus to someone coming from a public goods perspective to study clubs, namely, how many units of the good (nonrival within the club) to produce. That is, how big should the physical facility be? The second dimension is how big, in terms of membership, to make the club. The congestion costs obviously play a part in this latter decision. It is only a short step from noticing that added members may add to costs, to considering the possibility that a greater intensity of use by a given number of members may add to costs. From here, it is but another short step to the utilization dimension developed in Chapter 7.

Congestion

The models of congestion come closest to the generalization that this book offers.[4] The congestion models posit that the nonrival consumption characteristic goes only so far before crowding sets in, adding a degree of rivalry to consumption. The consideration of crowding grew naturally out of the economics of clubs. It is usually considered that crowding or congestion is the key feature that leads the club to have an optimal membership size less than the total population.

This crowding can be thought of in several different ways. In a club, for example, crowding may simply be related to the number of members. Alternatively, if the club provides Y units of the jointly shared good, where each individual can consume all or part of Y, that is, $y_i \leqq Y$, then crowding may be related to the summation of y_i taken over all members. In this case crowding increases because of added membership or because the members use more of the club's facilities. As a third possibility, each individual uses the totality of the club's facilities, Y, on each visit but may make multiple visits. Here, crowding is also related to the summation of y_i, but y_i need not be measured in the same dimension as Y. In this last possibility special forms of the congestion function are sometimes considered. One special form of the congestion function allows for congestion to be decreased through an increase in Y, the number of units of the jointly shared good.

The reason for this last linkage of the size of the club's facilities, Y, with a reduction in congestion is to link the optimal size of the club somehow to the individual's utilization of the club. This becomes crucial in the determination of optimal club size and optimal congestion-internalizing user fees. The result of the congestion models vary depending on the form of the congestion, but there are some regularities. The optimal user fee, not surprisingly, equals the sum of any direct costs the user imposes on the facility, called maintenance costs, and the external disutility caused to other users of the now more crowded facility. This latter cost is called the marginal congestion cost. Although maintenance costs and congestion costs enter into the setting of the user fee in the same way there is an important difference in these two types of cost. The producer, who bears the maintenance cost, presumably gets reimbursed out of the user fee, but the consumer, who bears the congestion cost, does not. That is, the members who suffer increased congestion are not reimbursed for their disutility. Instead, the money goes to funding the facilities in general. That maintenance costs are paid for out of user fees is not remarkable but that overhead costs might be paid for out of congestion-related user fees is. Most congestion models present conditions under which the optimal congestion-relieving toll also funds the production of the crowded good in the first place, thereby allowing the provision of such a crowded public good in the private sector. Whether or not these conditions will be met generally remains a contentious issue in the literature.

A still more surprising result is occasionally found. Depending on the connection of the size, Y, of the facility with the amount of congestion, and depending on whether the size of the facility enters directly into the consumer's utility function or only through congestion relief, the optimal facility size can sometimes be achieved through congestion-relieving tolls. My research shows that this is not generally the case. Like the congestion models, I allow for a separate utilization dimension in which pricing takes place and in which marginal costs are not necessarily zero. However, the relationship between this dimension and the public good or facility size dimension will be treated more generally than in the congestion models. This book considers the cost in the utilization dimension to be of the maintenance cost variety and not of the congestion cost variety. However, it will be clear that the addition of congestion costs to the general model will be no more difficult than the usual consideration of any external costs in a standard private goods framework.

Decreasing Cost

The nonrival consumption aspect of public goods has prompted some analysts to conclude that the public goods problem can be likened to the familiar private goods problem of decreasing costs or natural monopoly.[5] In particular, once the public good is produced, the relevant welfare economic question involves whether or not to allow people to consume it. If consumption truly is nonrival, then there are no added costs in allowing additional consumers. Therefore, all costs are overhead costs with respect to this decision. The large lump of overhead costs, that is, the cost of producing the public good, coupled with the zero marginal cost of allowing people to use it, certainly evokes the standard natural monopoly model. This connection was recognized early on but has been for the most part ignored. The attention has focused on how much of the public good to produce in the first place rather than on the consumption of the amount of public good that was produced.

A separate issue of decreasing cost in the dimension of public goods production can also be of interest. For example, if prices equal to marginal rates of substitution, possibly different for each person, are charged for each unit of the public good, there is no guarantee that total receipts will cover total costs. This claim holds even when the quantity of the public good is set where the summation of marginal rates of substitution equals the marginal costs of the public good. If marginal cost is less than average cost at this quantity, that is, when average cost is decreasing, then the total sum of all payments collected will be less than total cost. Most writers recognize that decreasing cost in this sense can be a problem and treat the potentially sticky point by assuming constant or increasing cost of public goods production.

Demand Revelation

For private goods, a consumer's action of choosing quantity given a price reveals information about the person's demand. However, given a quantity of public goods consumers will not ordinarily reveal their marginal rates of substitution. This is a significant problem because the marginal rate of substitution is likely to be different for each person. A profit-seeking producer will want to know these different marginal rates of substitution in order to establish an appropriately discriminating pricing scheme. A public sector, welfare-maximizing producer will want to know these marginal rates of substitution in order to establish the welfare-maximizing level of public goods production. Therefore, whether a public good is being produced in the public sector or the private sector, there is a demand revelation problem.

The demand revelation problem has been addressed from three directions. First, certain information-revealing mechanisms might be developed that would elicit truthful revelation about demand; second, in some instances observable information might be used to statistically arrive at demand curves; and third, experimental economics has been used to try to assess the importance of the demand revelation problem for public goods compared to that for private goods.

The first of these issues has been studied the most extensively. The pioneering work was laid out by Edward Clarke; the analysis since then has reached a high level of mathematical sophistication.[6] Basically, the demand-revealing models work in the following manner. Consumers each reveal a signal based on their preferences. The signals are used to determine both the provision level and the taxes paid by each person. It is the combination of the provision (which is good) and the tax (which is bad) that can bring about honest revelation. Essentially, all individuals pay a tax (receive a subsidy) that internalizes the net loss (gain) that their public good demands impose on the rest of the population. Two problems arise in this context. First, in general, there is no overall budget constraint that makes such tax collections equal to the cost of provision. Second, when a balanced budget constraint is added, the revelation scheme works only for a very restricted class of utility functions. Note that although most of these models are couched in terms of public sector provision, there is nothing to stop the private sector from using such schemes in a voluntary, precontracting sense to determine overall quantity and individual prices if the public good is an excludable one.

The statistical approach can use either market-generated data or survey data. Information about the demand for the public good can be gleaned from market-generated data for substitutes or complements to the public good.[7] Alternatively, there may be characteristics embodied in the public good which are also available in privately marketed private goods. If so, the value of these characteristics may be derived from the private good prices.[8] The use of survey data is similar to the demand-revealing processes discussed above, but perhaps only a sample of individuals are required to indicate their signals.[9]

Finally, experimental economics may be used to assess the extent of free-riding or the seriousness of the demand revelation problem.

Human subjects in a laboratory setting are confronted with economic decisions carrying real monetary payoffs. If the experiments are carefully run we may be able to draw an analogy from human behavior in the laboratory to human behavior when faced with corresponding real-life situations.[10] There are, however, many fundamental methodological problems with the approach of experimental economics.

Distinctness

Distinctness is necessary when multiple units of the public good are counted on the same axis. Due to the nonrival consumption property, if two units of a public good were identical, then there would be no need for the second unit since everyone can already consume the first. A desire for the second unit exists only if it is somehow distinct from the first. We could call this second unit a completely different public good with its own axis, but, if the goods are related, it seems natural to talk of two units of one public good, rather than one unit each of two public goods. The measure of relatedness usually remains unspecified, which is reminiscent of the unspecified relationship among the firms in a monopolistic competition group of related, but differentiated, products. As we shall see, the analytics of the number of firms in the group, or degree of product diversity, has a lot in common with the analytics of the number of units of the public good.

Diversity

Diversity is a term that comes from monopolistic competition models, where it has two meanings. As Chamberlin originally conceived diversity, it meant a departure from uniformity.[11] Differences in the cost structures of the monopolistically competitive firms or differences in the way consumers viewed the differentiated products meant that the firms were not all uniform. In this case, isolated pockets of monopoly profits might exist even in the face of competition from other members of the group.

A second meaning of diversity refers to the number of firms in the monopolistically competitive group. The extent of diversity or the degree of product differentiation is often measured by the number of different firms that exist in equilibrium. In general, the degree of diversity achieved at equilibrium by monopolistically competitive firms using simple monopoly pricing will not be the Pareto optimal amount. However, if firms can perfectly discriminate in their pricing, then perhaps optimal diversity is achieved.[12] Diversity in this second sense is relevant to the public goods analysis in that the generalization of public goods models developed in chapters 9 and 10 appears also to be a generalization of the optimum product diversity literature.

Externality

Externalities and public goods are often linked when nonexcludability is taken to be a feature of public goods.[13] Externalities occur when some production, consumption, or exchange activity that occurs between agents affects the utility function or production function of some noncontracting agent. As an example of a positive externality, perhaps something I produce, or some byproduct of my activity, positively affects your utility. If I do not take this into account, then I stop doing the activity when my personal satisfaction is maximized but have failed to take into account your benefit. From a Paretian viewpoint, this leads to an underproduction of this activity.

The link to public goods simply takes the external benefit as applying universally and in identical amounts (although possibly valued differently) to each consumer. It is the nonrival consumption characteristic that allows the benefit to be offered to everyone. Meanwhile, the nonexcludability characteristic possibly makes this benefit external to the decisionmaker. We get underproduction of the public good if the universal external benefit is ignored.

Of course, Ronald Coase has argued that externalities will not be ignored and that Pareto optimality can come about via bargaining or other exchange among the affected parties.[14] Indeed, as Coase shows, even though one party may naturally ignore the effect its actions have on another, the party that suffers the negative externality or misses out on increased production of the positive externality has an incentive to try to influence the behavior of the first party. Likewise, in the public goods setting, several authors have suggested that underproduction need not be the consequence of a situation with universal external benefit.[15] Indeed, once any externality is recognized, especially by the receiver of the benefit, strategic gaming behavior can even lead to superoptimal production,[16] and Kantian behavior can lead to optimal production.[17]

Since my treatment deals with public goods for which exclusion is possible, the connection between public goods and externalities plays only a minor role.

Free Rider

The free-rider problem is relevant in the case of nonexcludable public goods. Essentially, a consumer will be able to consume the public good without contributing toward its production, thus getting the good for free. When consumers free-ride, however, the optimal amount of the good may not be produced in the first place. Free-riding is usually thought to lead to underproduction of the public good.

A comprehensive treatment of free-riding was given by John McMillan.[18] McMillan identifies three separate issues relevant to free-riding. The first type of free-riding is simply that mentioned above, that consumers may not willingly pay for the good. If the good is excludable, or if a government can forcibly collect taxes for the provision of the public good, then this type of free-riding disappears. However, a second type comes into play. To decide on the optimal production level requires information on individual demand for the public good. By revealing false information about their tastes, consumers may hope to bring about a non-Pareto optimal equilibrium that gives them higher utility. Here, the free-rider problem naturally blends into the demand revelation problem. The third aspect of free-riding concerns what happens when the number of people in the economy grows large. The conventional wisdom is that free-riding and the associated under-provision worsen as the number of people grows. This would certainly be the view of Mancur Olson, for example, but the theoretical work of Cornes and Sandler and the experimental work of Christainsen and Brubaker challenge the generality of this conclusion.[19]

The first type of free-riding is relevant in the case of nonexcludable goods and, therefore, does not play an important role in this book. The second and third types of free-riding will make it difficult for a seller to establish discriminatory pricing schemes that accurately collect the value that a consumer places on a good. This essentially is an information cost problem which will make decisionmaking, with respect to the amount of the public good, difficult regardless of whether the good is produced in the public sector or the private sector.

Interchangeability

Interchangeability refers to the different units of the public good all being measured on the same axis. The terms *identical goods* and *homogeneous goods* are being purposefully avoided here. For private goods to be counted on the same axis, they must be identical. However, if two units of the public good are identical, then given the nonrival property, the second will be superfluous because everyone can already consume the first. So the units must be distinct from each other, but if so, then why are they on the same axis? Basically, the public goods models seek to establish just how many distinct units of the public good will or should be produced, and the quantity axis is the yardstick for this measurement. Interchangeability requires that the consumer be indifferent between situations in which the same number of units of the public good are consumed, even though the actual set of units consumed might be different.

Note the similarity between the number of units of the public good and the number of uniform, symmetrically differentiated firms as a measure of product diversity in monopolistic competition models. Indeed, in monopolistic competition, if the products are identical, then only one firm is needed. If the products are different, then why or how are they to be counted as belonging to the group? Chamberlin needed a term to capture the idea of different but related. He chose the term *differentiated*. In public goods analysis, this concept has been called *distinctness* and *interchangeability*.

Joint Supply

Joint supply was introduced to the study of public goods originally by James Buchanan and followed up by Harold Demsetz.[20] The basic import of the joint supply model was in demonstrating how different prices might be charged to different individuals without this being evidence of a non-Pareto optimal situation. In the familiar beef-and-hides joint supply model, the beef and hides sell for different prices without arbitrage acting to bring the prices into equality because consumption of beef is nonrival to the consumption of hides. In public goods, each individual's consumption is nonrival, so arbitrage will not bring prices into equilibrium. This is important, because if private sector production of public goods is to be optimal, different prices will generally have to be charged to each different individual according to the magnitude of the person's marginal rate of substitution. The fact that the diagrammatic models of both joint supply and public goods involved vertical summations of demand curves served to add credence to the analogy between the two models.

A considerable volume of literature soon emerged either extending the analogy, criticizing it, or containing warnings not to press the analogy too far.[21] One of the main bones of contention involved whether adding more people to the model aided or hindered the price determination process. In joint supply each additional person's demands for beef and hides are added horizontally to the rest of the demands for beef and hides. The increased rivalry in the beef market makes the demand side of that market more atomistic. This might make price determination easier but certainly it makes it no more difficult. Regardless of the number of people involved, there are only two markets, beef and hides, which must be summed vertically. In public goods, however, each person adds another market in which price determination is basically the outcome of a bilateral bargaining problem. There is no rivalry, no arbitrage, to help in price setting.

If it so happens that all consumers fit into a given number of "types," then the setting of price might become easier for the seller with the addition of more consumers. This is because the seller will now have more sources of information about the marginal rate of substitution of any one type and will also have greater incentive to try to measure those demands more accurately. This may lead to prices which are closer to marginal rates of substitution and to output which is closer to Pareto optimality. Beware, however, that this *if* is a big one and that the price-setting process hinted at here has little to do with what goes on in a standard private goods joint supply model.

Monopolistic Competition

Monopolistic competition refers to a class of models that study product differentiation and competition between firms selling close substitute goods. The firms that are considered to be competing with each other compose the "group," although the criterion on which one is determined to be in or out of the group remains nebulous. In the simplest versions, each firm has no control over the nature of its product, uses simple monopoly pricing, and earns zero profit in long-run equilibrium. The general public goods model presented in this book points the way to extensions of this simple monopolistic competition framework. In particular, endogenous quality choice and price discrimination on the part of the firm are indicated.

The consideration of issues in the public goods setting will aid in the extension of monopolistic competition. Simultaneously, by examining issues in a monopolistic competition model, the public goods framework can be illuminated. For example, the study of price discrimination in private good settings that are not pure monopoly (e.g., in a monopolistic competition setting) will help in the analysis of price discrimination in public goods settings. Meanwhile, this book shows how the incentive to practice price discrimination in public goods settings carries over to monopolistic competition.

Option Demand

Burton Weisbrod first broached the subject of option demand.[22] Starting from a cost-benefit project analysis perspective, he argued that the Samuelsonian rule of summation of marginal rates of substitution equal to marginal cost did not count all the benefits of the public good. The individual marginal rates of substitution captured only the value of the consumer's actual use of the public good; they did not capture the value that the consumer placed on the option to use the good. Weisbrod goes on to argue that user charges will not fund the efficient amount of the public good because they will not capture the option demand. Therefore, taxation to cover the cost of supplying the option to use the good is required.

The argument followed in this book views all benefits attributable to the public good as coming from the individual's consumption or utilization of it and not from the option to use it. Therefore, option demand is ignored. I might add that the option demand is a rather curious creature. Why does a person get utility out of the option to consume rather than the consumption itself? One possible answer is that the option demand stands for future consumption. In a one-period model, this possibility certainly has no place. Even in a multiple-period model, utility comes from using the good, in the present and in the future. The option demand may be a proxy for the discounted value of future consumption. If so, this could be made explicit without necessitating a novel construct. Perhaps there is an implicit uncertainty floating around in option demand models. Utility comes from current consumption and expected future consumption. Again, option demand models would be improved by modeling the phenomenon this way.

Overproduction

Overproduction and underproduction refer to comparisons between the equilibrium amount of the public good and the Pareto optimal amount. The Pareto optimum is characterized by the familiar equality between the summation of marginal rates of substitution and marginal cost. There are two ways of assessing whether overproduction exists. One way is to calculate and compare closed-form solutions for the amount of the public good in both the equilibrium and the optimum. The other way is to compare the conditions existing in the equilibrium with the conditions existing in the optimum. For example, if in the equilibrium it can be shown that the summation of marginal rates of substitution is less than the marginal cost, then overproduction has occurred. It would not be necessary in this latter example to actually calculate the solution values for the equilibrium amount and the optimum amount of the public good. The classic exposition of the overproduction of public goods is given by Thompson.[23]

Price Discrimination

There are two types of price discrimination that are relevant for the purposes of this book.[24] Interpersonal price discrimination, sometimes called third-degree price discrimination, involves different price schedules for different consumers. The standard example involves a separation of the market into segments with different demand elasticities. A different profit-maximizing price exists for each segment. When the assumption that consumers buy only one unit of a good is added, the demand elasticities are no longer relevant, but market segmentation can still exist based on the magnitude of the consumer's valuation for the single unit. Intrapersonal price discrimination, sometimes called first-degree price discrimination, involves different prices for different units of the same good to the same person. Multipart pricing, block pricing, two-part pricing, or in general any nonlinear pricing scheme represent the possibilities for this type of price discrimination. Perfect price discrimination often involves both interpersonal and intrapersonal price discrimination. For example, perfect price discrimination could take the form of a two-part pricing scheme with a different lump sum for each individual.

Price discrimination becomes relevant in public goods analysis because there is no requirement that marginal rates of substitution be equal across individuals. A Pareto optimal provision of public goods will generally require different prices for different individuals, or interpersonal price discrimination. In private goods markets different marginal prices would be evidence of a non-Pareto optimal distribution of goods, but this is not the case in public goods markets. Most authors implicitly recognize the distinction between price discrimination for public goods and private goods, although some confusion has occurred.[25] Harold Demsetz's exposition of the distinction is, perhaps, the most explicit.[26]

Several issues become relevant with the consideration of price discrimination in competitive settings. Some authors have considered only uniform pricing because of the informational requirements of price discrimination or the possibility of resale between consumers that will undo price discrimination. Others have considered quantity-dependent pricing, but with the same price function for each individual. Still others have considered full-fledged price discrimination. These models are discussed in Chapter 6. However, the pricing schemes that the received literature considers invariably revolve around pricing in the public good dimension for units of the public good. Chapter 7 will demonstrate what has been unappreciated until now—that ordinary price discrimination in a private goods setting is also relevant to the general public goods model.

Production Units versus Consumption Units

In *The Demand and Supply of Public Goods* James Buchanan highlighted a definitional distinction between production units and consumption units of the public good. For private goods the unit consumed is the same as the unit produced. Formally, the measurement of the good that enters the utility function is the same as the good that enters production or cost functions. Although this could be trivially assured in public goods analysis, perhaps it is more realistic to consider separate dimensions when considering production and consumption for public goods. Buchanan uses the example of the firehouse, which is consumed by separate individuals who live different distances from the firehouse. Production of the one firehouse involves costs, but once built, the firehouse offers firefighting services of possibly different amounts to different consumers. We could definitionally put "the firehouse" in the utility functions of the individuals who realize that they are consuming the same good in the production units sense. The consumers would have different marginal rates of substitution for this good, which would have to be added and compared to the marginal cost of producing the firehouse. Perhaps it makes more sense to explicitly recognize that the consumers are actually consuming different amounts of "firefighting services." Buchanan seems to be willing to go either way. He presents one set of marginal conditions which, variously interpreted, can cover either viewpoint. The analysis in this book shows that Buchanan's insight about the existence of the separate measures of production and consumption, although essentially sound, does not go far enough. Instead of being able to couch public goods problems in either production units or consumption units, the general model considers both dimensions simultaneously.

Pseudo-Demand Curves

Paul Samuelson labeled the individual demand curves that are summed vertically in the diagrammatic treatment of public goods "pseudo-demand curves," because the treatment of consumers in decentralized markets is different for public goods as against private goods.[27] In private goods markets, individuals react to market prices, assumed to be the same for all, and reveal their demands, possibly different for all, by choosing the quantity to purchase. The public goods problem is sometimes viewed as the dual of this private goods problem.[28] For public goods, quantities are the same for all, and if only individuals would reveal their possibly different demand prices, then an optimal equilibrium could result. Unfortunately, consumers will not voluntarily pay their full demand price for public goods in the same way they will consume their maximum quantities demanded in private goods. It is because consumers do not naturally reveal their demands in this sense that the curves are called pseudo-demand curves.

Presumably, if the demand curves were treated in the same fashion in the public goods case as in the private goods case, there would be nothing pseudo about them. For example, if prices, possibly different for each consumer, were established, then consumers would certainly reveal their demands by choosing utility-maximizing quantities. There are, however, two possible areas of distinction. First, in a competitive private goods market the equilibrium price and the different quantities for each individual are revealed in the market process, but there seems to be no analogous process through which the different prices in public goods markets will be discovered. Second, if price setting and quantity announcement are seen as information-gathering steps in deriving the different individual prices, incentives for gaming and strategic behavior may be introduced.

From a market process point of view, these same two problems also exist in a monopolistic private goods market. That is, once a monopolist sets an equilibrium price, the consumers will react and reveal their quantities demanded. However, the equilibrium price does not appear automatically. The monopolist must search for the correct price, and, consequently, consumers have strategic incentives while the searching in ongoing. Any difference between public goods and private goods with respect to the pseudo nature of the demand curve is primarily one of degree. The private goods monopolist has to find only one price, while the public goods supplier must find a price for each individual. Additionally, the consumer's strategic incentive is weaker (but not nonexistent) in the monopoly case, where the consumer is one of many, than in the public goods case, where each consumer essentially composes an entire market for a unit of the public good.

This book analyzes the price-setting behavior of the public goods producer. Whether the public goods are produced publicly or privately, this price-setting problem eventually must be addressed. Once the prices are set, however, price-taking consumers[29] would react by setting quantity, thus revealing their demand curves, which in this case, could no longer be considered pseudo-demand curves.

Public Factor

The extension from public goods models to public factor models is relatively straightforward.[30] Instead of summing individuals' marginal rates of substitution, we must sum individual firms' marginal rates of technical substitution. A further extension would allow some goods that enter into individual utility functions to also enter into firms' production functions. In this case we get a public good/factor, and summations of its marginal value must be added over individuals and firms. These wrinkles do not affect the argument in this book, and I use the term *public good* generically to stand for any of the above possibilities.

Quality Choice

Central to this book is the idea that product quality can be viewed as a public good.[31] Quality is nonrival in the sense that my consumption of a certain quality of product does not inhibit your consumption of the same quality. In fact, it is normally thought that all consumers of a certain product in private goods models consume the same quality of product. Since all consumers are getting the same quality, it would enter individual utility functions with the same value, and, therefore, optimum quality occurs where there is equality between the marginal cost of quality and the summation of marginal rates of substitution for quality. However, this decision and this discussion remain foreign to most private goods models where the nature of the good is immutably set from outside the model.

Spatial Competition

The economics of spatial competition arose naturally out of the economics of location. Competing sellers have the identical product for sale except for their location. The strength of the consumer's demand depends inversely on the distance between the locations of the buyer and seller. In location models, the distance between consumer and producer implies a transportation cost that either raises gross cost to the consumer or lowers net demand to the seller. However, it need not be a transportation cost and it need not be physical distance that distinguishes the sellers. It could, for example, be a characteristics space in which consumers and firms are located.[32] Regardless, spatial competition models are often lumped together with monopolistic competition models mainly because the metric that separates consumers and firms provides a convenient characterization of the relationship among all the products of the Chamberlinian group.

Since this book involves relationships between the generalized versions of public goods models and monopolistic competition models, we may also see some similarities between public goods and spatial competition. In *The Demand and Supply of Public Goods,* Buchanan even couched some of his elementary propositions about public goods in terms of a location problem with two consumers and one firehouse to be located between them. There is, however, one important simplifying assumption existing in spatial competition models that is relaxed in public goods models. The assumption is that in spatial competition the consumer buys, if at all, from only one firm. Only the "closest" or lowest cost supplier will sell to a given consumer. This assumption, if added to a model for competitive production of public goods, would be tantamount to saying that a consumer will buy the public goods supply from only one seller.

There is one other connection between spatial competition and public goods. It is often assumed that a consumer will purchase only one unit of the good if the price is lower than his demand price or else zero units of the good.[33] The same type of simplification is also used in competitive public goods models. That is, persons either buy the unit of the public good sold by the *n*th public good seller or do not buy it, depending on whether the price is less than or greater than their marginal rates of substitution. Realistically, however, the consumer may buy multiple units from one seller in the spatial setting or multiple units from one seller in the public good setting. (Here we are anticipating the argument of the book.) Should this be the case, the pricing practices applicable for these multiple purchases may importantly affect the outcome of the competition in the model and, therefore, should not be ignored. In both models improvements are possible through the consideration of price discrimination, nonlinear pricing, and other sophisticated pricing schemes used for multiple purchase items.

Two-Part Pricing

Two-part pricing is a form of nonlinear pricing that requires a lump sum payment, perhaps in the form of a membership fee, then a per unit price schedule for actual purchases of the good.[34] Two-part pricing is one possible form of perfect price discrimination with the per unit fee equal to marginal cost and the lump sum set to take away all consumer surplus. In general, this would require a different lump sum for each customer.

Several of the existing models of private provision of public goods consider perfect price discrimination simultaneously along with competition. This is unfamiliar ground for most economists.[35]

Underproduction

Underproduction and overproduction refer to comparisons between the equilibrium amount of the public good and the Pareto optimal amount. The Pareto optimum is characterized by the familiar equality between the summation of marginal rates of substitution and marginal cost. There are two ways of assessing whether underproduction exists. One way is to calculate and compare closed-form solutions for the amount of the public good in both the equilibrium and the optimum. The other way is to compare the conditions existing in the equilibrium with the conditions existing in the optimum. For example, if in the equilibrium it can be shown that the summation of marginal rates of substitution is still greater than the marginal costs, then underproduction has occurred.

Most treatments of public goods production conclude that underproduction will be the result. There are several different arguments that support this conclusion. First, if exclusion is not possible, then no firm has an incentive to supply the public good. Second, if exclusion is possible, then some customers with positive valuations for some units may be excluded from consuming them and, also, from paying for them. Consequently, their demands will not be counted on the margin by the producer. Third, since optimal provision may require different prices for each individual, and since revelation of those demand prices may not ordinarily be forthcoming, the seller has an information problem. In the extreme case the seller will have to charge everyone the same price, and this leads to underproduction. This book shows that the conclusion that private markets will underproduce public goods is not generally true. There is not systematic policy that government can use to deal with supposed market failures in the production of public goods.

Uniformity

Uniformity is a simplifying assumption that Chamberlin, in *The Theory of Monopolistic Competition*, added to aid in the original exposition of monopolistic competition. In uniformity, all firms in the group are assumed to have the same cost and demand conditions. Describing equilibrium for the firm therefore required only one set of cost and demand curves. Of course, market equilibrium still required the acknowledgment of a multitude of firms. Chamberlin himself stressed that the relaxation of the uniformity assumption was an important part of his theory. This book will illuminate the similarity between a Chamberlinian group composed of uniform firms and the quantity axis in a competitive public goods model, where the different units of the public good are distinct and interchangeable.

Utilization

This book devotes a whole chapter to the introduction and explanation of a dimension of consumption called utilization.[36] Briefly, individuals are assumed to get utility from using the public goods that are produced. Traditionally, this use, or utilization, has been assumed to be an all-or-nothing decision for each individual. This assumption vastly simplifies the consumption decision of the individual. This book argues that a sophisticated utilization dimension, in which multiple units can be consumed by each individual and in which pricing, exclusion, and demand revelation take place, helps immensely in understanding and extending the analysis of public goods.

Vertical Summation

Since public goods offer nonrival consumption, all individuals can consume the same unit of the good simultaneously. The total value of the good is, therefore, the summation of all the individual values. Diagrammatically, each individual's valuation is represented by the height of the respective demand curve, and the total valuation is represented by the vertical summation of demand curves.

Vertical summations are also relevant in joint supply models and externality models. In joint supply models, the demand for beef is vertically added to the demand for hides after each of these has been derived by horizontal summation over consumers. In externality models, the external cost or benefit associated with the consumption or production of any particular unit must be vertically added to or subtracted from the relevant demand curve or cost curve. This book shows how both horizontal and vertical summations are relevant in the general model.

CHAPTER FOUR

Public Goods, Private Goods, and Mixed Goods

Although the pure public goods case was of paramount interest originally as a stark contrast to the traditional private goods models, the pure cases, private and public, were soon seen to be too restrictive to encompass all of the possibilities. Some sort of mixed goods possibility, perhaps an impure public good, perhaps a private good with some jointness characteristics, was needed to fill the middle ground between the pure cases. In this chapter the goal is to review and criticize the surprising number of mixed good paradigms that have been offered. The extension of the ideas presented here leads to a new classification of mixed goods that will be presented in full in Chapter 7.

The characteristics of mixed goods will follow from the feature that distinguishes the pure private good from the pure public good. Not surprisingly, when different features are emphasized as the keys to distinguishing public goods from private goods, different characteristics of the middle ground come into play. Arguably, economists have overdone it by introducing too many paradigms.

Table 4.1 lists thirteen views of the feature that differentiates public goods from private goods. For most of the views there is an associated middle range of mixed goods. The characteristics are listed in three columns. Each one of the views is considered in turn.

Sector or Production and Consumption

The first distinction, the sector of production and consumption, is based on whether the good is produced in the public sector or the private sector. As a purely definitional matter, we could distinguish private goods as those produced under complete laissez faire and public goods as those produced under complete socialism. The middle range would have to include a number of possibilities, such as regu-

Table 4.1
Thirteen Views of Pure Public, Pure Private, and Mixed Goods

	Feature	Public Good	Mixed Good	Private Good
1.	Sector of production and consumption	public	regulated, taxed, or subsidized	private
2.	Sector of optimal production	public	depends on social welfare function	private
3.	Quantity choice for consumers	no	?	yes
4.	Relationship of individuals' consumption	equal for all consumers	equal for subset of consumers	generally unequal
5.	Demand curve aggregation	vertical summation	both? neither?	horizontal summation
6.	Size of sharing group	all consumers	subset of consumers	one consumer
7.	Range of externality	severe or universal	partial	none
8.	Algebraic relationship of production, U, and consumption, u_i	$U = u_i$	$U^{-p} = \Sigma(u_i^{-p})$	$U = \Sigma u_i$
9.	Crowding/congestion	none	after too much use	absolute after one consumer
10.	Cost of exclusion	infinite	positive	zero
11.	Marginal cost of wider consumption	zero		positive
12.	Presence of consumption dimensions	only public good dimension	both dimensions	only utilization dimension
13.	Rivalry in consumption	nonrival	both, but in different dimensions	rival

lated production and subsidized or taxed production. A further subdivision of public versus private provision would distinguish between the productive mechanism and the allocative mechanism because these need not be in the same sector. For example, nuclear warheads are demanded by the public sector but produced in the private sector, while public education is demanded privately (and also possibly publicly) but produced publicly. Neither warheads nor education would be a pure public or pure private good according to this view. On the surface, this approach pays little attention to why a good is produced in or demanded by one sector or the other. Underneath the surface of this approach, however, are the characteristics of the good itself that place it in one sector or the other or somewhere in between. The analysis of these characteristics constitutes a topic set squarely in the Public Choice domain. Indeed, what are the characteristics of a good that lead to collective or individual decisionmaking and what are the outcomes of these decisions? Presumably, these are the basic questions that these thirteen different views must address. As such, this first classification merely begs the question that the others are trying to answer.

Sector of Optimal Production

More often, however, the public/private distinction in determining where a good is to be produced takes on a normative aspect. Given some goal, should a good be produced publicly or privately? The answer might depend on the nature of exclusion costs, the possibility of free-riding, the distribution of income, differences in production costs, or a host of other criteria, some of which are addressed below. Of general interest, however, is the viewpoint expounded by John Head and Carl Shoup.[1] Head and Shoup argue that a pure public good is one in which a "nonmarketing mode" always leads to higher social welfare. By "nonmarketing mode" Head and Shoup essentially mean bureaucratic or administrative decisionmaking using some demand-revealing process and forced taxation. Alternatively, pure private goods are those for which the marketing mode leads to higher social welfare. The marketing mode is essentially voluntary exchange activity. The middle ground of "ambiguous goods" contains those goods that under some social welfare functions should be produced in the marketing mode but under other social welfare functions lead to higher welfare in the nonmarketing mode. The turning point for ambiguous goods revolves around the ability to redistribute income in a nonmarketing mode through tax policy. Of course, the inability to ever agree on a social welfare function makes this distinction vacuous in terms of policy relevance.

Quantity Choice for Consumers

Robert Staaf considers a good which might be produced either as a public good or a private good.[2] Consumers could consume the private good until their marginal rates of substitution equaled their cost. If the good is produced as a public good, each consumer must consume the same amount. The public good formulation basically adds an extra constraint, that all consumers must consume the identical amount, and, consequently, utilities are not as high in the public good formulation. However, the private formulation might have higher costs than the public formulation, because of an added cost of exclusion. Therefore, it is ambiguous as to where utilities are the highest.

Staaf is actually combining two notions of public versus private: excludability (number 10) and the relationship of one individual's consumption to another's (number 4). To privatize the possibly nonexcludable public good requires an extra cost to make the good excludable. The result of privatization is that consumers get to adjust quantity for the private good where they had not been able to do so for the public good. There does not seem to be a relevant middle ground in this formulation. You can either adjust quantity or you can't. The possibility that the distinction turns on the cost of quantity adjustment (i.e., zero quantity adjustment cost equals private good; infinite quantity adjustment costs equals public good; and, positive, finite quantity adjustment cost equals mixed good) can readily be discarded. Quantity adjustment will always be costly, even for private goods, except in the case of a free good. Neither will quantity adjustment ever be proscribed by infinite cost. Individuals always have the option to produce their own public goods, and thereby quantity adjust, while others possibly free-ride.

Relationship of Individuals' Consumption

A notationally motivated distinction between private and public leads to the well-known difference in the marginal conditions describing optimality. When a good enters into everyone's utility function identically, the summation of marginal rates of substitution must be compared to the marginal cost of its production. The argument entering identically into each person's utility function implies that each person must consume the same amount; therefore, this is certainly one of the things that Staaf had in mind. Private goods enter only one person's utility function, so only one person's marginal rate of substitution is compared to marginal cost. A middle ground for this characterization of public and private covers the possibility that a good enters identically into utility functions for only a subset of consumers. The difference in the marginal conditions is easily derived. A summation of marginal rates of substitution taken over only the relevant subset of consumers must be compared to marginal cost.

Unfortunately, there is nothing in the notation to tell us why a particular good will be consumed by just one consumer, a subset of consumers, or all of the consumers. The notational difference appears to be symptomatic of the distinction among public goods, private goods, and mixed goods but is not the cause of the distinction. Nevertheless, the power of this notation is evident in that, whatever the cause of the distinction, as addressed in the other twelve formulations, the pure polar cases will make use of the same notation.

Demand Curve Aggregation

The distinction between public and private based on whether demand curves are to be summed horizontally or vertically also appears to be a symptom or result of other considerations rather than a determinant of publicness or privateness. The middle ground, however, is intriguing. Is some other summation besides vertical or horizontal relevant? Or perhaps some combination of vertical and horizontal summation is necessary. Interestingly, both Evans and Head argue that, because of externalities, a vertical summation followed by a horizontal summation yields the correct analysis.[3] Alternatively, this book will argue that both horizontal and vertical summations are necessary for the analysis of mixed goods. However, the order is reversed—the horizontal summation will be followed by the vertical summation—and the summations are taken in different dimensions.

Size of Sharing Group

Following up on number 4, consider the size of the group that shares some good in common. Whether the good is to be shared by one, a few, or all is one of the themes addressed in the theory of clubs, as originally expounded by James Buchanan.[4] All club members consume the same good, so each member's marginal rate of substitution counts in the comparison of cost and benefit. Nonmembers, however, are ignored. The size of the sharing group can be one for a private good, the whole community for a public good, or any size in between. This view provides one motivation for the notational distinction between public goods and private goods given above in number 4. The theory of clubs gives a nice breakdown of goods as public, private, or mixed but still begs the question as to what determines the size of the sharing group. It could be exclusion costs, congestion costs, limits on the possibility for reciprocal externalities, or one of the other views enumerated here that lead to different club sizes.

Range of Externality

Another common theme in discussions of the distinction between public and private goods is ranges of externality.[5] If the externality is universal, then the notational analysis of it will be similar to that of a pure public good. For example, if my consumption or production activity affects the utility of every person in the society, then in assessing costs and benefits we would have to count everyone's marginal rate of substitution for the activity. In the case of reciprocal externalities the total consumption or production of all individuals may enter into everyone's utility function and, therefore, be analyzed like a public good. For example, if y_i is the *i*th person's consumption of some externality-producing private good, then Σy_i enters into all utility functions and the optimal marginal equalities will involve the familiar summation of marginal rates of substitution. If there were no externalities, then all goods would be private. Incomplete externalities give rise to mixed goods. It is evident that numbers 4 and 6 above can be motivated by this externality issue. Clubs of small size may form because of reciprocal externalities in the small group. Meanwhile, the summations of marginal rates of substitution for this externality will be taken only over the members of the club.

It is also clear that this view and the issue of exclusion costs are intertwined. With costless exclusion there will not be any external benefits bestowed. Nonpayers would be excluded from enjoying the benefits; meanwhile, any user's payment for benefits effectively internalizes them to the perpetrator's decisionmaking process. However, note that the marginal equalities describing optimality are unaffected by whether the benefits bestowed are externalities or are paid for by the recipient. Therefore, the issue of externality, like the issue of excludability, cannot be the key feature that defines public goods. While it is true that all (positive) externalities that affect the totality of the population are public goods, it is not true that all public goods are externalities of this kind.

As an aside, note that some scholars have been led astray by the connection between externality and public goods and what it implies about the normative issue of whether public goods should be produced publicly or privately. The misleading reasoning goes as follows. Since we know that the public sector has a role to play in correcting externalities through Pigovian tax/subsidy schemes and since public goods are extreme forms of externalities, it therefore follows that the public sector has a role to play in public goods provision. One might just as easily argue that since Coase demonstrated that the private sector does have the correct incentives with respect to dealing with and internalizing externalities, the public sector therefore has no role to play in correcting externalities and since public goods are externalities, the public sector has no role there either. Neither of these arguments goes anywhere because public goods are not externalities in the first place.

Algebraic Relationship of Production and Consumption

Jan Tinbergen's view is that the continuum of public to private can be captured by an algebraic expression with one parameter.[6] For private goods, the total production is the summation of the consumption of all the individuals, while for public goods, total production and individual consumption are related by equality. The expression given in Table 4.1 for the mixed goods case reduces to the private goods case when p equals -1. Alternatively, as p approaches (negative) infinity, the expression approaches the public good case. Tinbergen is attempting to get at a mathematical representation in consumption units of the difference between nonrivalry and rivalry, which he sees as partial rivalry. For public goods, given a fixed amount of production, one person's consumption does not reduce anyone else's. For private goods, however, with the same fixed production, one person's consumption must reduce someone else's on a one-for-one basis. In Tinbergen's mixed goods range, one person's consumption decreases someone else's but by less than the increase to the first person. Congestion might be one example of this phenomenon. Since partial rivalry of this sort is usually couched in terms of a cost measured in the numeraire, Tinbergen's approach couched in terms of consumption units has sparked little interest.

Crowding/Congestion

Crowded or congested public goods are often seen to fill the midrange between public and private goods. Oakland shows diagrammatically how private goods become completely crowded at a quantity of one, public goods never get crowded, and mixed goods suffer increasing crowding costs with increasing use.[7] Congestion models come closest to the treatment favored in this book in that they sometimes consider a separate dimension in which the individual consumes the good and, consequently, causes the crowding. Two things, however, detract from the generality of these congestion models. The first is that the cost in the crowdable dimension takes on the nature of an externality. In general, the cost in this dimension of consumption can be a resource production cost, an external cost, or any other kind of cost. The second is that often what would be the public good dimension in an uncrowded public goods model becomes solely a vehicle for congestion reduction. This makes the mixed goods case basically a capacity choice model in a private goods model with an external congestion cost. Under the congestion models there would be no reason to increase the public good if it were not crowded, whereas from the public goods perspective, more units of the public good, even if the existing units are uncrowded, are still valued by consumers.

Cost of Exclusion

The issue of exclusion was treated at length in Chapter 2. Suffice it to say at this point that exclusion has more to do with whether a good will be produced privately or publicly than with whether it is a private or public good in the sense of rival or nonrival consumption. Both private goods and public goods can be fully excludable, partially excludable, or nonexcludable. The models of excludable public goods clearly show that excludability and publicness are different problems. The economics of exclusion and the related area of property right formation are interesting topics, but it is unfortunate that the exclusion issue has become entangled with the economics of public and mixed goods.

Marginal Cost of Wider Consumption

One of the obvious distinctions between public and private goods involves the marginal costs of allowing additional consumers to enjoy the good. For a public good this cost is zero. For a private good this cost is positive. Apparently, there is no middle range in this instance.

Notwithstanding the zero marginal cost in the nonrival dimension, the public good must be produced, and this production will be costly. In the nonrival dimension this cost takes the form of an overhead cost.[8] The combination of an overhead cost and a constant per unit variable cost, be it zero or positive, is reminiscent of decreasing cost or natural monopoly models. Indeed, as mentioned above, several authors have been led to conclude that the public good represents a special case of extreme decreasing cost.[9] Sometimes unwarranted conclusions about public sector involvement have followed from this position. For example, Samuelson himself argued that "governments provide or regulate services that are incapable of being produced under the strict conditions of constant returns."[10] Presumably, therefore, government has a role to play in public goods since the public good problem can be likened to a decreasing cost industry. To counter the interventionist view, however, consider the free market economists' arguments that decreasing costs do not cause market failure.[11] In this view, private sector public good provision could certainly be possible.

Presence of Consumption Dimensions

From the discussion of crowding cost and from the zero marginal cost discussion, it is becoming apparent that there are actually two dimensions of consumption relevant in public goods analysis.[12] This is the view taken in this book, and it will be explained in full in Chapter 7.

Here, a brief mention of the basic idea will suffice. Essentially, there are two dimensions of consumption. One looks just like a standard private goods dimension where the marginal rate of substitution is set equal to marginal cost and demands are summed horizontally. The other looks just like the pure public good dimension in which marginal rates of substitution are added together for comparison with marginal cost and demands are summed vertically. In the pure public goods case the private-like dimension becomes trivial and is dropped from the analysis. Likewise, in the pure private goods case, the public goods dimension is trivial and is dropped from consideration. In the general mixed goods case, both dimensions are important.

Rivalry in Consumption

The notions of rival and nonrival consumption fit nicely into number 12. While at first it must seem that there is no middle ground (i.e., consumption is either rival or nonrival), in fact, an interesting middle ground can be examined. The good in question must simultaneously have rival consumption characteristics and nonrival consumption characteristics, in different dimensions of course, to be considered a mixed good. This book holds that most goods have precisely these aspects.

CHAPTER FIVE

The Private Provision of Public Goods: Preliminaries

Economists and students are often first exposed to public goods through "market failure" arguments: the private market undersupplies the public good because of free-riding, nonexcludability, demand revelation problems, and so forth. When nonpayers can be excluded, however, market institutions can provide public goods. This possibility leads to a very interesting and unsettled area in the literature in public goods. For starters, Thompson develops a model in which overproduction of the public good is the result of perfect competition. In an almost identical setting, Demsetz develops a model that leads to optimal production of the excludable public good. Finally, Oakland's model has an equilibrium characterized by underproduction of the public good.[1] In addition, several critical comments and extensions of these models have been offered.[2] It is the purpose of the next two chapters to review these arguments in the settings in which they were originally presented. In so doing, the stage will be set for the extension of these arguments to a more general setting where the special case nature of these models will clearly stand out.

One thing is clear already—there is little agreement in the conclusions of the models. Part of the problem is that public goods markets may resemble private goods markets in some, but not all, of their characteristics. Because of this, drawing analogies from private goods to public goods sometimes helps in the analysis but other times leads to errors in logic. For example, one characteristic treated identically in both public goods models and private goods models is the effect of competition on profits. Both areas assume that in long-run equilibrium, competition will lead to zero profits, at least for the marginal firm. If all firms have the same cost conditions, then all firms will earn zero profits in competitive equilibrium. Alternatively, consider an issue treated differently in public goods models and private goods models, for example, price discrimination. It is not surprising that price discrimination is one of the issues that has caused some problems in public goods models. The welfare economics of price discrimination differ between private goods and public goods. The market dynamics differ as well.

The combination of the issues of competition and price discrimination offers even deeper problems. Not only will this combination exhibit different characteristics in public goods models than in private goods models, but as an additional complicating factor, the economics of the combination in private goods models alone has not even benefited from extensive treatment. Traditionally, price discrimination in private goods models has been examined only in the monopoly setting. The conventional wisdom, although not entirely correct, is that the possibility of arbitrage and the competitive pressure from other suppliers will undo price discrimination in multiple firm settings. More recently, price discrimination and other sophisticated pricing schemes have been considered to varying degrees in multiple firm settings.[3] But these latter writings and viewpoints have all postdated the original expositions of Thompson, Demsetz, and Oakland. We should not be surprised that Thompson and Demsetz come to different conclusions regarding price discrimination in competitive public goods models or that Oakland's model rejects price discrimination outright, given that competitive price discrimination has not even received thorough treatment in private goods models. If my research fulfills the modest task of using public goods to draw attention to the treatment of price discrimination in private goods models, let alone in the general mixed good treatment, I will consider my efforts worthwhile.

The remainder of this chapter is organized into three sections. The first of these sections contains a discussion regarding the relevance and possibility of price discrimination in the public goods setting. Price discrimination in private goods markets is compared to price discrimination in public goods markets. These comparisons show which analogies between the two settings are relevant and which are not.

The second section discusses the positive and normative methodological background that is typical in models of private production of public goods. The third section sets out some of the assumptions of these models. Many of the assumptions are the same in each of the models and can be treated briefly. But a few important distinctions exist, and these must be explored in depth. Through the presentation of the assumptions, this last section acts as a springboard to the discussion of the actual models in the next chapter. Indeed, the purpose of the whole of Chapter 5 is to get us thinking about competitive production of public goods so we can dive right into the critique of the existing models in the next chapter.

Price Discrimination

The issue of price discrimination provides a convenient criterion upon which to divide the received literature. The two categories are obvious. Thompson and Demsetz allow price discrimination while Oakland does not. We must have an organized view of price discrimination to keep this division clear.

Typically, textbooks list several conditions that must be met before a firm can price-discriminate in an ordinary private goods market. These conditions include: the absence of competition, in the sense of multiple, noncooperative sellers; the prohibition of resale; and the availability of information about individuals' demands or demand elasticities. These issues, and their relevance in public goods pricing, will be treated in turn. In each instance, the issue will be introduced in its familiar private goods context, then followed by a discussion of any pertinent public goods considerations.

Absence of Competition

The first condition to be treated refers to the number of noncooperating firms in the industry. Notice the sense in which competition disallows price discrimination. It is not competition in the usual, zero profit sense; competition as used in the first condition means the opposite of monopoly. Since monopoly means single seller, competition as the opposite of monopoly means the presence of noncooperative, multiple sellers. Multiple sellers alone will not negate the possibility of price discrimination, because if the multiple sellers cooperate, then they can act just like a monopoly. Part of monopoly behavior can surely include price discrimination. It is the noncooperative behavior on the part of the multiple sellers that undoes any price-discriminating scheme. Therefore, the noncooperation among the multiple sellers is an important condition that must be absent for price discrimination to exist.

It is important to note that competition in the usual sense of zero profit in long-run equilibrium does not prohibit price discrimination. Neither does competition in the sense of contestability nor in the sense of potential competition preclude price discrimination. As an example, consider the case in which a uniform-pricing firm could not earn positive profits but in which a firm practicing price discrimination could. Price discrimination may be necessary for the firm to remain solvent; meanwhile, the effect of potential competition or contestability is to keep profits equal to zero by eliminating some, but not all, of the price discrimination.

In a multiple-firm setting, the firms' optimizing behavior and the consumers' optimizing behavior interact to undo any price discrimination. Consumers, of course, always seek to buy the product at the lowest available price. Because of this, in an industry composed of price-setting/quantity-taking firms, only those firms with the lowest price will exhibit positive sales quantities. But suppose firms are not pure price setters/quantity takers.[4] Then, might not price discrimination arise if all firms could place quantity restrictions on their low-price sales to force at least some consumers some of the time to purchase at higher prices? The answer is that noncooperating sellers could not sustain such a pricing system. Each firm would try to increase profit by undercutting the price in a rival's high-price market in an attempt to get extra customers. Even if constrained to hold overall output constant, each firm would try to undercut the competition, thereby replacing one of its low-price customers with a high-price customer. The attempted skimming of the high-price market will lower prices there, while the neglect of the low-price market will raise prices there. This incentive exists as long as any one firm has any low-price customers and any other firm has any high-price customers; therefore, this arbitrage will compete price to a uniform level.

In this regard, note than an industry composed of firms that could place maximum quantity limits on high-price as well as low-price sales could sustain the dual price system. Essentially, this is because arbitrage requires the ability of quantities to change without limit to eventually bring prices into equality. If quantity changes are somehow limited, arbitrage cannot complete its task. It is well known that enforceable quantity restrictions are one way of organizing a cartel. Production quotas and geographical market segmentation are two nice examples of this. Barring cooperation among the sellers, however, these quantity limits cannot be sustained in a private goods setting.

There are a couple of issues in the above private good setting that work against the possibility of price discrimination there but will not work the same way for public goods. The first of these involves the quantity limitation possibility discussed above. In public goods markets, there is a built-in limitation on the quantity that a seller can sell to any person. Usually this is assumed to be one unit. Therefore, a firm cannot take away units that it is selling at low prices to some consumers and sell them *instead* at higher prices by undercutting a rival seller. Basically, this is because of the nonrival consumption aspect of public goods. The first firm can sell a unit at a high price to any particular consumer only once. After this the consumer may still opt to consume the rival's public good, also at a high price. Both these sales take place while the first firm may still be selling a unit at a lower price to another individual. The low prices and high prices can exist simultaneously with no competitive pressure from other sellers to bring prices into equality.

The second issue distinguishing the public goods case from the private goods case involves an identical good assumption. Obviously, if the multifirm private goods market discussed above were made up of differentiated goods, the discriminatory pricing schemes of one firm may not unravel due to competitive pressure. In public goods markets, the different firms do sell products that are differentiated, at least in the sense of being distinct and interchangeable. The interchangeability assumption acts through potential competition to ensure that any one producer will not be able to earn positive profits. But as we have seen above, such a zero profit situation does not preclude price discrimination. Meanwhile, the distinctness of the units allows each firm to enforce a discriminatory pricing system without arbitrage competition from the rival firms.

The full force of this second point cannot be appreciated until after the presentation of the utilization dimension in Chapter 7. For now, the two points may seem redundant, but they should be thought of as differentiated. The first point above is that, because of a limit on the number of times a particular unit can be sold to any one person, arbitrage is not possible between units sold for different prices. Remember that in order for arbitrage to assure one common price, it requires limitless ability to take away a unit from a low-price payer and sell it instead to a high-price payer. The second point has to do with limits on arbitrage due to product differentiation, and it applies even when there is no limit on the number of sales made to any individual. In the utilization dimension there is no limit on sales, but price discrimination may still be sustainable essentially due to the distinctness of the units of the public good.

Prohibition of Resale

The second condition necessary for price discrimination in private goods markets is the prohibition of resale. The possibility of resale will negate any interpersonal price discrimination. With interpersonal price discrimination, consumers in the lowest priced market will have an incentive to overbuy, since they intend to resell the extra units to consumers in higher priced markets. The seller, realizing that all sales are being made at the lowest price, will raise the price to the uniform price monopoly level, and price discrimination of this sort disappears.

Resale will not necessarily undo intrapersonal price discrimination. Consider a two-part pricing scheme. If the seller imposes an ordinary two-part pricing scheme but resale is not prevented, then the incentive exists for only one customer to pay the lump sum and buy the consumption units for everyone at the low per unit price. This system may not unravel into a uniform price. The seller, for example, could increase the lump sum to capture not only the consumer surplus of the buying individual but also to capture any profit that the individual gets in the resale market. In the limiting case, the original seller may raise the lump sum to capture everyone's consumer surplus. Only one person will pay the grand lump sum, but that individual will set another two-part pricing scheme in the resale market. This person should also expect the resale possibility and will set the lump sum to capture the consumer surplus of everyone else (not including the seller). This process continues until the last person, who has no one left to sell to, simply pays a lump sum capturing the individual consumer surplus.[5] Instances of this extreme type may not exist. However, it is not uncommon for two or more people to share the cost of a membership fee. Even with only one membership, all the sharers might still be able to gain access to the facility. This is especially the case when members are allowed to bring guests who must pay the same per unit price as members. It would be expected that the seller take this type of purchase into account when setting the lump sum fee in the first place.

Generally, the resale possibility works the same way in public goods markets. If a public goods seller maintains different prices, then perhaps only the lower price buyer will buy the good intending to resell to the higher price consumer. If this cannot be stopped, the price discrimination will not last.

Realistically, if the good has any service attributes, or if consumption somehow requires the payer's presence, then resale will not be a problem. This service attribute is important in many goods and works the same way in public goods and private goods markets. As an example coming from the world of private goods, note that resale will not be a problem for haircuts or dental services. For public goods, resale will not be a problem for lighthouse services or bridge crossings.[6]

In one sense, the problem that resale poses to a supplier trying to price discriminate may be less severe in public goods markets than in private goods markets. This has to do with detection. How easy is it for the seller to know if resale is happening? It may be easier to spot resale in public goods markets than in private goods markets. This seems so in the received formulations of public goods markets because a person normally buys any unit of the public good only once. The act of buying the unit more than once, in order to resell it, may make resale more detectable by the seller.

Further inspection reveals some cases where detection of resale is harder for public goods. Detection is especially difficult when the public good is an item of information. Only one purchase is required to get the information which can be resold over and over again at no extra cost. In cases like this, resale is harder to detect in public goods markets. This possibility, however, is technically an example where exclusion of nonpayers is the problem rather than resale. If, at the time of the original sale, it is impossible to attach to the good stipulations forbidding resale or other misappropriation of it, then the market would not be expected to produce this good anyway. In this case we would be worrying not about price discrimination but about private provision in the first place.

Resale is a serious problem for public goods, but not an insurmountable one. Earl Thompson discusses the theory of patents and other market arrangements that will be forthcoming when the public good is an innovation.[7] Elsewhere, in a case study, I have discussed copyrights and other voluntary arrangements that have been developed in the news-providing industry when the public good is a news item supplied by a wire service firm.[8]

Information

The last condition required for price discrimination is information about the demands of the customers. The type of information required is different depending on whether interpersonal or intrapersonal price discrimination is considered. For example, to impose a nonlinear pricing scheme such as two-part pricing, the seller would like to know the demands of the individuals involved so the seller could set a profit-maximizing lump sum and per unit price. Of course, a seller using uniform monopoly pricing will also want to know the same demands for the reason of setting the profit-maximizing, uniform price. Nonlinear pricing actually requires a little more information than uniform pricing. Whereas uniform pricing can be implemented with information about the aggregate demand curve in the market, nonlinear pricing must take into account both the aggregate demand and the breakdown of that demand among individuals. If the breakdown among individuals is ignored, the lump sum may deter some individuals from buying any units at all. Once having set the pricing scheme, however, the seller need not know any more about the individual consumers.

Alternatively, the imposition of interpersonal price discrimination requires even more information. Information about individual demands, as well as information enabling the seller to distinguish one individual from another, is required. For example, the seller might try to impose a two-part pricing scheme with different lump sums for different individuals. To do so, the seller must be able to distinguish the high lump sum person from the low lump sum person. This is difficult, but not always as difficult as it first seems. The market has come up with a variety of mechanisms through which consumers will reveal to sellers which type of person they are. Sales, cents-off coupons, trading stamps, time-of-day or season pricing, option packages, block booking, tie-in sales, delivered pricing, and a host of other mechanisms serve simultaneously to segment the seller's market and charge different prices in the different segments.

There is little difference in how this informational requirement acts in private goods markets and in public goods markets. The biggest difference that does exist concerns whether price discrimination is required for optimal production. In private goods markets, it is usually seen as unnecessary, but in public goods markets it is usually held to be required. The flavor of the models presented in the next chapter is determined by whether the seller does or does not have the information required to practice interpersonal price discrimination.

The Oakland model does not allow price discrimination. The information required is assumed to be unavailable, so whatever the terms for which the seller offers the public good, the same terms must be available to all. The Demsetz and Thompson models allow perfect discrimination. The seller has perfect information about the individuals' demands and uses the information in the implementation of the pricing scheme. The Demsetz and Thompson models differ from each other on the basis of how the competitive firms and customers interact in using the perfect information.

Positive and Normative Methodological Issues

As positive economic exercises, both the perfect discrimination approach and the non-discrimination approach are useful. Presumably, reality lies somewhere between the no-information/no–price discrimination approach of Oakland and the perfect information/perfect price discrimination approach of Thompson and Demsetz. I have attempted the direct approach of pursuing an intermediate model of imperfect price discrimination.[9] However, this attempt was not wholly satisfactory because the extent of the price discrimination was determined exogenously. What is really required is the development of a model where the extent of the imperfect price discrimination is determined endogenously. This would lead one quickly into the highly technical area of the economics of information. To my knowledge this has not been attempted in a public goods setting, probably because the information setting and characteristics of the resultant model would quickly swamp the public goods considerations.

We are left with the pure cases of perfect price discrimination and no price discrimination. Hopefully, these bracket reality. Whether one believes that reality lies closer to the Oakland formulation or the Thompson/Demsetz formulation is somewhat a matter of taste, at least until convincing empiricism shows one formulation to be superior. So far, sparse evidence exists favoring the price discrimination approach; meanwhile, no realistic examples of the type of equilibrium derived by Oakland have been offered.[10] Ultimately, both approaches may prove useful. Which approach will serve best in any particular setting may have to be determined on a case-by-case basis.

As positive exercises, the above approaches are clearly useful as different attempts to describe the reality of private sector public goods provision. The models, however, clearly have normative aspects as well, evidenced in the comparison of the equilibriums calculated therein with the optimum described by Samuelson's marginal conditions. It is in this normative side that a subtle problem possibly exists with the interpretation of Oakland's no–price discrimination approach. The problem is that Oakland implicitly adds a cost that is not considered by either Thompson, Demsetz, or, most important, Samuelson. The cost is an information cost that disallows the private sellers from implementing price-discriminating marketing schemes. Oakland's equilibrium yields underproduction when compared with the Samuelsonian optimum. However, one must question whether the Pareto optimum embedded in Samuelson's marginal conditions is the correct welfare standard for Oakland's setting. The following example highlights the problem. However, a full exposition of the problem lies beyond the scope of this book.

Consider the marginal equalities describing optimality in a setting that satisfies all of the usual economic assumptions except for the addition of the simplifying assumption of zero energy costs.[11] A Pareto optimum could be calculated in this setting, but no one would be surprised that the equilibrium calculated in a market with positive energy costs was not the same. Neither would anyone say that a market failure had occurred. What they would say is that a wrong or misleading Pareto standard was being applied. Oakland's formulation would seem to be subject to this same criticism with information costs replacing energy costs. The criticism would not apply directly if information costs were somehow different from energy costs in the above analogy. However, the discussion and analysis of possible distinctions between these costs will remain beyond the scope of this book.

The Thompson and Demsetz formulations are clearly not beset with this problem. Both models assume that the cost of information required for perfect price discrimination is zero and calculate equilibriums for comparison with a Pareto standard that also ignores information costs. Whether or not this is a relevant comparison to make, it is, at least, a consistent comparison. Perhaps normative policy conclusions can be drawn from such a comparison in the Thompson and Demsetz models. However, to draw normative conclusions from Oakland's formulation would be treading on thin ice.

A different, more obvious, and therefore less dangerous, problem confronts the normative analyses of Demsetz and Thompson. Although both authors make the correct comparisons, the models lack a degree of realism that would instill confidence in applying the theoretical results to the real world. One might legitimately question the application of any direct policy conclusions that are developed in a free information model to a world with positive information costs.

The above considerations make it obvious that developing any normative policy implications from such models will be a tricky business. However, the methodology of comparing the Pareto optimum with the market equilibrium does not have to be scrapped completely. For instance, in comparing Oakland's results with Demsetz's we note that Oakland derives an underproduction result while Demsetz derives optimal production. If both analyses are correct, then we attribute the difference in the results to the differences in assumptions. In particular, the main difference involves whether the informational setting allows price discrimination to exist. The positive economic conclusion would be that the absence of price discrimination would lead to lower output. We draw this positive conclusion not because Demsetz and Oakland address each other's models but because they both compare their results with the Pareto optimum. If the Pareto standard is interpreted solely as a standard against which to measure other results, with no normative conclusions, then it can be a useful benchmark in drawing positive conclusions. The following types of questions can be addressed in such a manner: Using the Pareto standard as a benchmark, does the use of price discrimination decrease or increase production relative to uniform pricing? Or, using the same benchmark, does monopoly or competition yield greater production? Or, using the same benchmark, how does the conjectural variation in a multiple firm setting affect the equilibrium production?

In later chapters, I will make use of this methodology. Equilibria will be examined for various economic environments, and the results will be compared to the usual Pareto optimum. The goal is not as much to draw normative conclusions as it is to be aware of how different assumptions affect the equilibrium.

Assumptions

I now introduce the models analyzed in the next chapter by briefly examining the basic characteristics or assumptions of those models. (These assumptions are summarized in Table 5.1.) The purpose is not the explicit development and introduction of the assumptions so that they can be called upon later in the proofs of theorems. Rather, the

Table 5.1
Characteristics of Models of Private Provision of Public Goods

Characteristic	Oakland[a]	Demsetz[b]	Thompson[c]
1. Price discrimination	no	yes	yes
2. Consumers as price takers	yes	yes	no
3. Consumers with perfect information on firms' prices	yes	yes	yes
4. Distinct and interchangeable units	yes	yes	yes
5. Identical cost curves for firms	yes	yes	yes
6. Increasing cost for firms	yes*	yes*	yes*
7. Constant cost in industry	yes*	yes*	yes*
8. Zero profit competition	yes	yes	yes
9. Contestable market	yes/no	yes	no
10. Atomistic market	yes or no	yes or no	yes

* These assumptions can be relaxed. The simplest exposition has firms with increasing cost in a constant cost industry. Each firm will produce one unit, and marginal cost equals average cost.

[a] Oakland, "Public Goods and Underproduction."

[b] Demsetz, "Private Production of Public Goods."

[c] Thompson, "Competitive Production of Collective Goods."

goal is to offer a minimum specification of the market setting in which private provision of public goods takes place.

William Oakland pioneered the analysis of competitive public good provision when sellers do not price-discriminate. The assumptions of his model are designed to mimic the standard assumptions in competitive private goods models except, of course, for differences implied by the nonrival property of public goods. The assumptions will be presented first, followed by a discussion of some differences owing to the nonrival property of public goods. Along the way points of difference between Oakland's approach and the approaches allowing price discrimination will be noted.

The first two assumptions distinguish Thompson's, Demsetz's and Oakland's models from each other.

1. Price Discrimination

The assumption is that firms cannot practice interpersonal price discrimination. In Oakland's model each firm offers its public goods on equal terms to each consumer. Some individuals may value the good more than others, but the seller cannot distinguish the consumers. Consequently, the seller charges everyone the same price. This assumption is replaced with a perfect information assumption that allows price discrimination in the treatments of Thompson and Demsetz.

2. Consumers as Price Takers

The assumption is that consumers are price takers. That is, they treat price as a parameter and react by either buying or not buying. Whether the firm sets the price or the market sets the price is a moot point to the consumers if they actually are price takers. However, there is a possible distinction in the interpretation of firm behavior depending on whether the firm or the market is setting the price. Oakland and Demsetz both treat consumers as price takers. Thompson, however, argues that consumers can influence the prices they pay and should not be assumed to take price as a parameter. This one assumption turns out to be of utmost importance.

The next six assumptions are common to all three models.

3. *Consumers with Perfect Information on Firms' Price*

The assumption is that consumers have perfect information about the pricing of each firm. This issue is treated in the same way across all the models. The issues of searching behavior and price dispersion due to incomplete information are ignored.

4. *Distinct and Interchangeable Units*

The assumption is that units of the public good are distinct and interchangeable. Distinctness allows there to be a demand for multiple units of the public good. Meanwhile, interchangeability is, in essence, analogous to the homogeneous goods assumption in private goods models. This issue is treated in the same way in all of the models.

5. *Identical Cost Curves for Firms*

The assumption is that the firm's cost curves are identical. Each firm has equal access to the production technology and the input markets. In all but a trivial sense, this does away with the possibility of price leadership by a dominant firm. This issue is treated the same in each model.

6. *Increasing Costs for Firms*

The assumption is that the firm's marginal costs are upward sloping. This can be generalized to constant cost at the expense of the ability to derive a unique (with respect to the number of firms) equilibrium. With increasing cost, we are assured of an atomistic industry structure in which each firm will produce only one unit of the public good. This issue is treated the same in each model.

7. *Constant Cost in Industry*

The assumption is that industry cost is constant. This would follow as a result of assumptions 5 and 6 except for the possibility of positive or negative, pecuniary or technological production externalities. Actually, an upward- or downward-sloped industry cost curve caused by externalities poses no particular problems, given assumptions 5 and 6; therefore, constant cost can be seen as mainly a simplifying assumption. The problem that could arise with respect to industry cost is when industry cost is decreasing because the cost of an individual firm is decreasing. This leads to natural monopoly aspects in public goods production. This possibility is, correctly, ignored in the competitive provision case.

8. Zero Profit Competition

The assumption is that competition leads to zero profits. This innocuous-sounding assumption is actually the root of much of the controversy in public goods. Although each of the models reaches a zero profit equilibrium, there are, in fact, separate paths to it. One path involves small firms, while the other involves entry or potential competition. The first path is usually called atomistic competition; the second path falls under what has recently become known as contestable markets.[12] Atomistic competition yields zero profits in the limit as the number of firms approaches infinity, whereas in a contestable market, zero profits characterize the equilibrium even with only one firm. Oakland's equilibrium is basically a complex form of a contestable market constrained by the no–price discrimination assumption.[13] The model of Demsetz is, also, basically consistent with a contestable market. Zero profits arise in the Demsetz model, regardless of the number of competitors, basically because of the threat of entry by potential competitors. Thompson's model, however, is competitive in the sense of atomistic markets. Large numbers of independently acting sellers characterize the competitive market in Thompson's model.

In light of the above discussion I break down the competition assumption into two variants.

9. Contestable Market

The assumption is that the market is contestable. This applies for Oakland, in a constrained sense, and Demsetz but not for Thompson.

10. Atomistic Market

The assumption is that the market is atomistic. This is necessary in Thompson's analysis. For Oakland and Demsetz, the market may or may not be atomistic.

The list of assumptions could just as well describe a private goods market as a public goods market. It is in tracing the implications of the assumptions that differences arise depending on whether consumption is rival or nonrival. To complete this chapter I will consider just one instance where these same assumptions lead in different directions depending on whether consumption is rival or nonrival.

For example, assumptions 3 and 4 together imply that each consumer will always attempt to purchase at the lowest available price. That is, interchangeability ensures that all units are of equal value to the consumer and the information assumption ensures that the consumer knows where the best deal is. The consumer's desire to purchase each unit consumed for the lowest possible price holds equally for public goods and for private goods. Notwithstanding this, the nonrival consumption aspect in the public goods case leads to a totally different market dynamic than in the private goods case.

The difference in what it means to purchase at the lowest price is as follows. In a private goods market with consumers competing for the rival units of consumption, not everyone will be assured of being able to purchase from the lowest priced seller. Nevertheless, consumers will try to purchase all desired units and satisfy their total demand just by multiple purchases from the lowest priced seller. In a public goods market, however, everyone will be able to buy from the lowest priced seller because of the nonrival aspect of consumption. However, no one will be able to buy this lowest priced unit more than once. Except for people who become satiated with the public good after just one unit, no consumer's total demand can be satisfied by purchases from the lowest price seller.

CHAPTER SIX

The Private Provision of Public Goods: The Models

As mentioned in the previous chapter, the issue of price discrimination provides a convenient criterion upon which to divide the received literature. Thompson and Demsetz allow price discrimination while Oakland does not.

This chapter is divided into two sections to deal separately with the price discrimination view and no price discrimination views. We will examine the Oakland model first. Within each of the sections, we distinguish between the monopolistic case and the multiple seller case. As the preceding chapter's assumptions indicate, our interest is mainly with the competitive versions, but the marginal cost of briefly presenting the monopoly versions seems lower than the potential benefit.

The Oakland Model

The Competitive Case

The equilibrium in Oakland's model can be described without a high level of formality. Let the cost of any unit of the public good be C. Let there be n individuals. Let the price of the ith unit of the public good be p_i. Let m_i, where $0 \leqq m_i \leqq n$, be the number of individuals willing to pay at least p_i for the ith unit. Contestability and the zero profit condition dictate that $p_i = C/m_i$. That is, the cost of the unit will be equally divided among the m_i customers. Since the number of consumers jointly consuming any unit can differ, the price per unit will also differ. Price will be lowest when all n consumers buy the good. The highest possible price will obtain if only one person purchases a unit. Therefore, all prices must lie between C/n and C. Since the units are interchangeable, all consumers will purchase low-priced units before high-priced units. Consequently, the price function facing an individual is an increasing step function with the height of the steps drawn from the set C/n, $C/(n - 1)$, $C/(n - 2)$, . . . , C. Note that not all the steps have to exist, and that more than one unit may be sold on any one step.

Consider Figure 6.1, which illustrates a possible equilibrium in the three-person case. D_1, D_2, and D_3 represent the demand curves of three individuals for the public good. The vertical summation of these curves is given by *gheij*. Optimal production occurs at point *e* and quantity q^*, where the summation of marginal rates of substitution equals the marginal cost of the public good. The first person's marginal rate of substitution at q^* is zero. Oakland's equilibrium occurs at q_2, falling short of the optimum. First, q_1 units are sold to each of the

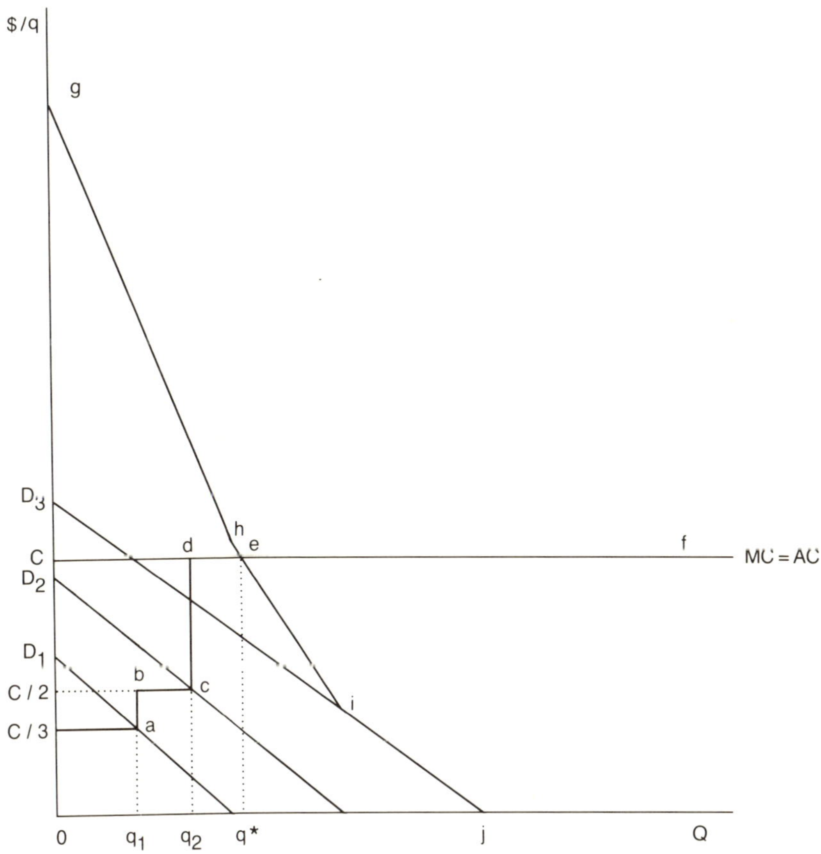

Fig. 6.1. Competitive public goods equilibrium with no price discrimination

three individuals at a price of $C/3$. Then, consumer 1 drops out and the remaining $q_2 - q_1$ units are sold only to persons 2 and 3 for a price of $C/2$ per unit. The price function is the rising step function $(C/3)abcdef$. Actually, only the first two steps are relevant in this particular case, because consumer 3 does not purchase any units at a price equal to the full cost, C.

In the language of the public goods models, consumer 1 and consumer 2 are being rationed by price. Given the market prices, these consumers are satisfied with the number of units that they can purchase. Alternatively, consumer 3 is being rationed by quantity. At the highest market price, this consumer has excess demand. If another unit were offered at a price of $C/2$, person 3 would buy it, but person 2 would not.

The firms in this market are indifferent as to whether they sell to all three individuals at the lower price or to just two of the individuals at the higher price. In either case, each firm makes zero profit. Furthermore, there is no action that an entrant can take to earn positive profits. An entrant coming in with a price below $C/3$ will sell to all three consumers but fail to cover cost. An entrant with a price between $C/3$ and $C/2$ will sell to two people but fail to cover cost. An entrant with a price above $C/2$ will sell either one or no units but still fail to cover cost. Finally an entrant with a price equal to $C/3$ or $C/2$ will cause a competition for the market, the result of which will be either failure for the entrant or exit by one of the incumbent firms. The nature of the equilibrium will remain unchanged. In this sense, then, the market is contestable. There is no possibility for hit-and-run entry by a potential competitor with uniform pricing.

Oakland draws two welfare economic conclusions from this equilibrium. Both of these are illustrated nicely in Figure 6.1. First, for the amount of the public good that is produced, some individuals may be inefficiently excluded from consuming the given production. In our example, consumer 1 misses out on consuming the last $q_2 - q_1$ units—units for which this consumer has a positive valuation. The usual argument is that since there is no extra production cost for these units, consumer 1 should be allowed to consume them. In terms of the production cost of these units, this is true. But as discussed in the previous chapter, there may be no production cost associated with allowing consumer 1 access to these units. However, there is an information cost in this model that is not being explicitly considered.

The second normative conclusion reached by Oakland is that the number of units of the public good actually produced is suboptimal. In this example, $q_2 < q^*$. Observe that at q_2 the sum of marginal rates of substitution is greater than the marginal cost of the public good. Underproduction will not necessarily result in this equilibrium. If all consumers are identical, then optimal production can ensue. Overproduction, however, can never result.

Two criticisms of this competitive model will be discussed before moving on to the monopoly case. The first criticism has to do with the stability of this equilibrium. The second, which is more important for our purposes, deals with the internal consistency of the assumptions, especially the assumption pertaining to information requirements and price discrimination.

Given the assumptions, this equilibrium apparently exists and is also apparently unique. There may, however, be some problem with regard to the stability of this equilibrium. Ekelund has claimed that such private market equilibriums for public goods are "fragile."[1] Given the no price discrimination stipulation, I argue that the equilibrium is stable but that the market-equilibrating process is much more complex than usual. Whether this added complexity makes the market process more fragile or not will be left an open question.

Given price-setting firms with no specific information about the nature of demands, how is the equilibrium described above to come about? If we suppose that the firms all know this model, then the task is simplified partly because all firms will know that in equilibrium all prices will be equal to the cost divided by some whole number between 1 and n. Profit-seeking activity, however, certainly will not ensure that prices are set equal to these possible equilibrium prices. Firms will be more likely to attempt to charge slightly higher prices, hoping to obtain a positive profit. It is up to the market contestability to ensure that only these equilibrium prices are charged. As noted above, this is fine once equilibrium is reached. Here, however, we are attempting to discuss the economic forces leading to that equilibrium.

Let us assume then, that the sellers know that these steps exist and therefore choose price aiming to contest the market and seek profits at any one of the steps. Presumably, if there are too few sellers at a step, then profits will be available to attract an entrant. If there are too many sellers, then losses and exit ensue. In this way equilibrium is reached at each of the steps. Since there are possibly as many as n

separate steps, the market process is, in this sense, n times as complex as is normally the case.

But there is a further problem. Suppose that some sellers are charging the lowest price, C/n, and selling to all n consumers. They will be breaking even. Suppose also that there is the equilibrium number of sellers at all of the other price steps. If the number of sellers charging C/n is the wrong number, it will throw off the equilibrium at all of the higher steps as well.

Consider the simple three-person example from above. Suppose there are $q_2 - q_1$ sellers charging $C/2$, which is exactly the equilibrium amount. Now suppose there are $q_1 + 1$ sellers charging $C/3$, that is, one seller too many. One of these lower priced sellers will only sell to persons 2 and 3 and will make a loss. Until this seller exits, however, one of the sellers charging $C/2$ will lose a customer and, therefore, will also be sustaining a loss. The problem exists at the $C/3$ step but will also affect the profitability of the sellers at every higher step.

That the market-equilibrating process is actually as many as n separate processes was noted above. Now an additional consideration becomes important. The n processes are undertaken sequentially rather than simultaneously. Establishment of equilibrium for each higher step must first await the completion of the market process at each lower step.

The incentives do exist to bring about this equilibrium, but depending on your view of the market process, these stability properties may seem rather weak. If you view the equilibrating process as instantaneous, then an n-step process taking n times as long is nothing particularly worrisome. The equilibrium is stable in this technical sense. However, if you view the market process as taking real time and costly effort, then certainly the market forces bringing about the Oakland equilibrium do not act as swiftly as is usually considered to be the case in other settings.

The second problem with this equilibrium is the no price discrimination assumption. This criticism seems to go outside the bounds of the Oakland model, which, motivated by the possible lack of information about consumer demands, explicitly examines only the uniform pricing case. The criticism of assumptions is not outside the bounds of the model, however, if the assumptions of the model are internally inconsistent. This may well be the case, because the equilibrium does, in fact, reveal enough information for price discrimination to be practiced. It is true that firms may not have enough information to practice price discrimination right at the start. However, since certain information is revealed in what Oakland calls the equilibrium perhaps it is impossible to logically maintain the lack of information assumption and the no price discrimination result that follows directly from it.

Consider once again the simple three-person model from above. Suppose we are in equilibrium. The market reveals which consumers purchase which units. Consequently, we know something about individual demands. While the equilibrium is impervious to entry by a uniform price firm, a price-discriminating firm could enter and earn positive profits as follows. If a firm were to produce one unit of the public good and sell it to both consumer 2 and consumer 3 for a price slightly below $C/2$, meanwhile offering it to consumer 1 for a price slightly below $C/3$, then this seller would sell the good to all of the consumers and earn a positive profit. It would be the first purchase of consumer 1 and it would be purchase number $q_1 + 1$ for consumer 2 and consumer 3. It now appears that Oakland's equilibrium is not an equilibrium in the contestable market sense, at least not when multiple price strategies are allowed.

The information needed by the entrant seems to be readily available, embedded in what we were calling the equilibrium. The number of units consumed by each individual and the prices paid for those units are observable data in the equilibrium. A discriminatory pricing scheme such as the one posed above might be most easily put in place by one of the sellers with a price of $C/2$. This seller will know automatically to whom to give the lowest price—it will be to the person not currently buying from that firm. Perhaps this is exactly what is going on when newspapers, for example, offer reduced rate subscriptions to new subscribers who have not been subscribers in the last three months.

Basically, the same type of interpersonal discrimination also will work to expand production beyond q_2. An entrant who raises the price to consumer 3 and lowers the price to consumer 2 will be able to expand production, profitably, beyond q_2. Persons 2 and 3 will be hard to distinguish on the basis of observable behavior in equilibrium since they both buy all the units offered at $C/2$. They will, however, be distinguishable in the market process approaching the equilibrium. How does the market reach this point? Since demands are unobservable before the fact, the market will not automatically stop at q_2. I presume that the market will have to overshoot this equilibrium to know when to stop. Some firm will have to offer the public good for a price of $C/2$ and then only sell it to person 3. This will provide the information that person 3 is being rationed by quantity and person 2 is being rationed by price. Although this will not be common information, someone will know, between person 2 and person 3, for whom to cut the price.[2]

The actions of these entrants will force losses on some of the existing firms, who will either be forced to exit or to copy the discriminating pricing themselves. For example, in our simple model one of the sellers charging $C/3$ will lose a sale formerly made to individual 1, who buys instead from the price-discriminating firm. The firm that loses the sale will either exit or lower the price to person 1 to keep the sale while raising price to persons 2 and 3 to make up the lost revenue. The latter course has the promise of profits and will most likely be chosen.

The profits obtained by these sellers will also attract copycat behavior. The outcome of this competition will preserve the interpersonal discrimination but lower the overall prices until zero profits are reached.

What will be the outcome of this market-information–revealing process? I believe that the ultimate result is the development, one iteration at a time, of perfectly discriminating prices. We shall see below how the equilibrium derived in Demsetz's model passes the test of contestability even when the hit-and-run entrants are allowed to use all available information and any pricing function. Interpreting the market behavior described above as the first step in the iteration, we can see that this first step is in the right direction. The prices to persons 1 and 2 go down while the price to person 3 goes up. These are the directions of change that would be expected in the movement from the Oakland equilibrium to the Demsetz equilibrium.

One objection should be made with respect to the above scenario. The objection concerns strategic behavior on the part of the consumers. Once the firms are seen to be using market-generated data in their future pricing decisions, the individuals have a strategic incentive to give false signals. Two comments are worthwhile. First, it is always the case, even when only uniform pricing is allowed, that information about consumer behavior is revealed in the market process and may be used to help determine future decisions. Therefore, strategic behavior might exist anyway. This reflects back on the difficulty in reaching the Oakland equilibrium in the first place. Second, even if the Oakland equilibrium could be reached without strategic behavior, the expectation that firms will use the information embedded in the equilibrium to price-discriminate means that the Oakland equilibrium itself will not come about. The iterations toward perfectly discriminating prices might be thrown off, but this does not mean that the Oakland equilibrium will result. Neither the Oakland nor the Demsetz equilibria will result. It is precisely this recognition of active behavior on the part of consumers that colors the results of Thompson's model.

To summarize briefly, the Oakland equilibrium no longer seems to be an equilibrium. It is a constrained equilibrium where the constraint is the forcing of uniform pricing. While this constraint seems reasonable at the outset of the market process, the movement to equilibrium actually reveals the information needed to price-discriminate. If the firms are allowed to act on this information, then entry by price-discriminating firms will alter the characteristics of the equilibrium developed by Oakland. The resulting characteristics of an equilibrium with price-discriminating firms are discussed below.

The Monopoly Case

Several offshoots of Oakland's competitive model have been offered for the monopoly case.[3] Interestingly, the monopoly case for the Oakland model is more complex than the competitive case. For the price-discriminating models reviewed below, this order of difficulty is reversed. The main supposition behind the monopoly versions of the Oakland model is that the seller cannot distinguish individuals from one another. As a consequence of this, any pricing function that will be offered must be offered identically to each person. There will be no interpersonal price discrimination; however, intrapersonal discrimination in various forms of nonlinear or quantity dependent pricing schemes is addressed. Brennan and Walsh address only the uniform pricing case. Brito and Oakland discuss both the uniform case and the nonlinear pricing case, using optimal control theory to derive properties of the best nonlinear pricing scheme. Meanwhile, Burns and Walsh analyze uniform pricing, all-or-none pricing, two-part pricing, and, what turns out to be the best, multipart pricing.[4]

Many interesting results come out of these models. Brennan and

Walsh even develop the possibility that an increase in marginal cost could lead to a decrease in the uniform price. In general, prices will be higher than in the competitive case. This leads to two conclusions. First, the inframarginal consumers, who were being rationed by price, generally consume less since prices are higher. Second, the individual with the highest demand, who was being rationed by quantity, not by price, may or may not consume less of the public good. This last result depends crucially on the income effects that are caused by nonlinear pricing.

A full-blown treatment of these results would serve only to reiterate the literature,. This is not the purpose here. If, however, we abstract from some of the complicating factors like income effects and intersecting demand curves, then the flavor of these results can be obtained from the analysis of multipart pricing in our simple, three-person case. The analysis will be kept on the diagrammatic level. After the presentation of the model, another discussion of the introduction of interpersonal price discrimination will be appropriate.

Multipart pricing is actually the easiest case to consider. With uniform pricing, whenever price is lowered in order to increase the quantity sold, revenue is lost on the inframarginal units. This must be taken into account. Alternatively, with multipart pricing there is never the need to consider lost revenue on previous units in the above sense. This means in some cases that the optimal pricing scheme can be determined one unit at a time. I present such a case below. It will become apparent why the general treatment is more complicated. A necessary condition for the simplest treatment is nonintersecting (except possibly at the vertical axis) individual demand curves. A sufficient condition, in addition to the above necessary condition, is that each individual demand curve be (weakly) steeper than all higher individual demand curves.

The goal in the simplest case is to earn the most revenue from each unit produced. This revenue will depend on the price for which the unit sells and the number of consumers who purchase it. Consider the first unit. If all n consumers buy it, then the revenue is n times the price. The highest price for which all n consumers would buy the unit is given by the height of the demand curve of the lowest demand individual. However, it is possible that higher revenue results from selling to only $n - 1$ consumers at a higher price. The price in this case is equal to the demand price of the second lowest demand individual.

The sharing group for the first unit could also be $n - 2$ consumers, $n - 3$ consumers, and so on. The possibility yielding the highest revenue will be chosen. The same calculations are made for each unit with the stipulation that once consumers are dropped from the sharing group, they may not be reinstated.

Consider Figure 6.2. These are the same three demands from the earlier competitive case. The relevant marginal revenue curve for this example is *nodpj*. This curve is the upper envelope of three different curves: (1) three times the demand of person 1; (2) two times the demand of person 2; and (3) one times the demand of person 3. The

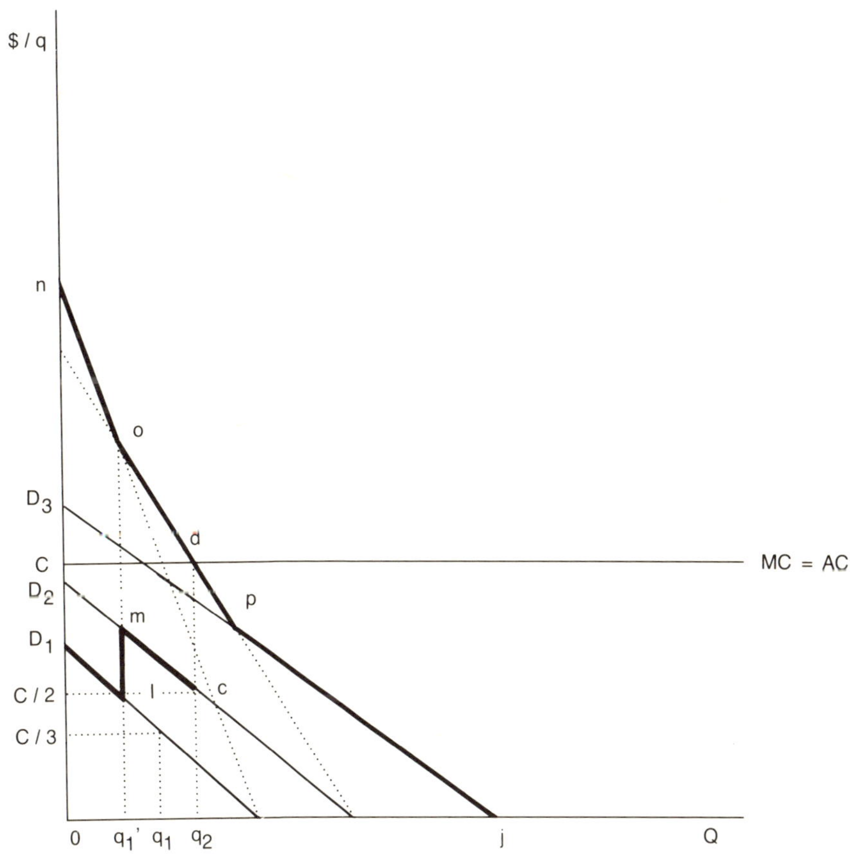

Fig. 6.2. Monopoly public goods equilibrium with no interpersonal price discrimination

profit-maximizing quantity is q_2, which is the same as in the competitive case. The multipart price schedule is given by D_1lmc. Along D_1l all three consumers are buying the good, while along *mc* only consumers 2 and 3 purchase at these prices. Overall output is the same as in the competitive case, q_2, but person 1 buys fewer units in the monopoly case, $q_1' < q_1$. In this sense, the authors claim that monopoly provision is even less efficient than the competitive case.

Two factors complicate this simplest exposition. First, income effects will alter the position of these demand curves from the competitive case. Actually, the analysis should be carried out with utility functions and indifference curves. This is precisely what Brito and Oakland do. Second, the upper envelope of the curves formed by multiplying the number in the sharing group times the lowest demand in that sharing group is technically only the upper limit on the marginal revenue curve, which in some instances may be lower. The problem is that once consumers are dropped from the sharing group, they cannot be reinstated. Suppose, for example, that the highest revenue for the first unit comes from sales to persons 2 and 3 at a price given by the height of person 2's demand curve. It is possible in this case that the highest revenue for the second unit (i.e., the point on the upper envelope) comes from sales to all three persons at a price equal to the demand price of the lowest demand individual. The seller cannot get both of these revenues. If the lowest demand person does not buy the first unit because the price was too high, he cannot later turn around and buy the second unit. The seller's choice in this case cannot be made on a unit-by-unit basis. The seller must essentially choose between the revenue gained by selling both the first and second unit to all three persons at prices given by person 1 and the revenue of the first two units from selling to only persons 2 and 3 at prices given by the demand of person 2. This is precisely the problem addressed by Burns and Walsh, using what they call the "demand distribution."

These authors all explicitly ignore the possibility of interpersonal price discrimination. But, as above for the competitive case, this pricing function does reveal who the low-demand and high-demand people are. The monopolist would be expected to act on this. For example, with the pricing scheme given by D_1lmc in the above example, consumer 1 stops consuming at q_1'. The seller could earn more profit by tailoring a special offer that would allow person 1 to consume more at lower prices while keeping the higher prices for persons 2 and 3.

The problem of not knowing which consumer is which is solved because the answer is revealed by the pricing scheme. Following up on this possibility leads to the monopoly models with price discrimination. These are discussed by Demsetz and Thompson. If the consumers act strategically to alter the implications that the monopolist draws from their revealed purchases, then the equilibria described in these models will still not come about.

There is one possibility in which these logistic problems and issues of price discrimination disappear. Suppose that pricing, production, and consumption were all one-shot deals that would not be repeated. Any information that is revealed in the equilibrium will be of no value because no second chance will be offered to either the seller or the consumers. Will the pricing scheme described above come about? It will only under the following unusual informational setting. The seller must know exactly the n demand curves of the n individuals but must be completely ignorant as to which consumer has which demand. The seller would then develop one multipart price schedule to be applied equally for all individuals. The assumption that the seller knows the exact distribution of demand without any individual particulars is awkward at best. Realistically, both types of information become available only through the market process, and the seller would not have one without the other. The extreme information conditions under which the results of these models are valid severely limit the potential application of these models. In defense of these models, however, they seem useful if they are correctly interpreted only as purely theoretical studies of the effect of a ban on interpersonal price discrimination while allowing perfect intrapersonal price discrimination.

Models with Interpersonal Price Discrimination

The Monopoly Case

This section deals with the models that allow price discrimination. Two basic models are of interest: the Demsetz model, which yields optimal production, and the Thompson model, which yields optimal production for monopoly and overproduction in the competitive case.[5]

For models with price discrimination, the monopoly case is easier to discuss and less controversial than the competitive case. Therefore, the monopoly case will be handled first. The scenario where the seller knows the demands of all the individuals is the simplest. The issue of whether this information is assumed to be freely available or revealed in the market process is addressed below. Remember, however, that the original development of these models was formally carried out only for the perfect information case.

The marginal revenue of the seller is precisely the vertical summation of the individual demand curves. The seller produces until marginal revenue equals marginal cost. This gives the Pareto optimal output as indicated by q^* in Figure 6.3. This marginal revenue is made up of different price schedules that are offered to each individual, each price schedule essentially tracing the consumer's demand or marginal valuation schedule.

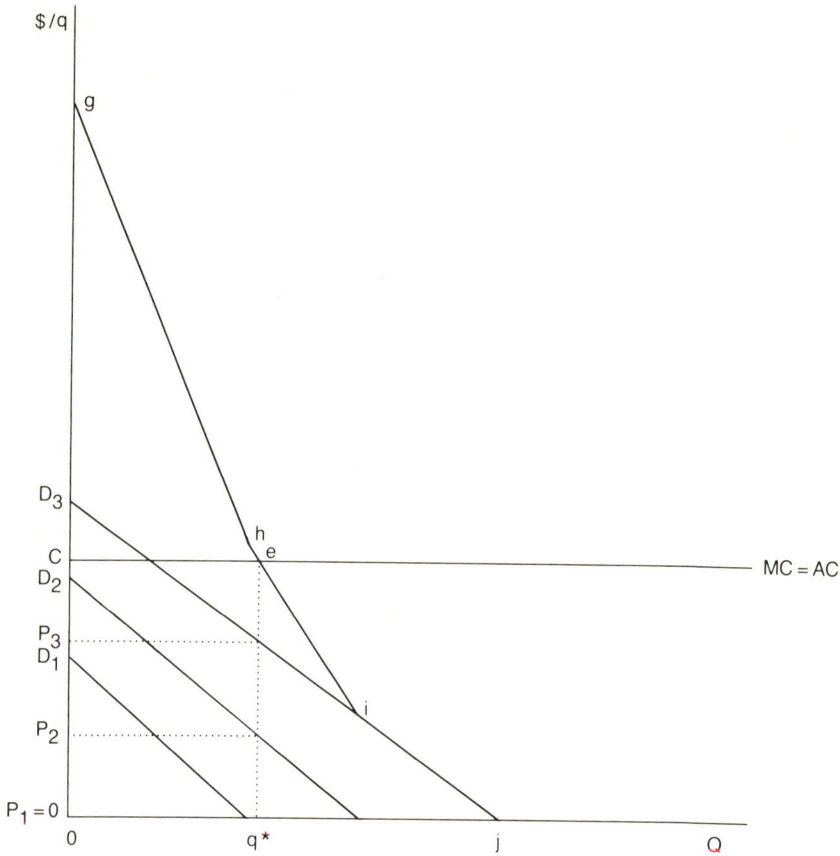

Fig. 6.3. Monopoly public goods equilibrium with perfect price discrimination

Actually, the monopolist need not know the whole demand schedule of each individual, only the height or marginal rate of substitution at the equilibrium quantity. In this scenario, a different uniform price for each buyer, equal to the buyer's marginal rate of substitution, will yield the same equilibrium production level. This price for the *i*th consumer is denoted P_i for (i = 1,2,3) in Figure 6.3. However, since the seller does not know what the equilibrium quantity is, information on the marginal rate of substitution in equilibrium may be tantamount to knowing the whole demand schedule of each individual. Therefore, this information requirement may not be any less stringent than the complete knowledge case. In any case, the monopolist seller would be expected to try to earn even more revenue by raising the inframarginal prices to each consumer.

In either of the above scenarios the optimality result comes about because, on the margin, price is equal to marginal rate of substitution for each individual and summed prices equal marginal cost.

In the case where the seller does not have this complete information, a different view will be required. One view is that a market process will reveal information about demands that will be used in refining the discriminatory price schedules. After possibly a series of refinements, the monopolist homes in on the perfectly discriminating prices. This view is hampered by the possibility of strategic action on the part of the buyers. The influence of this strategic action has not been extensively treated in voluntary, private provision models. Alternatively, in public sector monopoly provision models (the difference being the ability to forcibly collect taxes in the public sector) this issue has been analyzed. Some tentative conclusions in this literature indicate that the demand revelation problem can be solved.[6] Whether these results apply in a voluntary model is beyond the scope of this book.

In the models being discussed here, this strategic problem is either ignored or assumed to be solved nicely. The strategic behavior basically comes about because the seller is in a bilateral bargaining position with each buyer. In bilateral bargaining problems, the nice solution has buyers and sellers negotiating until they eventually find a way to jointly capture any gains from trade that can possibly be exploited. In the monopoly case addressed here, there are unexploited gains to be captured as long as production is less than q^*. The only way of capturing these gains all the way to the margin is to implement discriminatory (at the margin) pricing schemes. The sellers and buyers must, in a sense, reveal their marginal costs and marginal valuations in order for all the possible gains from trade to be exploited. It is in this sense that the second scenario above, the one where the seller knows exactly only the marginal valuations at the optimum, is relevant.

In this last case, the split of the inframarginal gains is generally indeterminate. The easiest case to consider is where the seller captures all the gains—that is, the perfect discrimination approach. This is the approach that is usually taken. The alternative case, where the buyer captures all the gains, is still indeterminate until more specification is added. For instance, which buyer captures all the gains? There are many joint purchasers of each unit. If one buyer only is to capture all the gains, then the seller must make zero profit and, in addition, all other buyers must be perfectly discriminated against, receiving no consumer surplus. This one buyer actually looks more like a perfectly discriminating seller who contracts production out to a zero profit producer. Looked at this way, this case is virtually the same as the case where the seller captures all the gains. Another possible interpretation of the buyer capturing all the gains has a zero profit producer while a cooperative collective of buyers splits the gains according to some predetermined rule.[7] The n-person, single-seller, noncooperative public goods game where all players are trying to capture the inframarginal gains has not been addressed in the past and will not be addressed in this book.

To summarize the monopoly model, let me reiterate the informational settings in which optimal production results from the discriminatory pricing schemes put in place by the seller. The first setting is where the seller knows the demand of each individual. This is the setting in which any formal analysis to speak of takes place in these models. Also, this will be the setting examined in the following discussion of the competitive case. The second setting is where the seller knows only the marginal valuations of the consumers. The third setting is where the market process reveals the information about individual demands without any strategic behavior by the consumer. The last setting is where any strategic bilateral bargaining problems are efficiently solved, usually in favor of the seller, in order to capture all possible gains.

The first setting is extreme, to be sure, but it does allow for the pure theory of monopoly and competitive public goods production. The second setting is possibly interesting not because the seller starts out with such information, but because the market process gives incentives for all to reveal their valuations at the margin in order to exploit all gains from trade. The third setting probably crosses a line into the area of irrational behavior on the part of the consumers. The fourth setting essentially assumes the strategic problem away.

The Competitive Case

Given that the sellers know or can find out the demand curves of all the consumers and, therefore, can price discriminate, we have finally arrived at the most salient issue. What does a competitive market with price discrimination look like? Demsetz and Thompson offer two divergent viewpoints, while Borcherding criticizes them both and offers a third.[8] The models diverge essentially because the meaning and application of competition is handled differently by each of the authors. The main interest of this section lies with the discussion of Demsetz and Thompson. These treatments will be followed by a brief presentation of Borcherding's argument.

There are two main differences between the treatments of Demsetz and Thompson that are indicated in Table 5.1. The first is that consumers are price takers in Demsetz's model but not in Thompson's. The second is related to the first. For Demsetz, competition most clearly aligns with what today is called contestability, whereas for Thompson, competition is in the independent behavior, atomistic sense. These differences are of minor consequence to the conclusions reached in private goods models, but in the public good context they lead to radically different conclusions.

I will first address the Demsetz optimality result. As Demsetz describes the equilibrium, each seller will set possibly different prices for each individual equal to the individual's marginal rate of substitution at the optimum quantity. These prices are just like the marginal prices in the monopoly case (see Figure 6.3). Consumers, acting as price takers, can do no better than to consume out to the optimal quantity, that is, to consume as long as their willingness to pay is above the price. The firms can do no better either. Since the sum of the prices just equals marginal cost, each firm earns zero profit. Any attempt to lower anyone's price will lead to a shortfall in revenue, while any attempt to raise anyone's price will lead to a loss of the customer because a potential entrant, charging prices equal to the marginal valuations, will take over the market. This scenario comes as close to saying "the market sets the price" as possible without actually saying it. Each firm actually does set price but is disciplined by the potential entrant, and the consumers react to these prices by setting quantity.

Apparently, this equilibrium exists and is unique. Given the contestability of the market and the price taking by the consumers, there is nothing that either firms, entrants, or consumers can do to enhance their position. The stability issues are more subtle but for the most part have been dealt with already. Supposing we were not at this equilibrium, what forces would exist? If a quantity greater than q^* were produced and if prices summed to marginal cost, then we would have excess supply. To relieve the excess supply, the sum of the prices required to induce consumers to buy a quantity greater than q^* would have to fall below marginal cost. But losses would be made in this case and exit would lower the quantity toward the optimum level. If production were less than q^*, then a profitable opportunity would exist for a firm to enter with discriminating prices slightly higher than the equilibrium prices. If production were equal to q^*, an entrant would earn exactly zero profits with prices exactly equal to the equilibrium prices. If perfect information is assumed, then finding these discriminating prices is no problem. Even if we do not have perfect information, some information may be revealed in the market process. In a free-entry market the most successful firms will be the ones that can best use this information and establish prices that are closest to being perfectly discriminatory.

As discussed above for the Oakland equilibrium, this information problem may lead to strategic behavior on the part of the consumers. If so, we can on longer maintain the price-taking behavior assumption. If consumers by their actions can influence the prices charged, they are not price takers. In this light, the Demsetz equilibrium is flawed like the Oakland equilibrium. Both models derive an equilibrium which, given the assumptions of their respective treatments, exists, is stable, and is unique. The problem is that each approach contains a possible internal inconsistency. For Oakland, it is the lack-of-information assumption, which is falsified by the equilibrium. For Demsetz, it is the price-taking assumption, which, given the public good, nonrival nature of consumption, saddles the consumer with an irrational behavior trait.

The inappropriateness of the price-taking assumption is the meat of Borcherding's criticism and the most important distinguishing feature of Thompson's original treatment. For Thompson, the nonrival nature of consumption puts each consumer in a position of monopsony with respect to each seller. That is, since consumption is nonrival, each person is in the position of being the single buyer of each unit produced. Each seller and buyer are in a small-numbers, bilateral bargaining game where price is jointly determined; neither buyer nor seller should be considered a price taker. Only in the closed-market monopoly case in which the seller unilaterally commits to a pricing scheme can the buyer be considered a price taker. This is precisely the case in Thompson's monopoly version, with the seller committing to perfectly discriminating prices and with optimal production as the result. In an open market, competitive situation, however, the consumer will not be a price taker.

Several important implications follow from the realization that the consumer is not a price taker. The first is that we now need a solution to the bilateral bargaining game that has developed. Thompson assumes that the seller will get all of the gains from trade. There are some arguments to support this. In a competitive market the best firms will be the ones to survive. In any given situation the firm that is better in bargaining with the consumer will be more profitable. Competition may be expected to weed out the firms that always give up the benefit in the bilateral bargaining, leaving the firms that drive the hardest bargains. On the margin, of course, all the benefit of exchange is squeezed out so both firms and consumers will simultaneously be giving up and getting all of the benefit. In the process toward equilibrium, however, the sellers that capture the gains will be the survivors, the ones that other firms try to emulate.

A second implication of the fact that consumers are not price takers involves the notion of competition that underlies the analysis. In particular, the market cannot be said to be contestable in the usual sense. There is free entry and free exit in Thompson's model, but contestability also requires a predetermined price policy by incumbents that entrants can potentially undercut with hit-and-run entry. This type of pricing necessitates price-taking behavior by individuals. Indeed, the timing of price setting and quantity setting in a contestable market must be the following. First, incumbents set price. Second, entrants can undercut that price if they want to. Third, consumers act to set quantity, taking all prices as given. Therefore, contestability requires price-taking consumers, and although Thompson's market has free entry, it is not a contestable market.

If the market is not contestable, then in what sense is it a competitive market? The answer is that it is competitive in the traditional, atomistic sense. Each firm is small relative to the market and ignores its influence on the quantity of all the other firms. In private goods markets this is essentially the Cournot model, which approaches the competitive ideal as the number of firms approaches infinity. This is the traditional meaning of competition in the "large numbers of independent actors" sense. This is the notion employed by Thompson. Note the difference between this idea and Demsetz's notion of competition. Thompson's model clearly requires large numbers to be called competitive. Demsetz's does not. In Demsetz's approach the same output obtains whether there are many sellers, two sellers, or even just one seller.[9] There are hints at this difference even in the titles of the two relevant papers. Demsetz calls his model "The Private Production . . ." while Thompson's is "The Perfectly Competitive Production. . . ."

The third and most important implication of the fact that consumers are not price takers is that the consumer's marginal valuation schedule, or marginal willingness-to-pay schedule, lies above the standard demand curve that traces out the marginal rates of substitution. When acting along this higher schedule, the market will oversupply the public good. The reason for the overvaluation is really quite simple. A person who consumes a unit of the public good in Thompson's setting gets benefits of two kinds. The first is the usual benefit of consuming the good. This is given by the consumer's marginal rate of substitution. The second benefit is the pecuniary effect of receiving lower prices from the other sellers offering imperfect substitutes. This pecuniary effect will be internalized into the demand price for the unit, thus raising that demand price over the marginal rate of substitution.

Let us examine this pecuniary effect more closely. The buyer has a downward-sloped demand for the public good—the more he consumes, the lower his marginal rate of substitution and demand price. Since the seller always wins the bilateral bargaining, the buyer will always pay his demand price. By planning to consume more units, the demand price falls, and the prices collectable by all other producers fall. This lowering of prices constitutes the pecuniary benefit. The consumer still gets the other units but at prices lower than would otherwise be the case. This benefit is incorporated into the demand for the marginal unit, thus raising the demand price above the marginal rate of substitution. Since all sellers are in the same position, this effect happens in the bargaining with each supplier. Indeed, each seller is the marginal seller and can collect the value of the pecuniary effect along with the marginal rate of substitution.

Notice that although Thompson has recognized each buyer's monopsony position, he is using the implication of monopsony in an unfamiliar way. Ordinarily, a monopsonist forces a lower price by consuming *less*, essentially pushing the seller back down the upward-sloped supply curve. However, if the seller uses perfectly discriminating prices, the way to get a lower price is to consume *more*, essentially moving down the demand curve. In either case, of course, the primary goal is not to get a lower price but to maximize profit or utility. The importance of the monopsony issue is simply that the buyer recognize his influence, whatever it may be, on price.

The effective demand curve of the individual turns out to be the average valuation schedule, which is above the marginal rate of substitution schedule. This makes sense. The consumer will end up paying prices equal to these average valuations, therefore earning no surplus. The possible potential surplus for any quantity of the good is always captured by the sellers. All the sellers are the same, so each one is able to price at exactly the average valuation. If the sum of these average valuations taken over all consumers is greater than the marginal cost of the public good, then the resulting profits will attract entry. The competitive equilibrium occurs when the summation of average valuations is equal to the marginal cost of the public good. Since the sum of the average valuations is greater than the sum of the marginal rates of substitution, this is an overproduction of the public good when compared to the Pareto optimum.

The same three-person case from the preceding sections is examined in Figure 6.4. The demand curves are again labeled D_i. The associated average valuation curves are the dashed curves labeled A_i. These curves are linear as long as the demand curves are linear. Their peculiar shapes are due to the kink that occurs when the demand curve

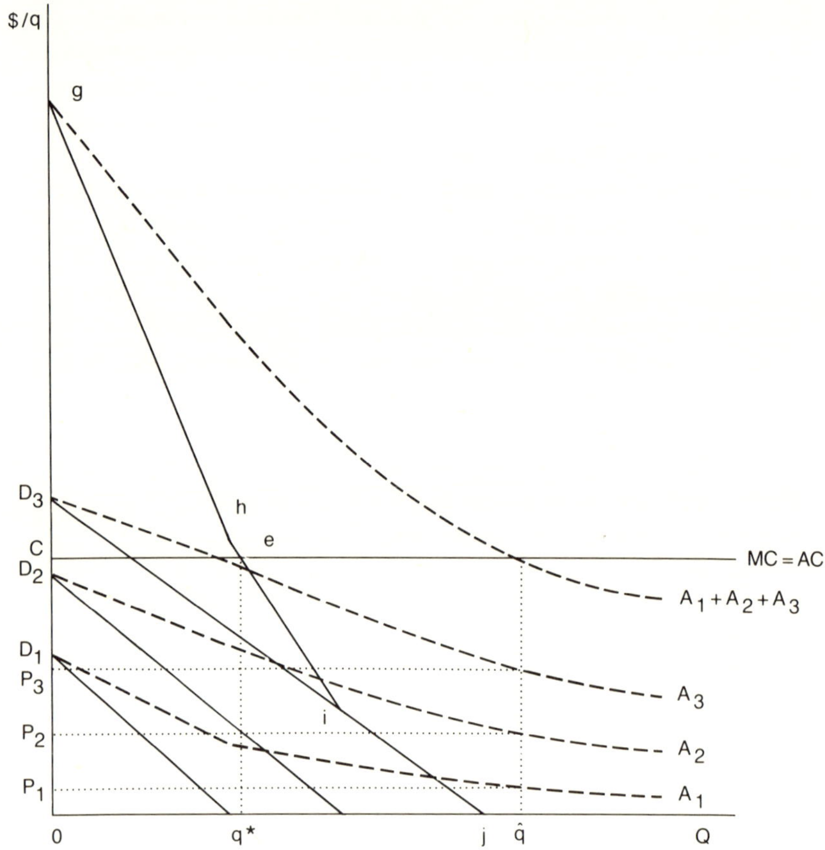

Fig. 6.4. Competitive public goods equilibrium with perfect price discrimination

hits the horizontal axis. The vertical summation of the demand curves is by now familiar. Optimal production occurs at q^*. Equilibrium production occurs at $\hat{q}$, the intersection of marginal cost and the dashed vertical summation of the A_i. The relevant individual prices are given by P_i.

It is tempting to think that this is not an equilibrium. Why would a consumer press consumption out past the demand curve as indicated by the A_i curves? A price-taking consumer would not, but that is not what we are dealing with here. This overproduction actually is a unique, stable equilibrium. If consumers wanted to consume lower amounts, their marginal willingness to pay would rise and the prices consumers would have to pay would rise. Consumers would not gain any consumer surplus by this action. Neither is there anything that a firm can do to increase profits. Increasing prices would drive away customers and lead to a loss. Decreasing prices would lead to a shortfall in revenue and a loss. Making commitments to these prices to try to thwart any pecuniary effect still just leads to zero profits. The equilibrium thus passes the test of an equilibrium, which is that there is no independent action that can be taken by any of the players to improve their individual situations.

The equilibrium also has good stability properties. On the one hand, if production is above $\hat{q}$, losses are made and firms exit. On the other hand, summed prices higher than marginal cost obviously attract entry if production is below the equilibrium.

The equilibrium is actually derived only for the perfect information case. However, Thompson does hint that similar mechanisms would operate in the case of imperfect information. The description of firm and consumer behavior remains essentially the same. However, the firm will not be able to capture all of the benefit. The consequence of imperfect discrimination is that the A_i curves will be lower than as pictured in Figure 6.4. The amount of the marginal rate of substitution that the seller will capture will be less than 100 percent. Consequently, the pecuniary effect may also be smaller, since when expanding their purchases, consumers may not be lowering the prices charged by competitors by the full amount of the decrease in the marginal rate of substitution. The A_i curves may even fall below the D_i curves. In this case the equilibrium would no longer evidence an overproduction.

Thompson concludes that with perfect information the competitive result is an overproduction of public goods. With less than perfect information and less than perfect price discrimination, production may be more or less than the Pareto optimum. According to Thompson, "realistic knowledge" leads to "approximate optimality." By this Thompson actually means that the model clearly indicates neither overproduction nor underproduction; there are forces acting in each direction. There is no across-the-board government policy that can be applied to nudge the market toward Pareto optimality. This is a curious type of laissez-faire result. The market may fail, but since we do not know in which direction, we can not formulate an effective policy. This result, however, seems susceptible to the criticism raised in the preceding chapter about comparing an equilibrium derived in a setting with positive information costs with an optimum derived in a zero information cost setting.

Borcherding claims that optimal production ensues in the setting with multiple public goods producers and consumers. We have noted above that Borcherding finds fault with Demsetz over the price-taking assumption. But Borcherding also claims that the Thompson equilibrium is not really an equilibrium. There may be no action that an individual consumer or firm could take to better its own position, but collusive or cooperative behavior might upset this equilibrium. Given that joint surplus is not being maximized at the Thompson equilibrium, most economists would expect that there would be some action, possibly joint, that could be taken to improve the welfare of the players involved. This situation is no exception. There is certainly the incentive for sellers to cartelize, restrict entry, and move toward the monopoly solution. There are also incentives for consumers and producers to collude to restrict entry, write efficient contracts, and split the surplus involved. From Borcherding's point of view, as long as the joint surplus is not being maximized there must be some other voluntary arrangements that could bring about a superior situation.

Thompson's reply to this critique convincingly notes that the types of contracts that Borcherding calls for are collusive and not competitive.[10] The *competitive* overproduction theorem still holds. But we are caused to question whether the competitive equilibrium will actually be an equilibrium. Indeed, doesn't the market process automatically generate forces toward the kind of complex contracts discussed by Borcherding? Won't these contracts eventually lead to the optimum?

It seems we have a problem with the Thompson model similar to the one we had with Oakland's and Demsetz's. Given the conditions of the model, an equilibrium is calculated. But do the conditions make sense? In Oakland's model it is nice to know that the lack of information needed for price discrimination will lead to underproduction. But, given the workings of the model, is the lack of information a maintainable assumption? In Demsetz's model it is nice to know that contestable markets with price-discriminating firms and price-taking consumers lead to optimality. But is the assumption of price-taking behavior consistent with individual consumer rationality? Finally, in Thompson's model it is nice to know that perfect competition and perfect price discrimination lead to overproduction. But is it really an equilibrium in the face of complex contracting or cartelization efforts?

Part of the problem is that the nature of pricing and competition in public goods models is a relatively new theoretical construct. Until the bugs are worked out, a variety of approaches will be taken to address different parts of the problem. The various approaches will not always be reconcilable. The whole question of the interaction of price discrimination and price-taking behavior in public goods models is a case in point. Another part of the problem is that real-world examples of pure public goods that could be used to inform the model builders are relatively rare.

The approach presented in the rest of the book combats both of these problems. By moving from a pure public goods format to a mixed goods format, many examples of how the market deals with public goods problems will become evident. These examples serve to guide our intuition in the model-building stage as well as to indicate that private production of public goods is an important concern, one not to be dismissed. In addition, the meaning of price discrimination and price-taking behavior will become clearer because these issues will be highlighted in more familiar situations. In the general mixed goods case to be developed below, the full impact of the public goods problem is not compromised by the mixed goods setting. All the familiar aspects of public goods still exist. However, an added dimension is addressed which allows the pricing, exclusion, and interaction among firms to be examined on familiar turf. The added dimension has the flavor of private goods. It is called the utilization dimension.

CHAPTER SEVEN

The Utilization Dimension

As the previous two chapters have shown, the received literature on the private provision of excludable public goods has not reached a consensus on the nature of the pricing in those settings. Neither has it reached a consensus on the nature of the equilibrium nor on the nature of the market process. At least part of the problem lies in the unfamiliar area being explored in this literature. Price discrimination is combined with competition, and both issues are examined simultaneously in a public goods framework. Part of the problem may also lie in the different conceptions of what constitutes a public good and in the different heuristic examples that support those conceptions. Different examples of public goods will bring to mind different types of pricing that might be relevant in those examples, thus hampering the integration of the divergent viewpoints.

The goal of this chapter is to generalize the pure public goods models discussed above to capture the mixed goods case. The generalization highlights specific, specialized assumptions, which are often hidden, thereby helping to unify the existing views. The generalization views the mixed goods case as a two-dimensional consumption problem—the public goods dimension and what I call the utilization dimension. As it turns out, the analysis of the utilization dimension is similar to that in a private goods model. Part of the analysis, then, takes place on familiar turf. Consequently, the analysis of the pricing and competition in the utilization dimension is facilitated. The two-dimensional nature of the problem is crucial, as we shall see. In fact, several of the received treatments of public goods and mixed goods are confusing precisely because explicit recognition of each dimension is lacking.

In the latter parts of this chapter, I introduce the basis for the formal analysis by developing the relationship between the public goods dimension and the utilization dimension. The formal analysis will then be continued in chapters 8 through 10.

Two Dimensions of Consumption

The point of departure, then, is the recognition of two distinct quantity dimensions. Consider, for example, bridges and parks, used as heuristic examples in public goods models. For the bridge, the quantity could be measured as the number of bridges, the number of lanes, or the number of crossings. For the park, we could measure the number of visits made to the park, the number of parks, the size of a park, the amount of time a park is open, or, in general, a quantification of any quality associated with the product, parks. There are two distinct categories into which all the above quantity measures fall.

One category contains all those quantity dimensions which define the actual good that all consumers receive. For example, suppose we were considering the public good, parks. If we measure the quantity of parks in acres, then all consumers consume, or at least have access to, the same number of acres of parks. If we measure the quantity in hours of operation, then all consumers have access to the park for the same number of hours. Perhaps different parts of the park maintain different hours of operation. If so, the amount of parks could be measured with the interactive acre-hours. Still, all customers, simultaneously, have access to the same good. The distinguishing feature of these kinds of measures is nonrivalry. Stated formally, because of the nonrival consumption aspect, this type of quantity measure of parks enters simultaneously into each individual's utility function. A good with such a dimensional measurement is usually thought of as a public good, and I will call such a dimension the public goods dimension.

The other category contains those dimensions in which the quantity may be different across individuals and over which those individuals have control. For example, individuals control the number of visits they make to the park, and each individual could have a different number. An individual's consumption of the park could also be measured by the amount of time the person spends in the park, or by the number of acres that the person actually uses, perhaps by walking through them or maybe just by visibly being surrounded by parkland. I shall call such a dimension of consumption the utilization dimension.

The public good dimension and the utilization dimension can be distinguished, although sometimes not so easily, in all of the usual examples of public goods. For parks and bridges we get a clear separation of the two dimensions. The public good dimension refers to the nonrival characteristics of the good that all people consume, while the utilization dimension refers to each individual's use of those characteristics. For highways the distinction is similar. The extent and quality of the network of highways is the public goods dimension and is the same for all users. Meanwhile, each individual's utilization of the highways may be different. But what about other traditional examples—national defense, the lighthouse, and television signals? Can the public goods dimension be separated from the utilization dimension in these examples?

For national defense, the public goods dimension is clear. The public goods dimension counts up how many tanks, how many jets, and so on. The utilization dimension is less clear; in fact, most of the time it is ignored. How much national defense does each person consume? The answer is usually thought of as, "all of it." Or, how often does an individual consume national defense? "All the time," is the usual reply. In such cases, the quantification of the consumption in the utilization dimension turns out to be the same for each individual. Since it is the same for each individual, it is either thought of as a public good dimension or ignored altogether.

But we could think of utilization of national defense as different for each individual. Iowans consume different amounts of Coast Guard services than Californians do, while international travelers do not consume national defense all the time. This may seem like a definitional splitting of hairs, but I believe it is more. Because our taxing institutions do not distinguish between Coast Guard services supplied to Californians and those supplied to Iowans and thus do not tax Californians more, the different utilization measures are ignored. The same goes for the difference between travelers and nontravelers in days in residence. However, if Coast Guard services were supplied on a fee-for-service basis, or if taxes were collected for national defense in proportion to the number of days a taxpayer was in the country, or if there were any marginal, or incremental, cost attributable to different individuals' different levels of utilization, then the different utilization measures should naturally be addressed.

The point here is to beware of simplifications that are sometimes made in the utilization dimension. Sometimes ignoring the utilization dimension is the natural way to analyze a public good. A slight change in institutions, however, may necessitate concentration on the utilization dimension. As in the above example, if Coast Guard services are supplied to all, automatically, with no charge, then there is no reason to highlight differences between the utilization levels of Californians and Iowans. If, however, user fees are charged for these services, then it becomes natural to highlight the differences in utilization.

Furthermore, in the case where it is natural to ignore the individual's utilization, care should be taken if the good is to be used as a prototypical example of a public good. Careless analogizing from the national defense example to other public goods could allow an unwanted hidden restriction on the utilization dimension to creep into the analysis. That is, as commonly construed, the national defense example does not distinguish among the different utilization levels of different individuals. All these levels are assumed to be equal. But this is certainly not necessarily the case.

The same point can be made from another direction. The consideration of a perhaps trivial utilization dimension in the national defense example may seem like an unnecessary complication of the analysis. Such a complication, however, is not without benefit. The benefit is in providing uniformity between the simple example and more complex examples where different utilization measures are important.

Consider the case of the lighthouse. The public good dimension could be thought of in various ways. The amount of the public good could be measured as the number of lighthouses, the strength of the light beam, or the number of hours of operation. A natural utilization dimension to consider is the number of times a person or a shipping firm passes the lighthouse while relying on its beam.[1] Obviously, this number could be different for each consumer. However, this dimension often is ignored. If the light is always on anyway, then there is no extra cost associated with another ship passing the lighthouse. In this case, there may be no reason to keep track of the utilization dimension, that is, no reason to count the number of passings. However, the simple change of allowing the light to be turned on or off depending on whether a ship is coming now means that costs of operation will depend on the number of passings and that the utilization dimension will capture an important economic variable.

In some cases it may be impossible or too costly to monitor the number of passings. In these cases, the utilization dimension reduces to a zero/one variable based on whether or not a shipping firm uses the lighthouse at all. This is so in the textbook example, where the lighthouse is always on the free-riding is possible while exclusion of nonpayers is not. Consequently, under these special conditions, individual utilization of the lighthouse is ignored. As soon as the cost of monitoring individual passes falls to an economic level, however, a sophisticated utilization measure will be appropriate. When monitoring and exclusion are possible, or if costs vary or pricing occurs in the utilization dimension, then the individual's utilization of the public good is an important economic variable.

Finally, consider the much discussed case of television signals.[2] The public good dimension is usually thought of as the number of programs broadcast. The shows, of course, must be distinct and interchangeable in order to be counted up on the same quantity axis. Alternatively, the public good dimension could be thought of as the quality of any one program. Meanwhile, the utilization dimension is ignored because of the implicit assumption that each show is watched, that is, utilized, once by each individual. This need not be the case. With today's technology, television signals can be taped for later viewing or repeated viewing of the same material. An individual may view a particular signal once, not at all, or multiple times. Currently, technology does not allow the producer to monitor and charge for repeated viewing of the same signal. In the future, however, this opportunity may be available and each individual's utilization of the material will become economically interesting.

Pure and Impure Goods

Armed with various examples of public goods and the associated dimensions of consumption, it is possible to review the distinction between public goods and private goods and between pure public goods and mixed goods. The usual taxonomy views mixed goods as being somehow intermediate to the polar cases of pure public goods and pure private goods. As Chapter 4 has shown, the precise nature of the continuum along which mixed goods lie between public goods and private goods has not been sufficiently pinned down. It is one thing to have a mental picture something like Figure 7.1. It is another thing to explicitly state what the axis in Figure 7.1 measures. To say the axis measures "degree of publicness" just begs the question. The attempt private good — mixed goods — public good

Fig. 7.1. Standard continuum of private, public, and mixed goods

here to pin down the nature of mixed goods involves the two-dimensional nature of consumption. I will first present the public goods/mixed goods/private goods taxonomy that is implied by the separation of the public goods dimension from the utilization dimension. With this viewpoint, we will be able to critically review several of the earlier attempts to describe the exact nature of the continuum along which public, private, and mixed goods lie. While Chapter 4 did comprehensively describe the many existing paradigms of mixed goods, this chapter, in light of the two-dimensional nature of consumption, will focus on criticizing, in depth, some of the more familiar formulations.

Given the two-dimensional nature of consumption, there are actually two economic problems in public good production: how much of the public good to produce in the public goods dimension, and how much to produce in the utilization dimension. In concrete terms, the problems translate into how many acres of parkland to build and how many visits to the park to provide for.

We may define the pure public good as a good for which only the public goods dimension is important. In the case of the pure public good somehow the utilization dimension disappears. Therefore, the only interesting question is how much of the public good to produce. Optimality is described by the familiar condition that sets the summation of marginal rates of substitution equal to the marginal cost of production.

Most of the original examples of public goods which came to be known as pure public goods do indeed have uninteresting utilization dimensions. As discussed above, for national defense each individual's utilization of the public good is "all of it," while each individual's utilization of the television signal is "one." Since, by construction, these measures cannot vary, there are no welfare economic considerations that apply to them. In fact, there are no considerations at all that apply to them because they are fixed from outside the model. Any marginal equalities or total conditions that might exist in the utilization dimension are irrelevant.

There is, however, at least a hinting at another dimension of consumption. Careful treatments do note that no individual should be excluded from the benefits of the amount of the public good that is produced. This introduces the possibility that the individual's utilization of the public good could vary, even if the choice is only of a zero/one, all-or-nothing nature. The welfare economics of the utilization dimension are reduced to an all-or-none decision, that is, a total decision as opposed to a marginal decision. Indeed, individuals either consume all of the public good or none of it. Optimality requires that individuals be allowed to consume all of it if they so desire, that is, that there be no exclusion.

There is a utilization dimension here, but there are no relevant marginal equalities because there is no marginal decision. There is, however, a total decision which is automatically satisfied as long as there is no exclusion. Therefore, once the no-exclusion proviso is mentioned, the utilization dimension is ignored and all attention rests on the public goods dimension.

If the marginal equalities were presented, as they will be below, they would indicate that optimality in the utilization dimension occurs when each individual's marginal rate of substitution in the utilization dimension is set equal to the marginal cost in the utilization dimension. This is identical to the condition that would exist for private goods. The marginal cost of utilization for the pure public good is given to be zero. Therefore, the consumer must be allowed to utilize the public good as long as positive benefits derive from such utilization. This, of course, will be the case if there is no exclusion. In the examples from above, however, this marginal condition is often obscured because of the all-or-none nature of the utilization decision. Actually, the optimum would be better described in incremental fashion. The consumer's incremental rate of substitution is a step function with a positive value at one and a zero value for utilization greater than one. Setting the marginal rate of substitution equal to zero translates to consuming as long as the incremental rate of substitution remains positive.

The special nature of the individual's utilization of national defense obscures the existence of marginal equalities that could exist in the utilization dimension if consumption in that dimension could be measured continuously. Although hidden for national defense, these marginal equalities can be brought out for the case of the lighthouse. Suppose for example, that the lighthouse is always on, with the marginal cost of a ship's passing and utilizing the light beam therefore being zero. Each ship may utilize the lighthouse over and over again. Optimal utilization would occur when the marginal rate of substitution in the utilization dimension equals zero. Here, utilization is not a simple zero or one variable, and, excepting an insistence that passings by the lighthouse be measured discretely, the standard calculus applies. This dimension, however, is usually ignored by assuming that there is no cost of utilization and no exclusion. Since consumers will automatically satisfy the marginal condition if there is no exclusion, attention rests only on the public good dimension.

Perhaps the case of the lighthouse should not qualify as a pure public good. It is true that as long as there is no cost in the utilization dimension, there is no economic production question in that dimension. There is, however, an economic distribution question revolving around exclusion. Once the no-exclusion proviso is assumed, the distribution question is automatically solved optimally. It is understandable that the utilization dimension might be explicitly ignored in this case once the zero utilization cost and absence of exclusion have been established. It is unfortunate, however, that the dimension has been implicitly ignored. The private good characteristics of the utilization dimension are well understood and could fruitfully be used to distinguish utilization from the public goods dimension. And most important for the purposes here, the utilization dimension supplies the link to the mixed goods case.

To recapitulate, the pure public goods case arises when, by definition, consumption in the utilization dimension is held constant. Since there is no possible decision to be made in this dimension, it can be ignored. National defense is, perhaps, the best example of this case. Besides national defense, there are other cases in which the utilization dimension is ignored. An example is the lighthouse that is always on, so there is no cost in the utilization dimension, with the added assumption of no exclusion. There is a utilization dimension in this example, but the welfare economic decisions in this dimension will always be made optimally. Because the only interesting questions are in the public good dimension, sometimes the lighthouse is also thought of as a pure public good.

In contrast to the pure public good, which ignores considerations in the utilization dimension, is the pure private good, which analyzes only the utilization dimension. This is what happens in the standard treatment of economies with only private goods. Indeed, the analysis of the pure private good case implicitly drops the economic consideration of the public goods dimension. Each individual's consumption (or utilization) of each private good is an interesting variable, but the characteristics of each good are set from outside the model and assumed to be immutable. Each person's utilization of each good may be different. Meanwhile, the characteristics of each good are public in that, for each good, all consumers consume the same quality. However, unless the model is one of product quality determination or spatial competition, the characteristics of the different private goods that are produced are held constant and no economic analysis applies. There are no summations of marginal rates of substitutions in private goods models because there are no possible changes in what would be public good dimensions.

Clearly, the pure private goods models and the pure public goods models lack a certain dimensionality. In each of these polar models one of the possible dimensions of consumption is ignored in order to focus attention on the other dimension. This is an admirable type of partial equilibrium analysis that allows concentration on the dimension at hand. However, it should be apparent that the general model is a mixed goods model, one in which both dimensions of consumption are important.

Recall once more the example of the park. The park could be analyzed as a pure public good, a pure private good, or a mixed good depending on what assumptions are made about the public goods dimension and the utilization dimension. For example, to analyze the park as a pure public good, we would assume that each individual utilizes the park exactly once. Thus, utilization is taken as a given and the pure public good question would be how big to make the park. Alternatively, analysis of the park as a private good would start by assuming that the park was a given acreage. With the public good dimension taken as given, the private good question would concern how to distribute visits to the park. Meanwhile, the mixed goods analysis of the park would take neither visits nor acreage as given but would try to determine both the optimal size and utilization of the park.

The mixed goods case is not so much "between" public goods and private goods as it is a rich mixture of the two separate dimensions of consumption that are used in standard models of pure public goods and private goods. Schematically, therefore, it takes two dimensions to characterize the relationship. Consider Figure 7.2. The horizontal axis measures a public good dimension, denoted *Y*. The vertical axis measures a utilization dimension, denoted Σy_i, where y_i is the *i*th individual's utilization of the good. A pure public good analysis implicitly holds Σy_i constant and only examines horizontal movements in the quadrant. A pure private good analysis holds *Y* constant and only examines vertical movements, both in the sense of Σy_i and also in the individual components of the summation, the y_i's themselves. A mixed goods analysis must consider both horizontal and vertical movements.

With this understanding of mixed goods, we can review some of the existing formulations of mixed goods. The literature on mixed goods has at times recognized a difference between individual consumption and the public good dimension but has not gone far enough. James Buchanan, for example, sought to distinguish the "production" of the public good from the "consumption" of the public good.[3] His example of the firehouse location showed that the public good that was produced, the firehouse of a particular size at a particular location, did not supply identical firefighting services to citizens located at different distances from the firehouse. The consumption measure was possibly different for each individual and different from the production measure. Nevertheless, when consumption is measured in production units, each individual gets the same good and the original pure public goods models apply. Buchanan develops the distinction mainly to draw the analogy from joint supply to public goods—the steer being like the firehouse—with different individuals consuming different goods, the beef and hides, much as the different citizens consume different

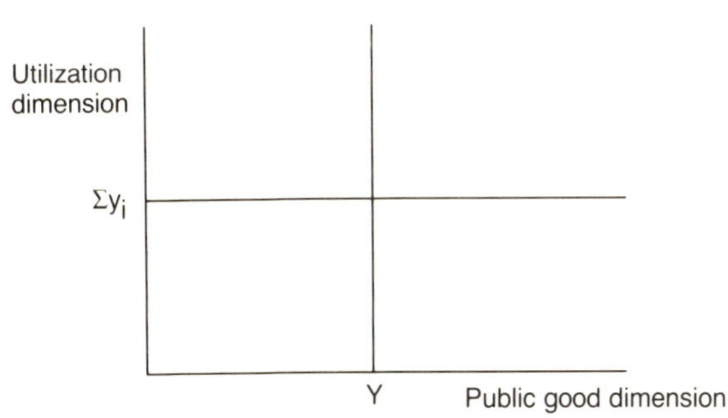

Fig. 7.2. Two-dimensional characterization of private, public, and mixed goods

amounts of firefighting services. Buchanan also uses the distinction to separate public goods that emerge via production indivisibilities from public goods that arise from consumption externalities.

Buchanan's attempts come close to the approach taken here but stop short of a complete analysis. In a general analysis, each separate dimension of production or consumption will have an associated marginal condition describing optimality. For Buchanan's example of the "location" of the firehouse and the consumption of firefighting services by two individuals, three equations are formally necessary. One equation must describe the location of the firehouse, and one equation each, for the two individuals, must describe the individuals' consumption levels of the firehouse. Buchanan, however, only supplies two equations. For the pure private good case, his two conditions work to describe the equality of each individual's marginal rate of substitution with the associated marginal cost. For the pure public good case, the two individuals' different utilization measures are ignored and the two conditions collapse into one which describes the optimal equality of the summation of marginal rates of substitution with marginal cost. For the mixed goods case, Buchanan realizes that there is another subsidiary condition that must be satisfied in addition to the two that are listed. Nevertheless, Buchanan stops short of formalizing this extra condition.[4]

Buchanan's failure to increase the scope of his formal analysis is unfortunate for two reasons. The less important reason is that the analysis was not pushed to its logical completion. This is quite understandable given that Buchanan was primarily interested in pure public goods rather than mixed goods and in institutions and public choice rather than mathematical theory. The more important reason is that Buchanan winds up obscuring the distinction that he laboriously draws with his verbal analysis. By allowing the same conditions, interpreted differently, to describe both the pure public good case and the pure private good case, the difference between what he calls production and consumption is masked rather than highlighted. When talking of individual i's marginal rate of substitution for the public good, Buchanan is left with only one equation, which must do double duty. Interpreted one way, we get the marginal rate of substitution in the public goods dimension; interpreted another way, we get the marginal rate of substitution in the utilization dimension. For pure cases we can flip back and forth, but for mixed goods we need separate marginal rates of substitution, one for each dimension of consumption. Certain types of errors and misinterpretations could have been avoided and other implicit simplifications would have been noted if the two dimensions were explicitly made distinct.

The most common type of mistake involves the possibility that price discrimination, by mixed goods sellers with the ability to exclude, leads to different marginal rates of substitution for different consumers. For private goods, of course, different marginal rates of substitution are evidence of nonoptimal distribution of the good. The same is true in the utilization dimension. In the public goods dimension, however, there is no necessity of equality between marginal rates of substitution, just an equality of the summed marginal rates of substitution with the marginal cost. The confusion arises if the two different marginal rates of substitution are not separated; if they are not, then the phrase "marginal rate of substitution" will have multiple, ambiguous meanings.[5]

The two-dimensional nature of mixed goods is also obscured in some of the mixed goods models that rely on pollution costs, congestion costs, or other types of externalities.[6] Suppose that y_i measures the *i*th person's utilization of some good and that additionally, Σy_i enters into each individual's utility function. Such would be the case, for example, if there were some externality associated with the consumption of good y. Since Σy_i enters identically into all utility functions, it can be viewed as a public good (or congestion cost or public bad in the case of a negative externality). There are two questions of consumption for individuals: how one's own consumption, y_i, is to be valued; and how one values the total consumption, Σy_i. Because of the nature of the example, however, one of the dimensions is finessed away. That is, both measures of consumption fall on the same quantity axis, and in certain situations, optimality in each individual's utilization can imply optimality in the public goods dimension as well. The public goods dimension and the utilization dimension get squeezed into the same dimension. In general, the two dimensions will not be measurable along the same axis. Explicit recognition of each dimension will be required.

When this explicit recognition is not made, the above approach leads to the conclusion that the public goods case is a subset of the economics of externalities, a kind of limit case of extreme positive externality.[7] Actually, the relationship is the other way around. Models of externalities are actually subsets of public goods or mixed goods models that contain a special arrangement whereby the public goods dimension and the utilization dimension can be combined.

The same problem is inherent in models that liken a pure or congestible public good to a capacity choice model.[8] There is a public good dimension, Y, and a separate utilization dimension, y_i. But in this variation, again, the two dimensions are forced to be compatible by adding the restriction: y_i is less than or equal to Y. Obviously, such a restriction is meaningless if Y and y_i are measured in different dimensions. Therefore, adding the restriction forces utilization and capacity to be measured in the same dimension. When the restriction is added, one set of marginal conditions applies when $y_i < Y$ and a different set applies when $y_i = Y$. But there is only one marginal rate of substitution doing double duty, once for the utilization question and once for the optimal capacity choice/public good dimension. Again, this is a simplification of the general case in which utilization and public good amounts require different axes.

An example will illustrate this point. Consider an entertainment park with Y distinct and interchangeable rides or attractions that make up Y units in the public goods dimension. If we add the assumption that each attraction will be utilized a maximum of one time by each consumer and if we consider separately pricing each attraction, then we are basically in the setting analyzed by Brito and Oakland and Brennan and Walsh.[9] Some people will be excluded from some units of the public good, and the demands of only those customers that attend all of the attractions will be considered in the decision to add another ride. What falls out of this analysis is a standard capacity choice model, where utilization and capacity are measurable in the same dimension. Alternatively, if we allow multiple visits to the park as a whole, y_i for the ith person, with one admission charge covering all attractions, then each time someone utilizes the park, that person gets to consume all Y attractions, all Y units of the public good. However, the person can still be excluded in the utilization dimension. To measure the ith person's utilization, y_i, or to discuss the exclusion question with respect to the ith person's utilization requires a different axis than that on which Y is measured.

Formal Analysis

The two dimensions of consumption must be conceptually kept separate, but they are related, as the following formal analysis shows. Let the *i*th person's utility function include: the public good dimension, Y; the person's utilization of the public good, y_i; and a private good numeraire, x_i. Therefore:

(7.1) $U^i = U^i(x_i, y_i, Y)$

Equation (7.1) is too general, however, in that there is nothing to specifically link the y_i to the Y for each consumer. The utility to the *i*th consumer is really a function of consumption of the private good and some composite function of the utilization of the public good. To highlight this we could write utility as:

(7.2) $U^i = U^i[x_i, g^i(y_i, Y)]$

With or without this change, there are a couple of properties that can be imposed on the utility function. The first property is that the marginal utility of the public good, $\partial U^i/\partial Y = U^i_Y$, equals zero when the person does not utilize it. That is, we will ignore any "option demand"[10] so that:

(7.3) $U^i_Y = U^i_{g^i} g^i_Y = 0$

when $y_i = 0$. Similarly, the marginal utility of utilization, $U^i_{y_i}$, equals zero if there is no public good to utilize. So

(7.3′) $U^i_{y_i} = 0$

when $Y = 0$. More will be said about the specification of the utility function in a later chapter upon the introduction of multiple public goods producers.

We can develop the model further by combining (7.1) or (7.2) with a nicely shaped transformation function:

(7.4) $F(\Sigma x_i, \Sigma y_i, Y) = 0$

where the summations are over all individuals, *i*. Maximizing the utility of each individual while holding the utility level of the others constant leads to the usual conditions:

(7.5) $$\left.\frac{-dx_i}{dy_i}\right|_{U^i} = \left.\frac{-dx_j}{dy_j}\right|_{U^j} = \left.\frac{-d\Sigma x_i}{d\Sigma y_i}\right|_F$$

for all *i*, *j*,

$$(7.6)\quad \Sigma \frac{-dx_i}{dY}\bigg|_{U^i} = \frac{-d\Sigma x_i}{dY}\bigg|_F$$

These expressions state, of course, that the marginal rates of substitution in the utilization dimension are equal across individuals and equal to the marginal cost and that the sum of the marginal rates of substitution in the public goods dimension is equal to the marginal cost of the public good.[11]

Using equation (7.1) as the utility function, equations (7.5) and (7.6) are open to the same interpretation as the original pure public good case of Samuelson. That is, Y is the pure public good and y is some unrelated private good. However, through equations (7.2) and (7.3) y is linked to Y. To highlight how the utilization dimension and the public good dimension are related, we can decompose the marginal rate of substitution in the public goods dimension and the marginal cost in the public goods dimension. First, for the marginal cost in the public goods dimension (the right-hand side of equation [7.6]), note that the right-hand side of (7.6) is evaluated for a fixed value of Σy_i, denoted, Σy_i^o. Thus,

$$(7.7)\quad \begin{aligned} \frac{-d\Sigma x_i}{dY}\bigg|_{F,\Sigma y_i^o} &= \frac{-d\Sigma x_i}{dY}\bigg|_{F,\Sigma y_i^o} + \frac{d\Sigma x_i}{dY}\bigg|_{F,\Sigma y_i = 0} - \frac{d\Sigma x_i}{dY}\bigg|_{F,\Sigma y_i = 0} \\ &= \frac{-d}{dY}\left(\Sigma x_i\bigg|_{F,\Sigma y_i^o} - \Sigma x_i\bigg|_{F,\Sigma y_i = 0}\right) - \frac{d\Sigma x_i}{dY}\bigg|_{F,\Sigma y_i = 0} \end{aligned}$$

where the second equality follows, since differentiation is a linear operation. The term inside the parentheses is the evaluation of the definite integral of the marginal cost in the utilization dimension for values of utilization from zero to Σy_i^o. Thus, equation (7.6) becomes:

$$(7.6')\quad \begin{aligned} \Sigma \frac{-dx_i}{dY}\bigg|_{U^i} &= \frac{-d\Sigma x_i}{dY}\bigg|_{F,\Sigma y_i^o} \\ &= \frac{-d}{dY}\int_0^{\Sigma y_i^o} \frac{d\Sigma x_i}{d\Sigma y_i}\bigg|_F d\Sigma y_i - \frac{d\Sigma x_i}{dY}\bigg|_{F,\Sigma y_i = 0} \end{aligned}$$

Essentially, the latter equality in (7.6′) says that a function can be expressed as the integral of its derivative plus a constant of integration that depends on a boundary condition. Equation (7.6′) illustrates that the marginal cost in the public goods dimension has two components. The last term of (7.6′) represents the marginal cost of the public good even before any utilization units are produced. This is analogous to the change in an overhead or fixed cost of supplying the utilization units of the marginally improved good, Y. The integral represents the variable cost of supplying Σy_i^o units of utilization of the public good, Y, and this variable cost may be altered by the change in the public good quantity. That is, the increase in the public goods dimension may increase (or decrease) the marginal cost in the utilization dimension, and if it does, the calculation of the marginal cost of Y when $\Sigma y_i^o = 0$ will not be the only cost.

This type of decomposition can always be made, even for unrelated goods. For example, consider the marginal cost of A when production of good B is B'. The marginal cost of A is the sum of the marginal cost of A when B equals zero and the change in the integral of marginal cost of B as B varies from 0 to B'. For unrelated goods, the change in the integral is zero, so the marginal cost of A is the same whether B equals B' or zero. In our case, however, the decomposition is interesting because the change in the public good quantity will often have an effect on the marginal cost of producing the utilization units of the public good.

The decomposition is even more interesting for the marginal rate of substitution. We can decompose the marginal rate of substitution in the public goods dimension in the same way that marginal cost can be decomposed. This will show how the marginal rate of substitution in the utilization dimension differs from, but is related to, the marginal rate of substitution in the public goods dimension. Consider one person's marginal rate of substitution for the public good, that is, one of the terms in the summation on the left-hand side of equation (7.6). This marginal rate of substitution is evaluated along a given utility surface, $U^i[x_i, g^i(y_i, Y)] = U^{io}$, and for a given level of utilization, $y_i = y_i^o$. Therefore, following the same steps as above for marginal cost we get:

$$(7.8)\qquad \left.\frac{-dx_i}{dY}\right|_{U^{io},y_i^o} = \left.\frac{-dx_i}{dY}\right|_{U^{io},y_i^o} + \left.\frac{dx_i}{dY}\right|_{U^{io},y_i=0} - \left.\frac{dx_i}{dY}\right|_{U^{io},y_i=0}$$
$$-\frac{d}{dY}\int_0^{y_i^o} \left.\frac{dx_i}{dy_i}\right|_{U^{io}} dy_i - \left.\frac{dx_i}{dY}\right|_{U^{io},y_i=0}$$

The interpretation of the consumption of the public good involves the individual utilization, y_i, of it. Therefore, by equation (7.3), the last term in the individual's marginal rate of substitution for the public good in equation (7.8) drops out. Thus,

$$(7.8') \quad \left.\frac{-dx_i}{dY}\right|_{U^{io},y_i^o} = \frac{-d}{dY}\int_0^{y_i^o} \left.\frac{dx_i}{dy_i}\right|_{U^{io}} dy_i$$

and only the integral term is left on the right-hand side. The integral of the marginal rates of substitution for utilization over values of zero to y_i^o is the total value placed on the utilization of the public good. Equation (7.8′) indicates that an individual's marginal rate of substitution for the public good is equal to the change in the total value placed on the utilization of the public good. This relationship can be illustrated diagrammatically. Figure 7.3 illustrates two projections (one for $Y = Y^o$, and one for $Y = Y^o + \Delta Y$) of the indifference surface defined by $U^i[x_i, g^i(y_i, Y)] = U^{io}$ into the x_i, y_i plane. Both indifference curves intersect the vertical, x_i, axis at the same point, A, illustrating the condition (7.3) that no benefits are gained from the enhanced public good without its utilization. The distance BA is the total value, measured in units of x, of y_i^o units of utilization of the public good, Y^o. Similarly, CA is the total value of y_i^o units of utilization of the improved public good, $Y^o + \Delta Y$. Thus, CB is the difference in value of y_i^o units of utilization of the public good due to the change in the amount of the public good from Y^o to $Y^o + \Delta Y$. This distance, CB, is also the value, measured in units of x, of the increment, ΔY, of the public good when starting at Y^o and y_i^o, as was proven in equation (7.8′).

This marginal rate of substitution for the public good which was calculated and illustrated above is just one consumer's valuation of the public good. There will be an equation such as (7.8′) for each con-

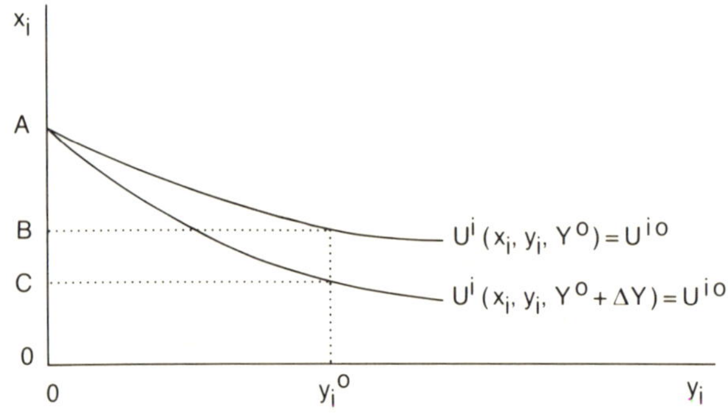

Fig. 7.3. Indifference curves illustrating the value of an increase in the public goods dimension

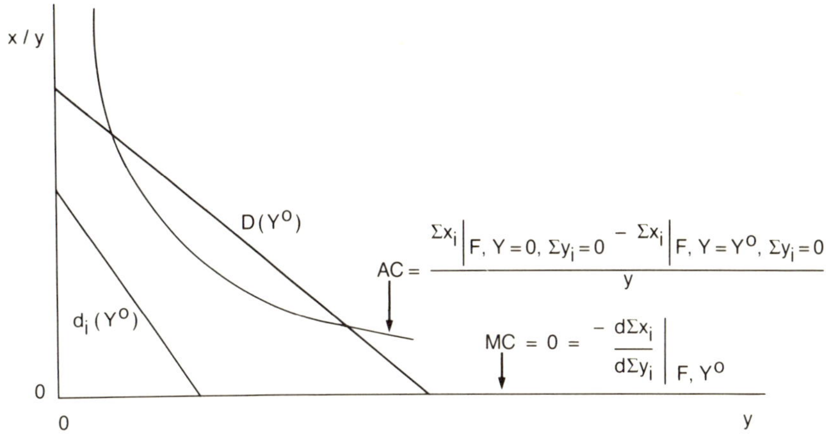

Fig. 7.4. The utilization dimension for a given amount of public good

sumer, and the condition describing optimality can again be rewritten by combining (7.8′) and (7.6′) to yield:

$$(7.6'') \quad -\Sigma \frac{d}{dY}\int_0^{y_i^o} \left.\frac{dx_i}{dy}\right|_{U^{io}} dy_i = \frac{-d}{dY}\int_0^{\Sigma y_i^o} \left.\frac{d\Sigma x_i}{d\Sigma y_i}\right|_F d\Sigma y_i - \left.\frac{d\Sigma x_i}{dY}\right|_{F,\Sigma Y_i = 0}$$

Another, slightly different, diagrammatic analysis can be presented as an approximation in a consumer surplus framework.[12] This is because equation (7.6″) states the marginal equality that characterizes the optimum in the public goods dimension in terms of the marginal rate of substitution, marginal cost, and overhead cost in the utilization dimension. Consider Figure 7.4. Demand curve $d_i(Y^o)$ is an individual's demand for utilization of a given amount, Y^o, of the public good. Demand curve $D(Y^o)$ is the *horizontal* summation of all $d_i(Y^o)$. For the pure public good case of Samuelson, the marginal cost curve for utilization is coincident with the horizontal axis. Optimal utilization by the individual and in the aggregate occurs where $d_i(Y^o)$ and $D(Y^o)$ intersect the horizontal axis. If each individual were to utilize the public good until no more benefits could be obtained from an additional unit of utilization, then condition (7.5) would be satisfied. An average cost curve added to this picture will be declining throughout. Now, it is evident that for this given amount, Y^o, of the public good, the supplier's position in the utilization dimension is analogous to that of the supplier facing decreasing average costs.[13] That is, marginal cost pricing will not yield enough revenue for the good to be privately produced. So marginal cost pricing will not persist in the utilization dimension without some sort of subsidy. Simple monopoly pricing may or may not yield enough revenue; indeed, sometimes discriminatory pricing schemes are necessary to make revenue cover costs. And monopoly and discriminatory schemes may lead to other departures from optimality.

The pure public good case with zero marginal cost of utilization can now be seen as a special case of a more general phenomenon which may involve a resource cost of utilization. As long as the marginal cost of utilization is below the average cost, so that average cost of utilization is downward sloping, the utilization dimension depicts the natural monopoly or decreasing cost situation described above. But, in general, the marginal cost of utilization may be rising. If the marginal cost curve rises steeply enough, marginal cost pricing will yield optimal utilization (condition [7.5]) as well as positive profits. That is, private, competitive firms will produce the public good and supply the utilization units of it without subsidies or price discrimination. Furthermore, for the amount of the public good they produce, they will supply the optimal amount of utilization.

As an aside, note that this conclusion is reached in a slightly different form in the models of congested public goods. In the present model, the cost in the utilization dimension is a resource cost which the supplier must cover. In the models of congestion the cost is an external disutility to other users of the crowded public good. In the models of congestion, prices equal to the marginal crowding costs will fund the production of the public good when those crowding costs are sufficiently high (that is, when the average social cost of utilization is no longer downward sloping). It must be emphasized that in the present, general model this optimality result for the utilization dimension is a conditional result depending on the amount of the public good that is produced. In the models of congestion where utilization and the public good are measured on the same axis, optimal utilization can also imply optimal public good production at the same time. In the present model, optimal utilization (7.5) is only half the story.

Indeed, the public good problem does not stop with the optimal pricing and allocation questions in the utilization dimension. There is still the problem of how much of the public good to produce. Consider Figure 7.5 which, like Figure 7.3, illustrates condition (7.8′). Remem-

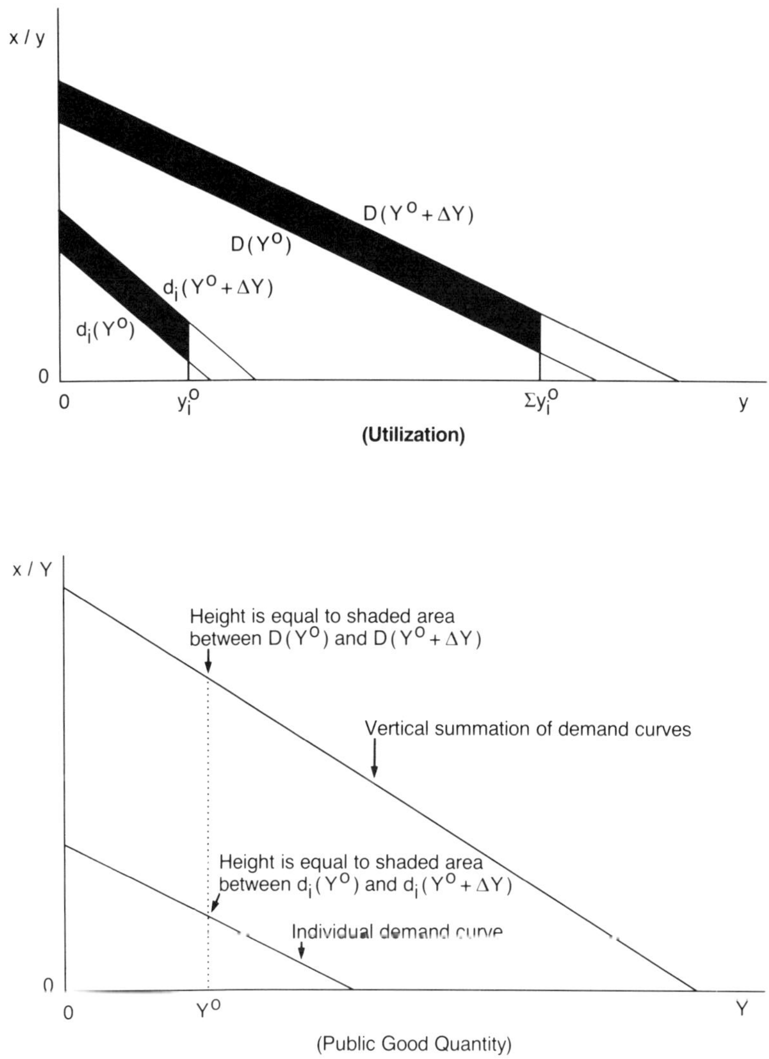

Fig. 7.5. Relationship of utilization dimension and public goods dimension

ber that curves $d_i(Y^o)$ and $D(Y^o)$ refer to a given amount of the public good. For an incremental increase in the amount of the public good (from Y^o to $Y^o + \Delta Y$), new demand curves for utilization will be relevant. Curve $d_i(Y^o + \Delta Y)$ is such a demand curve, evidencing the property that the improved good yields more satisfaction to the individual each time it is utilized. Curve $D(Y^o + \Delta Y)$ is the *horizontal* summation of all $d_i(Y^o + \Delta Y)$. The added consumer surplus to an individual consuming y_i^o units of utilization due to the increase in the quantity of the public good is the shaded area between $d_i(Y^o)$, $d_i(Y^o + \Delta Y)$, $y_i = 0$, and $y_i = y_i^o$. This area in the utilization dimension is translated into the height of an individual demand curve in the public good dimension at quantity Y^o as long as condition (7.3) holds. That is, the shaded area in the utilization dimension is the marginal rate of substitution in the public good dimension. This is the essence of condition (7.8′). The horizontal summation of all such areas for individuals in the utilization dimension is represented also as the shaded area between $D(Y^o)$, $D(Y^o + \Delta Y)$, $\Sigma y_i = 0$, and $\Sigma y_i = \Sigma y_i^o$. This same addition is done in the public good dimension by summing *vertically*. This sum measures the societal increase in welfare as presented in equation (7.6″).

This vertical sum of marginal rates of substitution must be compared with the marginal cost of the public good, presented in equation (7.6″) as a change in fixed and marginal costs of utilization. The nature of these costs, however, does not affect the relationship between the marginal rates of substitution in the utilization and public goods dimensions. That is, marginal cost in the utilization dimension can be zero, constant, or rising, either above or below average cost and either dependent on or constant with respect to the public good amount. Regardless, the relationship between the marginal rates of substitution will remain unchanged. The reason the public good has value is because of the consumer's utilization of it. Consequently, the marginal rate of substitution in the public goods dimension comes from a marginal change in the summation of marginal rates of substitution in the utilization dimension.

Marginal cost pricing in the utilization dimension will yield optimal utilization, as condition (7.5) states, and marginal cost pricing in the utilization dimension will yield enough revenue for private production if the marginal cost of utilization rises quickly enough. But marginal cost pricing does not collect as revenue the shaded area of extra consumer surplus from utilization, as illustrated in Figure 7.5. In order for private sector production to be efficient, this shaded area would have to be collected as revenue and set equal to cost at the margin in the public good dimension. This comparison is discussed and set out formally in the next chapter.

By examining the utilization dimension separately from the public good dimension we can clarify exactly what is meant by the price discrimination that is mentioned in most public goods models. But much of the public goods literature has been concerned solely with the public goods dimension. This is unfortunate because comparisons of public sector, monopolistic, oligopolistic, or competitive provision of public goods necessitate the specification of the interactions in the utilization dimension which should be explicitly modeled. Indeed, the pure public good looks like a natural monopoly in the utilization dimension, where the determination of the noncooperative equilibrium is far from being a trivial problem. It seems as if there would be benefits to emphasizing this utilization dimension, rather than ignoring it, in such public goods discussions.

CHAPTER EIGHT

Monopoly Producer

This chapter presents and discusses the equilibrium for a monopolist public good producer. The monopolist prices in the utilization dimension and, therefore, possibly excludes in the utilization dimension. Think of a single, uncrowded park as a heuristic example. It may be visited a multiple number of times by each individual, and consumers are charged on a per visit basis. Both the number of visits and the size of the park are economic variables that will be determined endogenously in this setting.

The direct antecedents for this chapter are in the two preceding chapters. The formal analysis from Chapter 7 provides the background for the formal presentation of the profit maximization of the monopoly firm. I will treat this technical material first, while it is still fresh in the reader's mind. The second part of this chapter is a verbal discussion of the equilibrium comparing it to the monopoly cases discussed in Chapter 6.

Formal Analysis

The analysis will present the optimization problems for the consumers and for the firm and piece together conditions that obtain in the private sector equilibrium. These conditions will be compared to equations (7.5) and (7.6″), which are the equations that describe Pareto optimality. In this technical sense, the comparisons will enable us to infer which private sector pricing schemes are consistent with optimality. Later, in Chapter 10, similar comparisons will be made for the multiple producer case. This will allow us to examine the effect of different market structures and different interaction assumptions on equilibrium production. The notation in this chapter for the monopoly case may seem a bit overdone, but the presentation of the simple case in this manner will assist in the presentation of the multiple producer case to come later.

There is one firm producing *Y* units of the public good and selling its utilization, *y*. The private good numeraire is *x*; x_i^o is the *i*th person's endowment. The utilization of the public good by the *i*th person is y_i, and total utilization is $\sum_i y_i$. Pricing is only in the utilization dimension. We want to allow the possibility of multipart pricing in the utilization dimension. Thus, the price of the *j*th unit of utilization to the *i*th person when that person consumes y_i units altogether is given by

$$(8.1)\quad p_{ij} = p_{ij}(y_i, \sum_i y_i, Y, j)$$

so that the budget constraint of the *i*th consumer can be written:

$$(8.2)\quad x_i^o = x_i + \int_0^{y_i} p_{ij}\,dj$$

Both the pricing function and the budget constraint are written to allow for individually tailored, nonlinear pricing schemes. The *i*th consumer will maximize utility (equation [7.1] or [7.2]), subject to this constraint by the selection of x_i and y_i. Note that here the consumer's decision is in the utilization dimension, not the public goods dimension. The consumer does not get to choose how big to make the park, only how many times to visit the park of given size, *Y*. In a later chapter, when consumers purchase utilization units from multiple producers, a choice in the public good dimension becomes possible, but for now, the consumer's only choice is in the utilization dimension. The first order conditions for this optimization are:

$$(8.3a)\quad \frac{\partial U^i}{\partial x_i} = \lambda\left(1 + \frac{\partial}{\partial x_i}\int_0^{y_i} p_{ij}\,dj\right)$$

$$(8.3b)\quad \frac{\partial U^i}{\partial y_i} = \lambda\left(p_{ij}\Big|_{j = y_i} + \int_0^{y_i}\frac{dp_{ij}}{dy_i}dj\right)$$

Equations (8.2) and (8.3) taken together represent three equations in the three unknowns, λ, x_i, and y_i. Usually, (8.3) is rearranged to eliminate λ, thus leaving two equations in two unknowns. This is easily accomplished if the consumer is a price taker, because the integral term inside the parentheses drops out of both equations when the price-taking behavior assumption is made. For equation (8.3a), the price-taking assumption presents no problem. By equation (8.1), p_{ij} does not depend on x_i, therefore, the integral term equals zero.[1]

For (8.3b), however, there is something to discuss. That equation states that the marginal utility of utilization must be proportional to the sum of the price charged for the unit and any inframarginal price effects. The factor of proportionality, λ, is the marginal utility of income, essentially transforming units of utility into units of the numeraire. There are two types of inframarginal effects. From equation (8.1) we see that generally the price for any unit may be a function of the individual's total utilization, y_i, and the economy's total utilization, $\sum_i y_i$. Since $\sum_i y_i$ depends on y_i, there are two avenues through which y_i affects the prices: the first, a direct effect of the consumer's purchases on inframarginal prices, and the second, the effect on prices due to the increase in total utilization. Thus, by assuming price-taking behavior at this point, we are denying two types of effects. Although the standard treatment in private goods models is to ignore both effects, we should address this issue more closely, especially in light of the different treatments of price-taking behavior in the received public goods models.

Usually, the integral term in equation (8.3b) is treated in one of two ways. First, if the consumer is the only buyer (i.e., a monopsonist), then the two effects merge into one, as y_i and $\sum_i y_i$ are the same thing. In choosing quantity, monopsonists will ordinarily take into consideration their own influence on price. Second, in standard private goods treatments, with uniform pricing, both effects disappear. There is no direct influence of y_i on price; the only influence occurs through the effect of the consumer's purchases on the total purchases made. This indirect effect of a consumer's purchases on price also disappears when an atomistic assumption is added. That is, when the consumer makes up only a small part of the market, the effect of the small change in total purchases brought about by a change in an individual's purchases is ignored by the consumer.

When price discrimination is considered, we should be careful about ignoring these two effects. It may be that the consumption of another unit of utilization will change inframarginal prices, especially in the multiple producer case. We will maintain the atomistic assumption so that the consumer ignores the indirect effect routed through the change in total purchases. However, we want to keep track of the influence of the individual's purchases on the prices that any seller charges, especially in the case of multiple sellers. Therefore, the integral term will not be dropped from (8.3b).

We continue by combining both of the equations in (8.3) to eliminate λ. The result is the familiar condition that the marginal rate of substitution equals the marginal expenditure of each individual. That is,

$$(8.4) \qquad -\left.\frac{dx_i}{dy_i}\right|_{U^i} = \left.p_{ij}\right|_{j=y_i} + \int_0^{y_i} \frac{dp_{ij}}{dy_i}dj\Big)$$

for all i. The marginal expenditure is made up of two parts: the price on the marginal unit and the integral of the changes in price on all inframarginal units. When the consumer is a price taker, this last integral term equals zero.

Equations (8.2) and (8.4) represent expanded forms of the budget constraint and the expansion path from elementary microtheory. Their intersection solves the two-equation system for the optimal values of x_i and y_i.

Note that a slight rearrangement of equation (8.4) gives us an opening to the Thompson overvaluation result introduced in Chapter 6. If we solve (8.4) for p_{ij}, then we can interpret the resulting equation as a statement of the consumer's willingness to pay for the *j*th unit. This willingness to pay consists of two parts, the consumer's marginal rate of substitution and any pecuniary effects represented in the integral term. If the effect of extra consumption is to lower inframarginal prices, this would be a benefit added to the usual marginal rate of substitution. As will be shown below, in the monopoly case this turns out to be of no import because the monopoly seller also internalizes the same pecuniary effects. Once multiple sellers are considered, however, the pecuniary effect will involve price changes for units from different sellers and will not be internalized.

In addition to equation (8.3) there are also second order and total conditions. These will not be presented formally here, but their interpretation is straightforward. The second order conditions essentially require the consumer's demand function to cross the nonlinear pricing function from above. This is always the case when a monopolist practices uniform pricing. However, the second order conditions become a potential problem for nonlinear pricing schemes. We will assume that the second order conditions hold.

The total conditions do two things. First, in the case of multiple interior solutions to (8.3), consumers will have to compare their utility at each of the multiple solutions and choose the one yielding the highest utility. With uniform pricing, multiple solutions do not come about, but once nonlinear pricing is considered, multiple solutions become a distinct possibility. The second thing that the total conditions do is to distinguish between the best interior solution and any possible boundary solutions. The total conditions essentially ensure that the consumer is no worse off at the interior optimum than at a boundary solution in which the consumer buys none of the public good. We will assume that the total conditions are satisfied.[2]

We now move to the profit maximization on the part of the seller. If we let π represent the profits of the firm, then

$$(8.5)\quad \pi = \sum_i \int_0^{y_i} p_{ij}\,dj - C(\sum_i y_i, Y)$$

where C is the cost of the production of the public good and of the utilization units. Since C is measured in x units, $dC/d\sum_i y_i$, the marginal cost of utilization, is

$$(8.6)\quad \frac{dC}{d\sum_i y_i} = -\left.\frac{d\sum_i x_i}{d\sum_i y_i}\right|_F$$

And dC/dY, the marginal cost of the public good, is

$$(8.7)\quad \frac{dC}{dY} = -\left.\frac{d\sum_i x_i}{dY}\right|_F$$

which can be rewritten:

$$(8.7')\quad \frac{dC}{dY} = \frac{d}{dY}\int_0^{\sum_i y_i^o} - \left.\frac{d\sum_i x_i}{d\sum_i y_i}\right|_F d\sum_i y_i - \left.\frac{d\sum_i x_i}{dY}\right|_{F, \sum_i y_i = 0}$$

The firm maximizes (8.5) by choosing Y and y_i for each individual. By examining the profit maximization with respect to the i'th individual, we get the following conditions:

$$(8.8)\quad \frac{d}{dy_{i'}}\sum_i \int_0^{y_i} p_{ij}\,dj = \frac{dC}{d\sum_i y_i}\,\frac{d\sum_i y_i}{dy_{i'}}$$

for all i', and

$$(8.9)\quad \frac{d}{dY}\sum_i \int_0^{y_i^o} p_{ij}\,dj = \frac{dC}{dY}$$

Since $d\sum_i y_i/dy_i$ equals one, in light of equations (8.6) and (8.7′), these conditions become

$$(8.8') \quad p_{i'j}\Big|_{j\,=\,y_{i'}} + \sum_i \int_0^{y_i} \frac{dp_{ij}}{dy_{i'}} dj = -\left.\frac{d\sum_i x_i}{d\sum_i y_i}\right|_F$$

for all i', and

$$(8.9') \quad \sum_i \frac{d}{dY}\int_0^{y_i^o} p_{ij}dj = \frac{d}{dY}\int_0^{\sum_i y_i^o} - \left.\frac{d\sum_i x_i}{d\sum_i y_i}\right|_F d\sum_i y_i - \left.\frac{d\sum_i x_i}{dY}\right|_{F,\sum_i y_i\,=\,0}$$

Equation (8.8′) basically says that marginal revenue equals marginal cost in the utilization dimension. The left-hand side is the marginal revenue. The unfamiliar look of the marginal revenue is due to the nonlinear and personally differentiated pricing schemes. Equation (8.9′) says that marginal revenue equals marginal cost in the public good dimension. We will return to the discussion of equation (8.9′) below. Combining the firm's profit maximization in the utilization dimension (equation [8.8′]) with the i'th consumer's optimization (equation [8.4]) we get

$$(8.10) \quad \left.\frac{dx_{i'}}{dy_{i'}}\right|_{U^{i'}} + \int_0^{y_{i'}} \frac{dp_{i'j}}{dy_{i'}} dj = \left.\frac{d\sum_i x_i}{d\sum_i y_i}\right|_F + \sum_i \int_0^{y_i} \frac{dp_{ij}}{dy_{i'}} dj$$

for all i'.[3] Equation (8.10) states that the sum of the marginal rate of substitution of the i'th person and any pecuniary effects internalized by this person is equal to the marginal cost of the unit plus any pecuniary effects internalized by the firm. These two amounts are set equal essentially because they are both equal to the marginal price. Equation (8.10) is comparable to equation (7.5), which describes optimality in the utilization dimension. It is clear that (8.10) is the same as (7.5) if and only if the integral term on the left-hand side of (8.10) cancels with the summation of integrals on the right-hand side. The integral on the left-hand side was discussed above. When the consumer is a price taker, this term is zero. For the monopoly case considered here, if the consumer is not a price taker so that the term is nonzero, the term will still cancel with a similar term on the right-hand side because if any pecuniary effect exists the seller will also internalize it.

To elaborate further, we need to examine more closely the integral term on the right-hand side. This integral represents any pecuniary effects internalized by the seller. As was the case for the consumer, there are two avenues of effects. The first is the direct effect of consumption by the i'th person on the prices charged. By equation (8.1) this effect is nonzero only for the prices charged to the i'th person. Therefore, for the direct effect, all the terms in the summation drop out except for the i'th person's. What is left is the same effect that the i'th person is internalizing on the left-hand side of equation (8.10). For the direct effect, whether the consumer is a price taker or whether the consumer and the seller jointly negotiate prices, on the margin both the buyer and seller consider the same marginal price and the same inframarginal price effects. Therefore, the direct influence consumers can exert on prices charged to them by a monopoly seller washes out with the monopolist's consideration of the same influence. Another way of saying this is that as long as total cost is the same, it does not matter to either the buyer or the seller whether the price for the marginal unit is high with a lowering of inframarginal prices or whether the price for the marginal unit is low with no inframarginal effects. Since both buyer and seller are internalizing the same inframarginal price effects, both are basing their decisions on the same total expenditure.

There is also the possibility of an indirect effect on inframarginal prices. The prices that the ith consumer must pay may be affected indirectly by the consumption of the i'th individual through the effect of $y_{i'}$ on $\sum_i y_i$. This effect is summed over all individuals. It is this effect which leads to the usual underproduction by the monopolist. In the textbook treatment of monopoly, this effect is captured more simply because the prices are the same for all individuals and the reduction in price on inframarginal units is the same for all individuals. In fact, it is the insistence in standard models that all units sell for the same price that leads to this inframarginal effect. When nonlinear pricing and interpersonal price discrimination are considered, this indirect effect disappears.

To summarize, two instances in which the integral terms in equation (8.10) generally disappear can be identified. The first instance is when the consumers and firms are price takers. In this case, they both ignore any influence on price and the integral terms drop out. The second instance is when the firm commits to individually tailored pricing functions (p_{ij}) such that the prices do not depend on $y_{i'}$ for any i'.

In light of the discussion of the integral terms in (8.10) and (7.5), we can highlight a pricing scheme that satisfies both equations. In fact, there are many pricing schemes that the seller could impose that satisfy both equations (8.10) and (7.5), because these conditions only specify the marginal equalities that characterize equilibrium. Indeed, there are many ways of splitting the inframarginal surplus, each with accompanying wealth effects and each still yielding optimal utilization. One such possibility is the perfectly discriminating price schedule:

$$(8.11) \quad p_{ij}\Big|_{j = y_i^o} = -\left.\frac{dx_i}{dy_i}\right|_{U^{io}, y_i = y_i^o}$$

for all i, where the term on the right-hand side has first derivatives with respect to y_i equal to zero. It is, of course, well accepted that perfect discrimination by a monopolist leads to optimal private good production. The utilization dimension, in fact, looks just like a private good in this regard.

However, there is more to the public good story than just the utilization dimension. Equation (7.5) is only one of the conditions that must be satisfied in a Pareto optimum. Equation (7.6″) describes the marginal condition that must hold in the public good dimension. Equation (8.9′) is the corresponding condition resulting from consumer optimization and the firm's profit maximization. Inspection shows that (8.9′) is the same condition as (7.6″) if and only if

$$(8.12) \quad \sum_i \frac{d}{dY}\int_0^{y_i^o} p_{ij}dj = -\sum_i \frac{d}{dY}\int_0^{y_i^o} \left.\frac{dx_i}{dy_i}\right|_{U^{io}} dy_i$$

The right-hand side of (8.12) is the summation of marginal rates of substitution for a public good expressed in terms of the utilization dimension as was derived in Chapter 7. The left-hand side is the summation over all individuals of the change in the utilization prices allowed by the change in the public good dimension. For each individual we get one term in each summation. On the right-hand side, an individual's term corresponds to the person's marginal rate of substitution in the public good dimension, while on the left-hand side this term corresponds to that consumer's "price" for the public good. Unlike the received models, however, the price is collected indirectly through the change in the producer surplus earned in the utilization dimension. While real-world examples of public goods being sold unit by unit with pricing in the public good dimension (as in the models of Thompson, Demsetz, and Oakland) may be rare, there is an abundance of examples of nonrival consumption in the public good dimension being sold by pricing in the utilization dimension.[4]

A pricing function equal to the marginal rates of substitution as in equation (8.11) would satisfy equation (8.12). This can be seen by a simple inspection of (8.12) on a term-by-term basis. Since the prices are the marginal rates of substitution, the changes brought about to each by a change in Y will be identical. A perfect two-part pricing scheme will yield the same result. The utilization charge would be a constant equal to $-d\sum_i x_i/d\sum_i y_i|F,\sum_i y_i^o$, that is, the marginal cost, and the lump sum fee (different for each individual) would be:

$$(8.11') \quad \int_0^{y_o^i} \left(-\frac{dx_i}{dy_i}\bigg|_{U^{io}} + \frac{d\sum_i x_i}{d\sum_i y_i}\bigg|_{F,\sum_i y_i^o} \right) dy_i$$

that is, the integral of the excess of their marginal rates of substitution over the utilization charge. That this pricing function satisfies equation (8.12) can also be seen by inspection. The first term in the integral in (8.11′) is the same as that in (8.12), and any changes in the per unit price due to changes in marginal cost of utilization are offset by equal changes in the lump sum as given by the second term in the integral in (8.11′).

The optimality of perfect price discrimination and perfect two-part pricing in the monopoly case are not new results. They are presented here as a springboard to the formal material to be presented in Chapter 10 for the multiple producer case. What is new is the interpretation given to this analysis along the lines of a generalization of public goods theory. Furthermore, what is useful about this interpretation is the light it sheds on the pure public goods models developed by Thompson, Demsetz, and Oakland and discussed in Chapter 6. We move now to a discussion of this equilibrium with and without perfect price discrimination and to a comparison of this model with the monopoly cases discussed in Chapter 6.

Discussion

The formal analysis presented above gives a basis for the discussion of the monopoly equilibrium in the generalized public goods setting. In this section, I wish to show the differences and similarities between the version presented above and the received public goods models presented in Chapter 6. I will discuss the Demsetz and Thompson formulations together, followed by the monopoly version of the Oakland treatment. Before these comparisons, however, I include a discussion of how the inability to practice perfect price discrimination may affect the equilibrium.

If equation (8.12) holds, then the public goods decision is being made optimally. Above, we have seen how perfect discrimination satisfies equation (8.12). Underproduction will occur, however, if the left-hand side of (8.12) is less than the right-hand side. That is, if the marginal revenue is less than the sum of individual marginal rates of substitution, then the marginal cost of the public good will be less than the sum of the marginal rates of substitution in the equilibrium. Any imperfectly discriminating pricing scheme will have the property that $p_{ij}|_{j = y_i^o} \leqq -dx_i/dy_i|U_i^o, y_i^o$, but this does not guarantee an underproduction result because it is the derivatives of the above expression taken with respect to Y that appear in equation (8.12). We will see that price discrimination need not be perfect in the utilization dimension for optimal public good production to be forthcoming. In fact, less than perfect discrimination in the utilization dimension may lead to underproduction, optimal production, or even overproduction in the public good dimension.

Overproduction would come about if the marginal revenue due to a change in the production of the public good was greater than the sum of the individual's valuations of the extra public good amount. This is possible if the seller, by producing the extra public good amount, could implement a more perfectly discriminating pricing plan. This overproduction is unusual in that less than perfect price discrimination is usually linked to underproduction in public good models. Heretofore, the special case nature of the usual results has not been sufficiently appreciated. This unusual overproduction result depends crucially on how the p_{ij}, the prices of utilization, are being determined and how they change with the increase in the public good. To determine the likelihood of this overproduction result, we must examine how a change in the public goods dimension affects the pricing structure in the utilization dimension.

In order for the overproduction result to ensue, the increments in the prices summed over all units of utilization must be greater than the increases in the marginal rates of substitution similarly summed. There are two factors which work against the possibility of overproduction. First, no one who was originally getting zero consumer surplus would continue to purchase units of utilization if the total payment rose more than the increase in the value of the units of utilization. To do so would be to violate the total conditions that ensure that consumers can at least do as well as if they had not purchased any utilization units. Second, all who were utilizing the public good, regardless of the amount of consumer surplus they had before the increase in the public good, would continue to consume units of utilization if the total payments they faced rose less than the increase in the value they place on utilization. These two effects lead to underproduction of the public good because, on the margin, the firm is not collecting the full value of the public good.

Notwithstanding these two effects that lead to underproduction, there are two more possibilities that lead to overproduction. First, suppose there is an individual that is not buying the good before the change in the public good dimension. This person does not buy because the utilization prices are greater than the benefit obtainable from utilization. With the increase in the public good amount, however, the consumer may decide to buy if the utilization prices increase by less than the increase in valuation in the utilization dimension. The consumer goes from not buying, because buying would lead to negative consumer surplus, to buying, because buying leads to positive consumer surplus. Meanwhile, the firm attributes all of the producer surplus to the increment in the public good dimension. Clearly, the revenue associated with the increase in the public good can be greater than the extra benefit that the consumer obtains. This effect leads to overproduction.

A second possibility also leads to overproduction. It is possible that a consumer who obtains positive consumer surplus before an increase in the public goods dimension will still earn positive surplus but of lesser magnitude after an increase in the public goods dimension. Still earning surplus, the consumer will therefore still purchase the good. The reason that the surplus diminishes, however, is that the firm increases the prices to this person by more than the increase in the consumer's valuation. This effect also leads to overproduction.

Actually, this type of overproduction has been noted before but in a different context. It is known that overproduction can occur when less than perfect price discrimination is explored in the context of all-or-none pricing. It is possible with all-or-none pricing that on the margin the cost of a good may be greater than the value of the good to the consumer. Because of the all-or-none pricing, however, decisions are not made marginally; only the total conditions influence the all-or-nothing decision. Nevertheless, overproduction exists if value is greater than cost on the margin. What is new here is the application of this type of overproduction to the public goods setting. The all-or-none issue surfaces here because the *i*th consumer either consumes all of the public good, Y (i.e., when $y_i > 0$), or none of it ($y_i = 0$).[5]

It should be clear that perfect discrimination in the utilization dimension is not required for the optimal public good amount to be produced. All that is required is an equality between marginal revenue of the firm and summed marginal rates of substitution. Price discrimination can be less than perfect in the utilization dimension and still capture as revenue the exact amount of the change in consumers' valuations due to an increase in the public goods dimension. For example, on the margin some consumers may have their prices increase by less than the increase in value of the utilization units, and other consumers may have their prices increase by more. This is imperfect price discrimination, but if these errors offset each other, optimality can be achieved in the public goods dimension.[6]

The possible optimality of public goods production in the monopoly case with less than perfect price discrimination has a parallel in the received pure public goods models. Recall that in both the Demsetz and Thompson treatments, perfect price discrimination by a monopolist leads to optimal public goods provision. However, perfect price discrimination is not required. Perfect, interpersonal price discrimination leads to different marginal prices for each individual—prices that are equal to the individual's marginal rate of substitution. Such perfect interpersonal price discrimination yields optimum production. However, perfect inframarginal price discrimination is not required. The consumer could pay the same price for each unit of the public good, thereby earning surplus on the inframarginal units, and the equilibrium could still be consistent with Pareto optimality. This is precisely what happens in the competitive version of Demsetz's model, although this is not necessarily what either Demsetz or Thompson has in mind by perfect price discrimination in the monopoly version. With respect to the price discrimination in the Thompson and Demsetz treatments then, the parallel between the presentation in this chapter and their models exists in two ways. First, perfect price discrimination leads to optimal public goods production. Second, perfect price discrimination is not required. All that is required is perfect price discrimination on the marginal decision in the public goods dimension. Beware, however, that the perfect price discrimination addressed by Demsetz and Thompson and the prefect price discrimination discussed here are taking place in different dimensions.

Although the model of this chapter is consistent with the analyses of Thompson and Demsetz for perfect price discrimination as explained above, the different dimensions give rise to a couple of important differences. I have shown that even with less than perfect discrimination, overproduction in the public goods dimension is possible in the model of this chapter. When pricing takes place in the public goods dimension, however, overproduction ordinarily will not come about in the monopoly case. When consumers are allowed to choose the number of units of the public good that they wish to consume, they will never purchase a unit on the margin which costs more than it is worth. Indeed, if the monopolist charges a price that is greater than the consumer's marginal rate of substitution, the consumer forgoes consumption and the seller loses the potential revenue. Alternatively, if the monopolist charges a price that is less than the marginal rate of substitution, then the seller is not collecting the full value of the good on the margin. Both of these effects lead to underproduction of the public good. The overproduction possibility in the present chapter comes about because of the all-or-none nature of the decision in the public good dimension.

Note that a similar overproduction could exist in the Demsetz and Thompson formulations if imperfect all-or-none pricing, or imperfect two-part pricing, were used in pricing the public good. The main distinction between my results and the received models is that when pricing is done in the utilization dimension, the pricing scheme automatically looks like an all-or-none pricing scheme in the public good dimension. Alternatively, in the received models, all-or-none pricing is just one of a variety of pricing schemes that could be used in the public goods dimension. Regardless, the overproduction possibility in the public goods dimension seems to have been overlooked in the literature, because the traditional models assert that less than perfect discrimination leads to underproduction.

There is one more parallel between the received models of Thompson and Demsetz and the treatment of this book that may be introduced for the case of two-part pricing. If the per unit charge in the utilization dimension is equal to the marginal cost of the utilization units, then the lump sum charge is analogous to an all-or-none price in the public goods dimension. The pure public good case implicitly has both a zero marginal cost and a zero price in the utilization dimension. Therefore, the usual pure public good treatments can be seen as simplified versions of the two-dimensional model with two-part pricing. In the simplification, the per unit price becomes zero and the economic decisions in the utilization are ignored. As the utilization dimension disappears, the lump sum price becomes the price in the public good dimension.

All of these results for the public goods dimension are conditional results given the level of utilization. That is, we have been comparing equations (8.9′) with (7.6″). Actually, (7.6″) and (7.5) are solved simultaneously to yield optimal production, while (8.9′) and (8.8′) are solved simultaneously to yield equilibrium production. When we look only at (8.9′) and (7.6″), we are implicitly holding the level of utilization constant. This approach arguably provides the closest parallels to the received pure public goods literature because in that literature the utilization level, which is ignored, is implicitly being held constant.

So far, the similarities and differences have been addressed for the Thompson and Demsetz approaches but not for the Oakland approach. This is because in Thompson and Demsetz, and in the treatment of this book, all consumers obtain all units of the public good. That is, there is no inefficient exclusion of consumers from the units of the public good that are produced. In Thompson and Demsetz, this basically comes about because of a perfect information assumption through which no one with a positive valuation for a unit of the public good will be excluded. In my model, this comes about because the firm sells, to each person, utilization units of the total amount of the public good that is produced. In the Oakland approach, however, different consumers may consume different amounts of the public good, thus leaving some consumers inefficiently excluded in the public goods dimension. For the monopoly version of the model of this book the setting is not rich enough to capture this possibility.[7]

Brito and Oakland, as well as Brennan and Walsh, present the monopoly version of Oakland's public good model.[8] Interpersonal price discrimination is not allowed, but intrapersonal discrimination in the form of nonlinear pricing is addressed. The monopolist uses nonlinear pricing but must present everyone with the same pricing function. Unlike the model of this chapter where the consumers make an all-or-none decision in the public goods dimension, in the Oakland model consumers choose how much of the public good to consume. A heuristic example may help make the distinction. Consider an entertainment park with various distinct and interchangeable rides or attractions. In my model, consumers make multiple visits to the park and consume each ride in the park on each visit. In the Oakland tradition, consumers make only one visit to the park and must decide how many of the rides to go on.

This distinction colors the results of each model. Exclusion takes place in each model but in different dimensions. In my model exclusion takes place in the utilization dimension; because of an admission price a consumer may be discouraged from making another visit to the park. In the Oakland tradition, because of a price in the public goods dimension a consumer may be discouraged from going on all the rides.

If we apply an Oakland-type information assumption to my model and disallow any interpersonal price discrimination, do the results derived in the Oakland variant of public goods models hold up? The answer, in general, is no. In my model, because pricing takes place in the utilization dimension, different consumers, with different utilization levels of the public good, end up paying different prices for the same amount of the public good. Alternatively, when pricing and exclusion take place in the public goods dimension, any two people consuming the same amount of the public good end up paying the same price. The underproduction results that are derived in Brito and Oakland and in Brennan and Walsh are based on the fact that no interpersonal price discrimination exists in the public goods dimension. In my model, even if the same pricing function must be offered to each consumer in the utilization dimension, a form of interpersonal price discrimination in the public good dimension can take place.

A real example of this type of pricing existed in the renting of mainframe computers that were priced in the utilization dimension through the use of a metering device like computer cards. Each user faced the same pricing function and each user got the same computer, yet different users paid different amounts depending on their utilization. While in this particular example the tie-in of the cards may have been technologically unnecessary, and therefore illegal, technological settings do exist in which the tying device, that is, the utilization dimension, is essentially inseparable from the public goods dimension. Consider a time-sharing computer system in which users have access to all the hardware, software, and data (these make up the nonrival, public good dimension) in the system but are charged for their access by minutes of usage (which constitute the utilization dimension). Again, all users consume the same amount of public good and all users face the same pricing function in the utilization dimension, but different users pay different amounts.

Because different users of the same amount of the public good end up paying different amounts, one of the main conclusions of the Oakland-type models will not follow through to the general public goods setting of this book. The conclusion that does not stand up is that of private market underproduction of the public good. In all of the Oakland-type models, except in the identical consumer case, some consumers get excluded from consumption of some of the units of the public good, and too few units of the public good get produced. Yet we have seen earlier in this chapter how even imperfect price discrimination can lead to overproduction in the public good dimension. We must beware of the policy conclusion that argues in the following manner: (1) this good is a public good, or has aspects of nonrival consumption which makes it "like a public good"; (2) due to imperfect information we have imperfect price discrimination, an extreme form of which would be no interpersonal price discrimination; (3) following Oakland, such a setting leads to underproduction of the public good; (4) subsidization of production may remedy this market failure. This argument may hold when pricing takes place in the public goods dimension, but for many examples of private sector public good provision, pricing takes place in the utilization dimension and, therefore, the argument is not generally valid.

There is a sense in which the Oakland-type perspective does lead to underproduction. The underproduction, however, is in the utilization dimension, not the public goods dimension. When price discrimination is imperfect, the textbook examples in private goods models generally show that underproduction results. Traditionally, in order to achieve the optimal quantity, the monopolist must perfectly discriminate, both interpersonally and, perhaps, inframarginally. Since the buyer will always purchase at prices less than but never at prices greater than marginal rates of substitution, mistakes in pricing by the seller generally lead to suboptimal consumption and production.[9]

This distinction leads to an important difference in the types of policies that would be applied. To go back to the example of the entertainment park, if you believed in the possibility that government intervention could correct market failures and if you followed an Oakland-type model, your policies would be to make sure that all consumers could go on all rides and to subsidize the production of rides. Alternatively, if you believed that government could correct market failure, but you intended to follow the approach of this book, your policy would be to subsidize admissions to the park in general but to be silent about the number of rides that existed.

What has been demonstrated in this chapter is that under certain conditions, the profit-maximizing behavior on the part of the private sector firm leads to optimal public goods production along the lines of the theory presented in Chapter 7. The conditions, not surprisingly, entail perfect price discrimination. Price-taking behavior on the utilization level may yield optimal utilization, but to obtain the optimal provision in the public goods dimension at the same time requires the firm not only to choose the correct utilization but also to capture on the margin as revenue any increment in value of that utilization to its customers. Uniform monopoly pricing leads to underproduction in the utilization dimension and a possible overproduction or underproduction in the public goods dimension. The same result is true for imperfectly discriminating pricing schemes.

In terms of the utilization dimension, this is precisely what we already knew from the textbook treatments of price discrimination: the monopolist will keep price too high and quantity too low. But a public goods or quality dimension has been added to the familiar story. Here, too, perfect price discrimination or perfect two-part pricing schemes will lead to optimality. But it is not necessary for the pricing schemes to be "perfect," as imperfectly discriminating schemes can be consistent with optimal production, underproduction, or overproduction in this dimension. In the models of quality choice by a monopolist these results are, again, the standard ones. It has not generally been appreciated, however, that this analogy between quality choice and public goods exists. And once the analogy is made, several of the results in the received public goods treatments are seen from a new perspective and, possibly, contradicted.

In the preceding analysis, the issues of price discrimination and quality choice have helped to clarify some of the issues in public goods models, at least insofar as the monopoly versions of private goods and public goods models are concerned. In the remainder of the book some of the more sophisticated issues and results in the competitive public goods models will be used to enlighten the treatment of price discrimination and product quality determination in noncooperative, multiple firm settings. In a nutshell, we can use what we now know about public goods to improve upon the usual analysis in monopolistic competition settings.

CHAPTER NINE

Multiple Producers: Public Goods and Monopolistic Competition

The previous chapters have shown how recognition of the utilization dimension enriches the received public goods models. So far, however, the analysis has been restricted to the monopoly case. In this chapter, we make the extension to the multiple producer case. It is in the consideration of multiple producers that the connection to monopolistic competition models becomes apparent. Monopolistic competition becomes relevant because the extension to the multiple seller case essentially brings us to a model of competing producers who sell substitutable products of variable quality. This resultant model certainly reminds us of the monopolistic competition setting in which competing firms sell differentiated substitutes. The exact nature of the relationship between monopolistic competition and the generalized public goods model is explained in this chapter.

Actually, the model of this book turns out to be richer than the standard monopolistic competition models in two ways. First, standard monopolistic competition models do not allow the sellers to vary their product quality, while the public goods approach adopted here does encompass product quality choice in what we have been calling the public goods dimension.[1] Second, the standard models employ uniform pricing, while models from the public goods perspective naturally consider price discrimination.

In addition to describing the link between public goods and monopolistic competition, this chapter also sets the stage for the formal consideration of the multiple producer case. The nature of the consumer's utility function is addressed first. Following this, the discussion turns to the presentation of the transformation function and the first order conditions describing Pareto optimality. The formal analysis is completed in the next chapter, which discusses the nature of the equilibrium and compares the incentives existing in equilibrium with the conditions describing optimality. In setting out the formal analysis, the links between public goods and monopolistic competition will be pointed out along the way.

In order to analyze the multiple producer case we must keep track of both the amount of the public good produced by each firm and the number of utilization units sold by each firm. Let Y_k be the amount of the public good produced by the kth firm, $k = 1, \ldots, K$. The total production of the public good is $\sum_{k=1}^{K} Y_k$. However, it is no longer appropriate to simply add together the outputs of the various firms because of the possibility of different utilization amounts for each firm. It will become clear below in what sense we can talk about the aggregate public good production. We must also keep track of the utilization level of each firm and each individual. Let y_{ik} stand for the total utilization of the kth firm's public good amount by the ith individual. The general utility function of each individual may now be characterized as:

$$(9.1)\quad U^i = U^i(x_i; y_{i1}, \ldots, y_{ik}, \ldots, y_{iK}; Y_1, \ldots, Y_k, \ldots, Y_K)$$

As in Chapter 7, we may describe how the Y's are linked to the y's in the utility function. We rewrite equation (9.1) as:

$$(9.1')\quad U^i = U^i[x_i, g^i(y_{i1}, Y_1; \ldots; y_{ik}, Y_k; \ldots; y_{iK}, Y_K)]$$

There are several conditions motivated by the public goods scenario which can be imposed on g. These conditions will be presented and discussed in turn.

Condition 1: g is symmetric with respect to the ordered pairs (y_{ik}, Y_k). That is, any permutation of the k ordered pairs (y_{ik}, Y_k) will leave the value of g unchanged.

The first condition ensures that on the demand side all the goods are treated equally. This is an implicit assumption in both competitive public goods models and in Chamberlinian monopolistic competition. In the public goods models, the units produced by different firms are added on the same horizontal axis, in no particular order, indicating that each unit has a symmetric effect upon utility. In the Chamberlinian version of monopolistic competition, again, the products of the individual firms are symmetrically or uniformly differentiated. In fact, one of the margins of interest in these models is simply the number of firms.

Note that in spatial competition, the symmetry assumption does not hold in general. In spatial competition, the products of the K firms will have different impacts on any individual's utility. For each firm, the size of the impact depends on the distance between the firm and the consumer.

Condition 2: g reduces to the model of chapters 7 and 8 if only one firm has a positive output of the public good and its utilization. That is, $g^i(y_{i1}, Y_1; 0,0; \ldots ; 0,0) = g^i(y_i, Y)$.

The second condition guarantees that the only change we are adding from the previous analysis is the consideration of multiple sellers. When we simplify the multiple seller example we should arrive back at the same monopoly model already discussed. An outcome of condition 2 is that all the assumptions about the utility function of the monopoly case still hold here. In particular, we will still be ignoring any option demand as evidenced in the next condition.

Condition 3: A consumer does not benefit from an increase in public goods production if he or she does not utilize it. That is, $U^i_{Y_k} = U^i_{g^i} g^i_{Y_k} = 0$, for any pair (i,k) if $y_{ik} = 0$.

As in previous chapters, subscripts on the U and g functions indicate partial differentiation. Remember that exclusion takes place in the utilization dimension. If the consumer utilizes the public good from any particular firm, then the consumer gets the whole amount of the public good produced by that firm. However, if the consumer does not utilize a particular firm's product, then the consumer gets no benefit from an increase in the public good level of that firm. Condition 3 implies that individuals' marginal utility in the public goods dimension, and therefore their marginal rates of substitution in the public goods dimension, are both zero if the utilization of that good is zero.

The next condition also follows from the monopoly case.

Condition 4: A consumer does not benefit from the utilization of nothing. That is, $U^i_{y_{ik}} = U^i_{g^i} g^i_{y_{ik}} = 0$ for all i, if $Y_k = 0$ for any k.

By condition 4 the firm must supply some nonrival public good quantity in order to be able to sell the utilization units. If no public good amount is supplied, then the marginal utility and the marginal rate of substitution in the utilization dimension are automatically zero.

The first four conditions have done little to distinguish the public goods dimension from the utilization dimension. Conditions 1 and 2 discuss only the ordered pairs and do not address the two dimensions separately. Meanwhile, condition 4 essentially makes the same point for the public goods dimension that condition 3 makes for the utilization dimension. Differences between the two dimensions will be developed in the last three conditions.

The next condition is actually implied by symmetry.

Condition 5: A unit of utilization is interchangeable with another unit of utilization when the two units of utilization refer to a like quantity of the public good and when the utilization levels of those like quantities are equal to begin with. That is, $g^i_{y_{ik'}} = g^i_{y_{ik}}$ if $Y_k = Y_{k'}$ and $y_{ik} = y_{ik'}$.

For example, if two different amusement parks each had the same number of rides and if you had visited each park the same number of times, then you would get the same benefit out of another visit regardless of which park you chose. As stated formally above, this means that an individual's marginal utility in the utilization dimension for one firm's output is equal to the marginal utility of utilization for another firm's output when certain equalities exist across firms in both the utilization dimension and the public goods dimension.

The implication in this condition does not go both ways because it could be possible for marginal utilities to be equal if both the amount of public good and the utilization levels were different to start with. It is possible, for example, for the first unit of utilization of a firm's product with a small public good amount to yield the same increment to utility as, say, the fifth unit of utilization of a different firm's product that contains a larger public good amount. This equality would purely be a coincidence. Nevertheless, its possibility falsifies the converse of condition 5.

Note that symmetry also ensures a result similar to condition 5 for the public goods dimension. That is, if the public good amount and the utilization amount from two different firms were equal, then the marginal utilities in the public goods dimension must also be equal. This interchangeability of different firms' outputs in the public goods dimension, however, actually holds with fewer restrictions than are required in condition 5. We will address interchangeability in the public goods dimension in condition 7, below.

The final two conditions really capture the essence of the relationship between the public goods dimension and the utilization dimension in a competitive public goods model. The first of these goes hand in hand with condition 5.

Condition 6: Units of utilization are distinct in the sense that when two different producers supply the same number of units of the public good but the utilization measures of each are different, then increasing the utilization of one is not the same as increasing the utilization of the other. That is, $g^i_{y_{ik}} \neq g^i_{y_{ik'}}$ if $Y_k = Y_{k'}$ and $y_{ik} \neq y_{ik'}$.

It is not the same, in general, to utilize one unit of a public good twice as it is to utilize two different units one time each. It is usual to assume a taste for diversity so that $g^i_{y_{ik}} > g^i_{y_{ik'}}$ if $Y_k = Y_{k'}$ and $y_{ik} < y_{ik'}$. This taste for diversity is hidden in the literature on competitive provision of public goods because the utilization dimension itself is absent in those models. In the received models, for example, after an individual consumes a unit of the public good from one seller, the consumer's only choice is to get a different unit of the public good either from the same seller or from another firm. This is because in received models the nonrival consumption aspect applies only across consumers but not within one person's consumption. Therefore, the choice of utilizing one unit of the public good twice is not a feasible possibility in these models.

In the model of this book, multiple utilization of any unit of the public good is possible. In the absence of a taste for diversity and of utilization costs,[2] only one unit of the public good from one firm will be required in the optimum. Indeed, two units of utilization of one unit of the public good will be cheaper than one unit of utilization of each of two units of the public good. And without a taste for diversity, the former yields the same utility as the latter.

Again, using the example of the amusement park with rides, if there were no taste for diversity, then two rides on the same roller coaster would be just as good as one ride each on two interchangeable roller coasters. Unless the cost of providing rides on a given roller coaster rises sufficiently, the rides will be supplied most economically by one roller coaster. If the cost of providing rides on a given roller coaster does rise, it may do so abruptly, due to a capacity constraint, or gradually, due to congestion costs or normal production or maintenance costs. In these cases, more than one roller coaster may be desired even if the consumers exhibit no desire for diversity. Standard oligopoly models are capable of addressing this situation. Once a taste for diversity is considered, however, we leave pure oligopoly models and enter the realm of differentiated oligopoly or monopolistic competition.

Condition 7: The units of the public good are interchangeable in the sense that the value of an extra unit of the public good does not depend on the source of the public good if and only if the utilization of the extra unit of the public good is equal across all units of the public good. That is, $g^i_{Y_k} = g^i_{Y_{k'}}$ for all Y_k and $Y_{k'}$ if and only if $y_{ik} = y_{ik'}$.

In condition 7, note that it is not required that the public good amounts be equal between the kth and k'th firm; only utilization must be equal. As long as the extra unit is utilized the same number of times, the source of the extra unit is irrelevant to the person's utility. The equality in the utilization dimension is met by default in the received public goods models where the utilization dimension is ignored. It is implicitly assumed in those models that the utilization of each unit of the public good that a person consumes is unity. Therefore, in the received models, the separate units of the public good are always interchangeable. They can be aggregated on the same quantity axis to constitute the total production of the public good even when that public good is produced by different firms.

In the model of this book, however, one can talk about the competitive provision of *the* public good, $\sum_{k=1}^{K} Y_k$, by examining *the* marginal utility of *the* public good, $(dU^i/dg^i)\,(dg^i/d\Sigma Y_k)$, or *the* marginal rate of substitution of *the* public good, $-dx_i/d\Sigma Y_k|U^i = (dU^i/dg^i)(dg^i/d\Sigma Y_K)/(dU^i/dx_i)$ if and only if $y_{ik} = y_{ik'}$ for all k, k'. This is because we can define

(9.2) $\quad g^i_{\Sigma Y_k} = g^i_{Y_{k'}}\, dY_{k'}/d\Sigma Y_k)$

for all k' if and only if $y_{ik} = y_{ik'}$ for all k, k'. That is, when $y_{ik} = y_{ik'}$, the right-hand side of equation (9.2) does not depend on which firm's public good amount is increased. When the utilization levels are equal, the marginal utility of the public good can be defined unambiguously regardless of which public good supplier expands. That this special condition in the utilization dimension is required is not fully appreciated in the traditional public goods models, where the utilization dimension is left in the background. In the traditional models, the interchangeability of the units of the public good is implicitly assumed with little or no discussion of the consequences of the imposition or the relaxation of the special condition.

The last three conditions address the issues of distinctness and interchangeability in both the public good dimension and the utilization dimension. Distinctness essentially means that the marginal utilities of units of consumption, either utilization units or public good units, from different firms are unequal. Interchangeability means that the marginal utilities for different firms' products are equal. Table 9.1 summarizes the possibilities for equality or inequality of the marginal utilities depending on the relevant equalities or inequalities in the utilization dimension and the public goods dimension.

In the northwest quadrant of Table 9.1, the public good levels of the kth and k'th firms are equal and the ith person's utilization levels of the two firms' public good amounts are also equal. The marginal utilities are equal essentially because of the symmetry of the utility function with respect to the different firms' output levels. In the southeast quadrant, the marginal utilities are not equal because the starting utilization and public good levels are not equal. In the northwest and

Table 9.1
Interfirm Comparisons of Consumption Levels and Marginal Utilities

	$Y_k = Y_{k'}$	$Y_k \neq Y_{k'}$	row
$y_{ik} = y_{ik'}$	$U^i_{Y_k} = U^i_{Y_{k'}}$	$U^i_{Y_k} = U^i_{Y_{k'}}$	1
	$U^i_{y_{ik}} = U^i_{y_{ik'}}$	$U^i_{y_{ik}} \neq U^i_{y_{ik'}}$	2
$y_{ik} \neq y_{ik'}$	$U^i_{Y_k} \neq U^i_{Y_{k'}}$	$U^i_{Y_k} \neq U^i_{Y_{k'}}$	3
	$U^i_{y_{ik}} \neq U^i_{y_{ik'}}$	$U^i_{y_{ik}} \neq U^i_{y_{ik'}}$	4

southeast quadrants the results are the same for the utilization dimension as for the public goods dimension. That is, either the marginal utilities in the utilization dimension and the public goods dimension are both equal across firms or both are unequal. Therefore, there is still nothing to differentiate the treatments of the two different dimensions. The difference between the treatment of the utilization dimension and the public goods dimension becomes apparent from examination of the southwest and northeast quadrants.

Note, especially, the asymmetric treatment of the utilization dimension and the public goods dimension evidenced by the equality of marginal utilities in the public goods dimension in the northeast and the inequality of the marginal utilities in the utilization dimension in the southwest. In the northeast, we see that the interchangeability of units of the public good requires only equality in the utilization dimension. In the southwest, however, equality only in the public goods dimension does not lead to interchangeability in the utilization dimension. This is the essence of conditions 5, 6, and 7.

Table 9.1 also shows how the utilization dimension enriches the received literature. In the public goods literature without the utilization dimension, only the top row of Table 9.1 is relevant. The received models implicitly consider utilization equal, which eliminates the bottom two rows of the table, and never discuss the marginal utility in the utilization dimension, which eliminates row 2. Row 1 shows that the marginal utilities in the public good dimension are always equal to each other, regardless of the source of the extra public good amount. It is natural to talk of *the* public good in this setting. It is also natural to add the different amounts of the public good, produced by different firms, on the same quantity axis. Once utilization is considered, the aggregation of the public good amounts from different firms is no longer a simple matter.

The problem of aggregation in the public goods dimension, although new to public goods analysis, is reminiscent of the problem of specifying the nature of the Chamberlinian group. It is essentially the same problem. It has always been recognized in monopolistic competition that the idea of the group of firms selling related but differentiated products is a slippery concept. The group could be the whole economy or just one firm; there is nothing in the theory to divide the firms in the group from those in the rest of the economy. Whenever group size is treated endogenously in a monopolistic competition model, it is done so only after the introduction of symmetry and uniformity assumptions that allow all the members of the group to have the same costs, price, and, most important, output. Then, the aggregation takes the form of counting the number of firms in the group. The number at a zero profit equilibrium is usually compared to the number in the welfare optimum.[3] Since all the firms are selling the same number of units of output, it makes sense to aggregate the firms in the monopolistic competition model in this way. In the past, however, this has only been appreciated at the intuitive level. The conditions listed above and summarized mathematically in Table 9.1 make it clear when and when not to aggregate in the public goods dimension by simply counting the number of firms in the group.

While the public goods tradition glosses over this aggregation problem, the received monopolistic competition framework is also too restrictive. Each producer in monopolistic competition is not allowed to alter the nature of its product. Therefore, each producer essentially produces one unit in the public goods dimension. The possibility where some firms can alter or augment the nature of their output, thereby producing more than others in the public goods dimension, is never considered. When this possibility is allowed, we get a richer model. In this richer model, however, it does not make sense to simply count the number of firms. The margin of interest will not simply be the number of firms; rather, it will be the number of firms weighted by their output in the public good dimension. As Table 9.1 indicates, however, this weighted addition is allowable only under certain conditions, that is, when the utilization measures are equal across firms.

Table 9.1 does much to clarify and highlight some of the hidden assumptions in the received literature in both the public goods arena and in monopolistic competition. This, of course, is one of the goals of introducing and pursuing the model of this book. The usual public goods approach is to take a special case in which the utilization levels of each firm's public good amount are implicitly equal to each other. Aggregation in the public goods dimension follows simply by adding the possibly different public good amounts from each firm. The usual monopolistic competition approach is a special case in which each firm is constrained to produce the same amount in the public goods dimension. Aggregation in this model follows simply by counting the number of firms, assuming that the quantity of output in the utilization dimension is identical for each firm.

The relationship between public goods and monopolistic competition can be stated clearly at this juncture. The regular quantity dimension in monopolistic competition models is the same as what we have been calling the utilization dimension. Meanwhile, the other margin of interest in monopolistic competition, the number of firms, is actually a nonrival, public goods dimension. Indeed, in Chamberlinian monopolistic competition, all consumers have access to each seller. Received public goods models simplify one dimension while monopolistic competition simplifies the other. On the one hand, the utilization dimension, which is treated generally in monopolistic competition, is constrained in public goods models so that utilization is always equal to unity. On the other hand, the nonrival public goods dimension is treated generally in public goods models but constrained in monopolistic competition so that each firm produces exactly one unit of the public good. Therefore, public goods and monopolistic competition are different dimensional simplifications of the same general model.

We should probably demonstrate that the seven conditions listed above are not mutually exclusive. A function which satisfies these seven conditions, and at the same time incorporates diminishing marginal utility, is the following:

$$g^i(y_{i1},Y_1; \ldots ; y_{ik},Y_k; \ldots y_{iK},Y_K) = (y_{i1}^{a/A}\, Y_1 + \ldots + y_{ik}^{a/A} Y_k + \ldots + y_{iK}^{a/A} Y_K)^A \tag{9.3}$$

where $1 > A > a > 0$. The restriction on the parameters, A and a, ensures a positive but diminishing marginal utility in both the public good dimension and the utilization dimension. Of course, it is conditions 1 through 7 which are important, while the functional form offered in equation (9.3) is done so as just one possibility. However, note the similarity of this formulation to that of Dixit and Stiglitz. Dixit and Stiglitz start with a utility function of the form $u = U[x_{o'}, (\sum_i x_i^p)^{1/p}]$.[4] The second argument in this utility function is what we have been calling the g function. To translate notation, note that Dixit and Stiglitz use subscript i to denote firms where we use k. Therefore, x_i in Dixit and Stiglitz is the same as y_{ik} in our notation. Except for the fact that Dixit and Stiglitz implicitly set equal to unity[5] the public good amount of each firm, and, therefore, have no variable analogous to our model's Y, the formulations are practically identical. This form for the utility function leads to constant elasticities and so is often employed in mathematical models. The important point here is that although our formulation looks like a generalization of the Dixit and Stiglitz monopolistic competition model, we have actually arrived at our formulation by trying to generalize the public goods models, not by trying to generalize the monopolistic competition models. In the generalization of the public goods models we have been led to a model which is also a generalization of monopolistic competition models. This further illustrates one of the central themes of the book: that public goods models and monopolistic competition models are different simplifications of the same general model.

We turn now from a discussion of the nature of the utility functions to the societal transformation function and the first order conditions describing optimality. The transformation function has the form

$$F(\sum_i y_{i1}, Y_1; \ldots ; \sum_i y_{ik}, Y_k; \ldots ; \sum_i y_{iK}, Y_K; \sum_i x_i) = 0 \tag{9.4}$$

Combining (9.4) with the utility function (9.1′) and maximizing the utility of each individual while holding the utility level of the others constant leads to the following conditions:

$$\left.\frac{dx_i}{dy_{ik}}\right|_{U^i} = \left.\frac{dx_{i'}}{dy_{i'k}}\right|_{U^{i'}} = \left.\frac{d\sum_i x_i}{d\sum_i y_{ik}}\right|_F \tag{9.5}$$

for all i, i', and k,

$$\sum_i \left.\frac{dx_i}{dY_k}\right|_{U^i} = \left.\frac{d\sum_i x_i}{dY_k}\right|_F \tag{9.6}$$

for all k.

These conditions are the same as those described in Chapter 7, except there are k times as many. Equation (9.5) expresses that for each k, each consumer's marginal rate of substitution must equal the marginal cost in the utilization dimension. These are precisely the marginal equalities we expect in a standard private goods model. Equation (9.6) expresses that for each k, the sum of consumers' marginal rates of substitution must be equal to the marginal cost in the public goods dimension. These equalities are precisely what we expect in ordinary pure public goods treatments.

Conditions (9.5) and (9.6) can be interpreted in several different ways. For example, we could interpret the conditions as describing optimality in K private goods and K different public goods. However, we have been interpreting the model as linking the utilization dimension and the public goods dimension. That is, the public good amount gets sold automatically along with the utilization, and pricing takes place in the utilization dimension. Therefore, as in Chapter 7, we rewrite (9.6) to focus only on the utilization dimension:

$$(9.6') \quad \sum_i \frac{d}{dY_k} \int_0^{y^o_{ik}} \left.\frac{dx_i}{dy_{ik}}\right|_{U^{io}} dy_{ik} = \frac{d}{dY_k} \int_0^{\sum_i y^o_{ik}} \left.\frac{d\sum_i x_i}{d\sum_i y_{ik}}\right|_F d\sum_i y_{ik} + \left.\frac{d\sum_i x_i}{dY_k}\right|_{F, \sum_i y_{ik}} = 0$$

Equation (9.6′) is the same condition as (9.6). The left-hand side is the summation of marginal rates of substitution in the public goods dimension expressed as summations of increased areas under individual demand curves in the utilization dimension. The right-hand side represents the marginal cost in the public good dimension as the changes in variable and overhead costs in the utilization dimension. This is precisely the same condition as equation (7.6″), only now there are K times as many equations.

Once we have linked the utilization and public goods dimensions so that we no longer have K private goods and K different public goods, there are still two possible interpretations to equations (9.5) and (9.6). These K sets of conditions could be interpreted as the optimal marginal equalities in the public goods dimension and the utilization dimension for K separate public goods. Alternatively, we could think of one industry or group composed of K independent, competing firms. In the former interpretation, each firm would essentially be a monopoly producer of a public good, just like in the monopoly case introduced in Chapter 7. Partial equilibrium analysis might be used on each firm independently, as was the case in Chapter 7. In the latter interpretation, however, the K firms are interdependent. A partial equilibrium analysis looking only at one of the firms will be inadequate to capture the interrelatedness which is really the focus of our interest in the multiple producer case.

The approach adopted here actually causes us to embark upon a very ambitious voyage. The extension of public goods theory leads naturally to the discussion of competing, price-discriminating sellers with endogenous quality in a close-to-general equilibrium setting. The setting is not completely a general equilibrium one because the numeraire good, x, is still treated as outside the group of K competing public goods firms. A complete description of the equilibrium in this setting is beyond the scope of this book. Nevertheless, progress of a sort is made just by reaching this point. Not only is the setting to be studied an extension of public goods theory, it is also an extension of monopolistic competition. This realization alone helps to synthesize two disparate literatures. The techniques used and advances made in each of the separate literatures will eventually be exploited in the complete analysis of this model. Even short of a completely general analysis, there are issues that can be addressed simply by comparing the optimum marginal equalities with the marginal equalities existing for interdependent profit-maximizing producers. This is the goal of Chapter 10.

Before moving on to Chapter 10, there is one more issue that deserves discussion. The issue is that conditions (9.5) and (9.6) describe the welfare optimum as an interior solution, but corner or boundary solutions might be relevant. For example, if indivisibilities or nonconvexities exist, or if there are cost differences between the supply of the kth and k'th firm, then the overall maximum might have y_{ik} for all i and Y_k both equal to zero for some k. Alternatively, when the number of firms, K, is made endogenous, then the corner solution of zero output automatically becomes relevant for any firms that do not produce positive amounts in the equilibrium. The boundary conditions also become relevant in still another way. Since price discrimination is being considered, the limit on the ability of the firm to price-discriminate is given by the consumer's possible utility level in the relevant corner solution where the consumer completely drops consumption of the price discriminator's good. Essentially, the consumer's utility level in the relevant corner solution becomes the constraint on the ability of any one of the firms to price-discriminate. This quickly becomes a difficult problem because the number of possible market configurations, or corner solutions, expands geometrically with the number of firms, K.[6]

In Chapter 10, only the interior solutions will be treated. That is, given that K firms exist, we will analyze the public good output and the utilization output of these profit-maximizing sellers. Since K is not quantified except that it is given as greater than one and since none of the results depend on the magnitude of K, the treatment is still fairly general. The results are derived for all K greater than one and hold for all K greater than one, but they are still conditional results in this sense.

Note that the models starting from the monopolistic competition perspective usually allow the number of firms to vary. These studies pose the question of how many firms will and should produce positive amounts of utilization.[7] To answer that question requires two potentially problematic assumptions. The first has been discussed above. For the number of firms to be a margin of interest there must be the very strict assumption that firms cannot vary Y_k, the output in the public goods dimension. Therefore, firms only consider whether to produce zero or positive quantities of utilization. The second assumption is that industry equilibrium can be characterized by a zero profit condition. However, as Demsetz has argued, the zero profit condition in monopolistic competition is inconsistent with the notion of uncopiable product differentiation.[8] The analysis in the next chapter, in focusing exclusively on interior solutions, begs the question of how many firms will exist but allows discussion of the ability of the firms to vary their product.

In actuality, leaving the number of firms exogenous is not as problematic in our setting as it normally might be. In standard monopolistic competition the number of firms is actually a simplified version of what we have been calling the public goods dimension. This dimension does not go unexamined in the model of this book. The profit-maximizing amount in the public goods dimension is examined in the firm's internal optimization in that dimension. Chapter 10 will compare the condition describing the profit-maximizing choice in the public good dimension to equation (9.6) or (9.6′) of this chapter. Whatever results are derived in monopolistic competition for the number of firms can also be addressed in the approach of this book by examining the optimal public good amount of each firm.[9] In fact, perhaps an improvement is inherent in the approach of this book. Whereas monopolistic competition allows endogenous treatment of the number of firms through the use of the potentially troublesome zero profit equilibrium condition, the model of this book will employ only the well-accepted notion of internal profit maximization (zero profit at the margin) to analyze the public good amount of each firm.

CHAPTER TEN

Multiple Producers: Equilibrium

This chapter examines the equilibrium for the model set out in Chapter 9. The organization of the formal analysis follows along the lines of Chapter 8. The consumer's optimization is presented first. Each firm's profit maximization is presented second, the details of which are relegated to an appendix following this chapter. This is followed by a comparison of the conditions existing in equilibrium to equations (9.5) and (9.6). The chapter concludes with brief comparisons of the model to conventional results reached in models of monopolistic competition and public goods.

Although the analysis follows along the lines of Chapter 8, it is quite different here because of the added element of multiple firms. Whenever a firm considers changes in its production in either the public goods dimension or the utilization dimension, the firm will want to consider the many possible reactions of its rivals. A rival could react by changing prices, changing the quantity in the utilization dimension, and/or changing the quantity in the public goods dimension. Furthermore, different rivals could react differently. The analysis in this chapter will remain at a general level so that all of the possible reactions are considered. One plausible scenario is developed in the text and alternative scenarios are covered in the appendix. Closed-form solutions will not be sought because that would go beyond the level of generality. To obtain exact, closed-form solutions for the equilibrium values of public good production and utilization quantity would require stringent assumptions about the possible reactions of the firms. For the most part, this is not attempted.

It is possible to pursue the calculation of closed-form solutions for a variety of special cases. Nash reactions could be assumed for price, utilization, or public good quantity.[1] Predatory responses and matching behavior could also be considered. An example of this type of approach taken to the limit is in a paper by Koenker and Perry.[2] Koenker and Perry present a taxonomy of the types of reactions that might occur and then calculate the resulting equilibria for each reaction assumption in an oligopoly setting. Of course, Koenker and Perry are only considering uniform pricing in the presence of exogenous quality determination. The Koenker and Perry approach would be more difficult here because of the multiple dimensions in which the rival might react. Nevertheless, attempts to calculate the equilibrium for the model in this book by exogenously imposing a reaction condition will probably be useful exercises to undertake.[3]

A more difficult approach is to endogenously determine what the reaction of the rivals will be. This is an area of research in industrial organization that is still in its infancy. Even in relatively simple duopoly settings, the game theory aspects of the problem become difficult. The completely general endogenous treatment of reaction functions for the setting described in Chapter 9 would quickly involve multiperson, multistrategy games of an optimal control theory nature.[4] Such a treatment is beyond the scope of this book.

The analysis in this chapter will settle for a comparison of the conditions describing the internal optimization of the firm with the conditions describing Pareto optimality. Following the formal analysis, a verbal discussion will clarify how the incentives existing in equilibrium are affected by differences in the expected reactions of the rival firms. Since this chapter is mainly concerned with the competitive or noncooperative provision of public goods, the types of reactions that are considered most plausible for noncooperative sellers are highlighted. The characteristics of equilibrium in the presence of these plausible reaction assumptions are treated in the text. Alternative (e.g., collusive) reactions are treated in the appendix. Beware, however, that the discussion of these reactions is somewhat ad hoc in nature. There is no attempt herein to derive the rational reaction assumptions existing in such a rich setting as this. This job must be left to future research.

We turn first to the presentation of the consumer's maximization of utility. The ith consumer maximizes U^i, given by (9.1) or (9.1′) and conditions 1–7, over the choice of x_i and y_{ik}, for all k, subject to a wealth constraint:

$$(10.1) \quad x_i^o = x_i + \sum_k \int_0^{y_{ik}} p_{ikj} dj$$

where

$$(10.2)\quad p_{ikj} = p_{ikj}\,(y_{i1}, Y_1, \sum_i y_{i1}; \ldots ; y_{iK}, Y_K, \sum_i y_{iK}; j)$$

is the price of the jth unit of utilization from the kth firm to the ith consumer when $y_{i1}, \ldots, y_{ik}, \ldots, y_{iK}$ are purchased overall. The pricing function and budget constraint are written in the most general format to allow for both price discrimination and the effect of the consumption of the rival firms' output on the prices charged by any one of the firms. The first order conditions for the maximization are:

$$(10.3)\quad U^i_{x_i} = \lambda\left(1 + \frac{d}{dx_i}\sum_K \int_0^{y_{ik}} p_{ikj}\,dj\right)$$

for all i,

$$U^i_{y_{ik'}} = \lambda\left(p_{ik'j}\Big|_{j\,=\,y_{ik'}} + \sum_K \int_0^{y_{ik}} \frac{dp_{ikj}}{dy_{ik'}}\,dj\right)$$

for all k', i. By (10.2), p_{ikj} does not depend on x_i for any k, so the summation of integrals in the first equation of (10.3) drops out. In short, the prices that the K public good firms charge are not affected by the individual's consumption of the numeraire good. Therefore, there is no pecuniary effect related to the consumption of the numeraire good. However, the summation of integrals in the second equation of (10.3) does not generally disappear. Thus, when combining the two equations of (10.3) to eliminate λ, the result is

$$(10.4)\quad -\frac{dx_i}{dy_{ik'}}\bigg|_{U^i} = p_{ik'j}\Big|_{j\,=\,y_{ik'}} + \sum_K \int_0^{y_{ik}} \frac{dp_{ikj}}{dy_{ik'}}\,dj$$

Equation (10.4) states simply that individuals consume until their marginal rates of substitution for output from the k'th firm are equal to the marginal price paid for the unit from the k'th producer plus any inframarginal pecuniary effects on the utilization units of any of the K firms. When these pecuniary effects are ignored, the summation of integrals in (10.4) drops out and we get the standard result of an equality between marginal price and marginal rate of substitution, as in

$$(10.4')\quad -\frac{dx_i}{dy_{ik'}}\bigg|_{U^i} = p_{ik'j}\Big|_{j\,=\,y_{ik'}}$$

Equation (10.4′) comes about essentially because of a price-taking assumption on the part of the consumer. Care should be taken here, however, because such a price-taking assumption is not generally valid, especially in the face of price-discriminating sellers.

The price-taking assumption was examined above in Chapter 8 for the monopoly producer case. In consideration of the existence of multiple producers, it would do well to examine this assumption once again. There are several scenarios under which some or all of the integral terms in (10.4) vanish. First, in the ordinary textbook treatment of uniform pricing, a single price is established for all units, y_{ik}, regardless of consumer. Therefore, an individual's consumption of a utilization unit has no direct effect on any price. That is, $\partial p_{ikj}/\partial y_{ik'} = 0$ for all pairs k,k'. Since p_{ikj} also depends on the total consumption of utilization units, there is also the indirect effect routed through the effect of the individual's consumption on total consumption. By the chain rule, this can be represented as $(dp_{ikj}/d\sum_i y_{ik})(d\sum_i y_{ik}/dy_{ik})$, where $d\sum_i y_{ik}/dy_{ik} = 1$. Although this term is nonzero, it is typically ignored when an atomistic assumption of a large number of consumers is added.

A second scenario in which the price-taking assumption is valid is if the firms make commitments to their pricing schedules such that the consumers cannot affect those prices through any actions. Such pricing schedules need not be linear, nor need they be the same for each individual. All that is required is that the individual consumer have no control over any variable that will affect the pricing schedule. If the kth firm makes such commitments, consumers will act subject to those commitments, therefore assuming that they cannot change prices, so $dp_{ikj}/dy_{ik'} = 0$ for all k'. Note, however, that if the k'th firm does not also make such commitments, then consumption of a unit of utilization from the kth firm may affect the prices charged by the k'th firm, that is, $dp_{yik'j}/dy_{ik} \neq 0$.[5] Note also that if sellers make commitments to pricing schedules that the consumers cannot influence, those schedules could be discriminatory but not perfectly so. This is because perfect price discrimination would require that the prices be adjusted depending on the consumer's purchases of substitutes or complements. If, however, the prices are so adjusted, then the consumer can affect the prices by buying substitutes or complements, and the pecuniary effect represented in the integral terms in equation (10.4) returns.

A third scenario, in which some of the integral terms in equation (10.4) disappear, develops if the firms are set up as perfectly discriminating entities that are noncompeting. Such would be the case if the customers are divided among the firms so that they can deal with only one firm. In this case, $y_{ik} > 0$ for only one k, and $dp_{ik'j}/dy_{ik} = 0$ for all $k \neq k'$.[6] Of course, there still remains the pecuniary effect on infra-marginal units sold by the kth firm. In essence, this scenario takes us back to the model of Chapter 8, which considered the monopoly case.

Unless one of these scenarios is envisioned, the proper treatment of interrelated, price-discriminating sellers must consider the pecuniary effects captured in equation (10.4). I believe that such consideration of the pecuniary effects goes to the heart of the problem with conventional treatments of monopolistic price discrimination. In the monopoly situation, all interfirm pecuniary effects disappear. But such an analysis errs too much in the direction of partial equilibrium. Monopoly, or rather, price-searching firms do not operate in a vacuum, and such interfirm effects should be considered. This is perhaps the most important feature to be taken from Thompson's analysis of price discrimination in the case of pure public goods.[7] My analysis shows how this consideration is also relevant in the generalized public goods model and in monopolistic competition.

Moving on to the firm's profit maximization, the profits of the kth firm, π_k, are:

$$(10.5) \quad \pi_k = \sum_i \int_0^{y_{ik}} p_{ikj} dj - C_k(\sum_i y_{ik}, Y_k)$$

for all k, where C_k are the costs of the kth firm. The particulars of the firm's profit maximization are presented in the appendix to this chapter.[8] The first order conditions for the k'th firm's maximization of equation (10.5) are:

$$(10.6) \quad p_{i'k'j}\Big|_{j = y_{i'k'}} + \sum_i \int_0^{y_{ik'}} \frac{dp_{ik'j}}{dy_{i'k'}} dj + \sum_{k \neq k'} \sum_i \left(\sum_{i^*} \int_0^{y_{i^*k'}} \frac{dp_{i^*k'j}}{dy_{ik}} dj \frac{dy_{ik}}{dy_{i'k'}} \right) + \sum_{k \neq k'} \left(\sum_{i^*} \int_0^{y_{i^*k'}} \frac{dp_{i^*k'j}}{dY_k} dj \frac{dY_k}{dy_{i'k'}} \right) = \frac{dC_{k'}}{d\sum_i y_{ik'}}$$

for all i', and

$$(10.7) \quad \sum_i \frac{d}{dY_{k'}} \int_0^{y_{ik'}} p_{ik'j} dj + \sum_{k \neq k'} \sum_i \left(\sum_{i^*} \int_0^{y_{i^*k'}} \frac{dp_{i^*k'j}}{dy_{ik}} dj \frac{dy_{ik}}{dY_{k'}} \right) + \sum_{k \neq k'} \left(\sum_{i^*} \int_0^{y_{i^*k'}} \frac{dp_{i^*k'j}}{dY_k} dj \frac{dY_k}{dY_{k'}} \right) = \frac{dC_{k'}}{dY_{k'}}$$

Equation (10.6) describes the profit-maximizing level of sales of utilization units to the i'th consumer. There is one such equation for each consumer. Equation (10.7) describes the profit-maximizing level of public good quantity. There is only one such equation because each consumer jointly consumes the same public good quantity. These equations are the counterparts of equations (8.8) and (8.9). Of course, in the present multiple producer case, the equations are much more complex. The intuition surrounding these conditions will be discussed verbally when they are compared to the characteristics of the optimum as presented in equations (9.5) and (9.6′) of the last chapter. Condition (10.6) is discussed first.

By substituting (10.4) for the i'th consumer, that is, the i'th consumer's optimum, and (10A.1), from the appendix, into (10.6) we derive:

$$(10.6') \quad -\left.\frac{dx_{i'}}{dy_{i'k'}}\right|_{U^{i'}} - \sum_{K}\int_0^{y_{i'k}} \frac{dp_{i'kj}}{dy_{i'k'}}dj + \sum_{i}\int_0^{y_{ik'}} \frac{dp_{ik'j}}{dy_{i'k'}}dj$$
$$+ \sum_{k\neq k'}\sum_{i}\left(\sum_{i^*}\int_0^{y_{i^*k'}} \frac{dp_{i^*k'j}}{dy_{ik}}\,dj\,\frac{dy_{ik}}{dy_{i'k'}}\right) + \sum_{k\neq k'}\left(\sum_{i^*}\int_0^{y_{i^*k'}} \frac{dp_{i^*k'j}}{dY_k}\,dj\,\frac{dY_k}{dy_{i'k'}}\right)$$
$$= -\left.\frac{d\sum_i x_i}{d\sum_i y_{ik'}}\right|_F$$

for all i'. Equation (10.6′) must hold in equilibrium. It says that the consumer's marginal rate of substitution for utilization units, the first term on the left-hand side, plus four more terms equals the marginal cost in the utilization dimension as represented by the right-hand side of (10.6′). Inspection reveals that equation (10.6′) is the same as the condition describing optimality, equation (9.5), except for the four extra terms on the left-hand side, which may be nonzero.

$$(10.8) \quad \text{(a)} -\sum_{K}\int_0^{y_{i'k}} \frac{dp_{i'kj}}{dy_{i'k'}}dj$$

$$\text{(b)} \sum_{i}\int_0^{y_{ik'}} \frac{dp_{ik'j}}{dy_{i'k'}}dj$$

$$\text{(c)} \sum_{k\neq k'}\sum_{i}\left(\sum_{i^*}\int_0^{y_{i^*k'}} \frac{dp_{i^*k'j}}{dy_{ik}}\,dj\,\frac{dy_{ik}}{dy_{i'k'}}\right)$$

$$\text{(d)} \sum_{k\neq k'}\left(\sum_{i^*}\int_0^{y_{i^*k'}} \frac{dp_{i^*k'j}}{dY_k}\,dj\,\frac{dY_k}{dy_{i'k'}}\right)$$

If these terms are negative, then the marginal rate of substitution must be greater than the marginal cost, indicating an underutilization. Alternatively, if these terms are positive, then the marginal rate of substitution will be less than the marginal cost indicating overutilization. Each of these terms will be discussed in turn.

The term in (10.8a) is the pecuniary effect internalized by the consumer. Verbally, (10.8a) is the negative of the summation over all firms of the inframarginal price effects on all units of utilization purchased by the *i*th consumer, where those price effects are brought about by the additional consumption of a unit of utilization from the k'th firm. This is the effect originally highlighted by Thompson for pure public goods but commonly ignored when the consumer is assumed to be a price taker. If the consumer is a price taker, then the derivative inside the integral is zero and the term disappears. However, if the consumer can use the consumption of the utilization units from the k'th firm to bargain for lower prices from the other firms, then the derivative is negative, making the whole of (10.8a) positive. As such, (10.8a) represents an overproduction incentive existing in this scenario. Intuitively, since the purchase of a unit of utilization from the k'th firm allows the purchaser to both consume the unit and to obtain lower prices elsewhere, the consumer will continue to purchase such units past the point where the marginal rate of substitution falls below the price of the unit.

Equation (10.8b) represents the pecuniary effect internalized by the k'th firm. Indeed, (10.8b) is the sum of the inframarginal price changes for all units of the k'th firm to all individuals, where such price changes are due to the expansion of sales to the i'th consumer. As such, (10.8b) is the same term that appears in (8.10). This term is typically less than zero if the firm has to lower inframarginal prices in order to expand utilization. Only under perfect competition (or atomistic competition as an approximation) or perfect price discrimination will this term be zero. In typical cases this term is less than zero, thus leading to a condition where each individual's marginal rate of substitution for utilization is greater than the marginal cost of utilization, and this is a characteristic of underutilization of the public good. The more perfect the price discrimination, the smaller this term is and the less the underutilization incentive. Indeed, the term in (10.8b) is essentially the generalization of the argument that marginal revenue is less than price for the uniform pricing monopolist.

Note that the i'th term in the summation in (10.8b) cancels exactly with the k'th term in the summation in (10.8a). The inframarginal price changes for the utilization units bought by the i'th consumer and sold by the k'th firm are internalized by both parties. This makes sense. Anything over which the i'th individual and the k'th firm are bargaining that affects both parties will be taken into account by both parties. Except for the one term that cancels, the essence of (10.8a) is that there are some benefits, in the form of lower prices from other firms, that the consumer gets that do not affect the profitability of the firm. Again, except for the one term that cancels, the essence of (10.8b) is that there are some costs, in the form of lower prices from other consumers, that the firm incurs that do not affect the utility of the i'th consumer. The benefits that the consumer gets lead to overutilization while the costs that the firm incurs lead to underutilization.

The terms in (10.8c) and (10.8d) capture the interaction effects with the other suppliers. If these two terms are negative like (10.8b), then a further underproduction incentive exists in the utilization dimension. However, (10.8c) and (10.8d) may be greater than zero and together with (10.8a) may provide overutilization incentives that may even be greater than the underutilization incentive in (10.8b). Of course, there are many different types of interactions that can be discussed in the analysis of (10.8c) and (10.8d), and because of this the terms can take any sign. I will argue that under realistic information assumptions and noncooperative interaction, the resulting types of reactions exhibited will imply the existence of overproduction incentives. The scenario resulting from conjectures of price constancy will be discussed in the text. For the alternative situations of Cournot type interactions or collusive interactions, see the appendix. Condition (10.8c) is discussed first.

The term in (10.8c) captures the effect on all the inframarginal prices of the k'th firm due to the competitor's change in utilization level. Since the competitor's utilization units are substitutes, the effect on the k'th firm's prices is negative, that is, $dp_{i*k'j}/dy_{ik} < 0$. Therefore, the sign of (10.8c) is the opposite of the sign of $dy_{ik}/dy_{i'k'}$. This whole term could be zero if the competitors react as in a Cournot model, because then, $dy_{ik}/dy_{i'k'} = 0$ for all firms (see the appendix). But this may not be a realistic assumption. Firms are usually viewed as price setters, letting quantity and inventories adjust. This possibility is taken up here.

An Edgeworth or Bertrand type price constancy reaction implies that $dy_{ik}/dy_{i'k'} < 0$ for all firms. This follows because when the k'th firm increases utilization (by lowering its prices), the kth firm suffers a decrease in demand. Thus, holding Y_k, the public good quantity, constant (which [10.8c] does) and holding p_{ikj} constant, a decrease in demand must lead to a lowering of the utilization output of the kth firm. Therefore, the term in (10.8c) is positive overall, and this type of interaction leads to overutilization of the output of the k'th firm.

I believe this type of price constancy reaction to be plausible as a first approximation or short-run reaction on the part of the kth firm. After all, if the kth firm is setting prices, and if the kth firm is not able to observe the price or output change by the k'th firm, the first indication to the kth firm that something has happened is in the decrease in its sales. As noted above, this decrease in sales leads to overproduction by the k'th firm.

In the case where the kth firm can observe the price cuts by the k'th firm, the effect is still analyzed as a decrease in the price of a substitute good and therefore a decrease in demand as well. Under all but extremely unusual circumstances, a decrease in demand leads to a decrease in output. Therefore, $dy_{ik}/dy_{i'k'} < 0$, and the situation is still one of incentives for overutilization.

Note that these arguments will not apply if the firms are assumed to be perfect discriminators. If the rival firms are perfect discriminators, then the k'th firm could not expect price constancy from its rivals. Indeed, if perfectly discriminatory rival firms were to keep prices constant, then the customer receiving the expanded utilization of the k'th firm will totally drop utilization of the rival firm. Indeed, the customer, who is receiving no surplus to begin with, suffers a decrease in demand for the rival firm's utilization and, if prices do not change, will not continue to purchase the rival firm's product. Quite simply, perfect price discrimination and price constancy reaction functions are not compatible. What this means here is that if the customer does not stop buying the rival firm's output, (when the rival firm holds price constant), then the rival firm could only have been imperfectly discriminating so that some surplus is left for the consumer after demand falls.

These examples illustrate that the response of other firms to one firm's change in output is to change their outputs in the opposite direction. In fact, the negativity of this derivative, $dy_{ik}/dy_{i'k'}$, is often seen as the distinctive criterion for a competitive, or rivalrous, interaction. The opposite case, $dy_{ik}/dy_{i'k'} > 0$, occurs for coordinated, collusive interaction, or for a predatory reaction. These are taken up in the appendix.[9]

There is one quick, final note about (10.8c) and its relationship to (10.8b). In standard, pure private goods models with homogeneous goods and no price discrimination, it is possible to prove that the overproduction incentives in (10.8c) can totally offset but will never dominate the underproduction incentives in (10.8b). Remember that (10.8b) represents the monopoly distortion effect through which inframarginal prices are lowered when the firm expands. This effect causes underproduction. Meanwhile, (10.8c) represents the positive effect on inframarginal prices due to the contraction of rivals. As Koenker and Perry show for the limiting case, when $\sum_K \sum_i dy_{ik}/dy_{i'k'} = -1$, these two price effects exactly cancel and the k'th firm acts as a price taker.[10] There is no reason for the rival firms to contract more than this, however, because it is the prospect of lower prices which is causing them to contract in the first place. If prices do not fall, then the rival firms will no longer contract. Therefore, (10.8c) cannot dominate (10.8b) in such a setting. This argument, however, requires the homogeneity and uniform pricing assumptions which are absent in this model. Therefore, although an overproduction incentive from the combined effects of (10.8b) and (10.8c) is never possible in standard models, it is a possibility in the generalized model considered here. Indeed, as the price discrimination approaches perfection, then (10.8b) approaches zero. However, (10.8c) may still be positive. Intuitively, if the marginal price is lowered by the k'th firm in order to expand, then the kth firm will suffer a decrease in demand, and, in general, will lower output, thus establishing the existence of a net overproduction incentive.

So far, we have not considered the response that the kth firm might make in the quality or public goods dimension. The expression in (10.8d) captures this element of the interaction. Equation (10.8d) is the effect on all the inframarginal prices of the k'th firm due to the changes in the public goods dimension of each of its competitors. Since the effect on prices of the k'th firm of an increase in the kth firm's public good amount is negative (i.e., $dp_{i*k'j}/dY_k < 0$), the sign of (10.8d) is the opposite of the sign of $dY_k/dy_{i'k'}$. This means that overproduction incentives exist for the utilization dimension of the k'th firm if the kth firm responds with a decrease in public good production when the k'th firm increases its utilization. This is the plausible reaction of a firm that can observe the price cuts by the k'th firm. That is, the price cuts by the k'th firm cause a decrease in demand to the competitors who respond by lowering the price and quality (public good amount) of their products.[11] Notationally, $dY_k/dy_{i'k'} < 0$, and an overproduction incentive exists.

If the kth firm cannot observe the price decrease by the k'th firm, then they will hold price and quality constant and suffer a decrease in utilization as discussed above in regard to (10.8c). In this case the kth firm holds the public good amount constant and (10.8d) is zero.

I would consider either of these cases to be a plausible interaction, the difference depending on whether the price cut by the k'th firm is observable. In the observable case, the kth firm recognizes the decrease in the price of a substitute and reacts by cutting production in the public goods dimension, giving the k'th firm an overproduction incentive in the utilization dimension. In the unobservable case, the kth firm leaves price and public good amount constant and suffers the decrease in sales in the utilization dimension mentioned in the discussion of (10.8c).

Furthermore, there is no presupposition that (10.8a), (10.8c), and (10.8d) taken together cannot dominate the underproduction incentive in (10.8b). Indeed, since (10.8b) approaches zero as the price discrimination gets closer to being perfect, it is likely that these overproduction incentives dominate whenever price discrimination is an important factor in an industry.

We move now to the discussion of the firm's decision regarding the public good output. By using (10.A2′), from the appendix, and by adding and subtracting,

$$(10.9) \quad \sum_i \frac{d}{dY_{k'}} \int_0^{y^o_{ik'}} \left.\frac{dx_i}{dy_{ik'}}\right|_{U^i} dy_{ik'}$$

from the left-hand side of (10.7) we get:

$$(10.7') \quad \begin{aligned} &\sum_i \frac{d}{dY_{k'}} \int_0^{y_{ik'}} p_{ik'j}\,dj - \sum_i \frac{d}{dY_{k'}} \int_0^{y^o_{ik'}} \left.\frac{dx_i}{dy_{ik'}}\right|_{U^i} dy_{ik'} \\ &+ \sum_i \frac{d}{dY_{k'}} \int_0^{y^o_{ik'}} \left.\frac{dx_i}{dy_{ik'}}\right|_{U^i} dy_{ik'} + \sum_{k \neq k'} \sum_i \left(\sum_{i^*} \int_0^{y_{i^*k'}} \frac{dp_{i^*k'j}}{dy_{ik}}\,dj\,\frac{dy_{ik}}{dY_{k'}} \right) \\ &+ \sum_{k \neq k'} \left(\sum_{i^*} \int_0^{y_{i^*k'}} \frac{dp_{i^*k'j}}{dY_k}\,dj\,\frac{dY_k}{dY_{k'}} \right) \end{aligned}$$

$$= \frac{\partial}{\partial Y_k} \int_0^{\sum_i y^o_{ik}} - \left.\frac{d\sum_i x_i}{d\sum_i y_{ik}}\right|_F d\sum_i y_{ik} - \left.\frac{d\sum_i x_i}{dY_k}\right|_{F, \sum_i y_{ik}} = 0$$

This condition describes the equilibrium in the public good dimension for the k'th firm. Inspection indicates that (10.7′) is the same as the condition describing Pareto optimality in this dimension, (9.6′), except for the following three expressions on the left-hand side:

$$\text{(a)} \sum_i \frac{d}{dY_{k'}} \int_0^{y_{ik'}} p_{ik'j} dj - \sum_i \frac{d}{dY_{k'}} \int_0^{y^o_{ik'}} \left.\frac{dx_i}{dy_{ik'}}\right|_{U^i} dy_{ik'}$$

$$\text{(10.10)} \quad \text{(b)} \sum_{k \neq k'} \sum_i \left(\sum_{i^*} \int_0^{y_{i^*k'}} \frac{dp_{i^*k'j}}{dy_{ik}} dj \, \frac{dy_{ik}}{dY_{k'}} \right)$$

$$\text{(c)} \sum_{k \neq k'} \left(\sum_{i^*} \int_0^{y_{i^*k'}} \frac{dp_{i^*k'j}}{dY_k} dj \, \frac{dY_k}{dY_{k'}} \right)$$

The first expression, (10.10a), is the derivative, taken with respect to the public good amount of the k'th firm, of the difference between the total revenue of the firm and the total amount that all consumers would pay to acquire $\sum_i y_{ik'}$ units of utilization. It is true that $p_{ik'j} = dx_i/dy_{ik'}|U^i$ at the margin, as this is ensured by the utility maximization of each individual. But unless the price discrimination is perfect, the inframarginal prices will generally be less than the corresponding marginal rates of substitution. In any realistic setting, the revenue collected will be less than what the consumers would willingly pay. This, however, does not ensure that the expression (10.10a) is less than zero because it is the derivative of this difference with respect to $Y_{k'}$ that appears there. This, of course, is the same point that was made in Chapter 8 with regard to equation (8.12). The present analysis is inconclusive with respect to the impact of (10.10a) as a discrepancy between conditions describing profit maximization and optimality. Since this expression can take on any sign, it can be consistent with either overproduction or underproduction in the public goods dimension.

The expressions in (10.10b) and (10.10c) correspond to the same types of interaction discussed in (10.8c) and (10.8d) above. These two terms capture the effects on the inframarginal prices of the k'th firm due to the responses on the part of the kth firm in both the utilization and the public good dimensions. Above, in (10.8c) and (10.8d), those changes made by the kth firm come about because of the increases in utilization (brought about by decreases in prices) of the k'th firm. Here, the changes come about because of the increase in the quality or public good amount of the k'th firm. As in (10.8c) and (10.8d), $dp_{i*k'j}/dy_{ik} < 0$ and $dp_{i*k'j}/dY_k < 0$, so the signs of (10.10b) and (10.10c), respectively, are the opposites of the signs of $dy_{ik}/dY_{k'}$ and $dY_k/dY_{k'}$. Overproduction in the public goods dimension occurs, then, when these last two derivatives are negative, whereas underproduction results when they are positive. One plausible scenario is discussed below, and alternative cases are treated in the appendix.

Arguably the most plausible information scenario is when the kth firm cannot directly and immediately observe the public good output level of the k'th firm. Thus, when the k'th firm increases its output in the public goods dimension, the kth firm will hold price and quality level constant but lose sales of utilization units to customers who are now being better served by the k'th firm. This leads to a Cournot assumption in the public goods dimension, $dY_k/dY_{k'} = 0$, representing the passive reaction by competitors to a change in the quality of the k'th firm. This implies that (10.10c) is zero. But the kth firm suffers a decrease in sales of utilization units, $dy_{ik}/dY_{k'} < 0$, which leads to overproduction in the public goods dimension by the k'th firm according to (10.10b).

To briefly summarize this presentation of the comparison of the equilibrium and optimum levels in the public good dimension I would like to point out that there is no clear case made for underproduction of the public good. The expression in (10.10a) suggests an unsigned bias in the public goods dimension similar to that existing in the monopoly case. In addition, examination of the terms in (10.10b) and (10.10c) suggests that overproduction incentives may exist in a plausible scenario once the effects of the rivals' reactions are considered.

I conclude this chapter with brief comparisons between the model set out in this chapter and models of traditional monopolistic competition, pure public goods, and the monopoly version of the model that was presented in Chapter 8. The comparison with monopolistic competition, to be presented first, is the lengthiest. This will be followed by briefer comparisons to public goods models and the monopoly version of the model of this book.

The results that we obtain from the examination of the profit maximization of the firm that sells utilization units of the public good can be compared to the traditional results in the theory of monopolistic competition. Indeed, the settings are similar. In both the generalized public goods model presented here and in monopolistic competition models, there are several producers supplying units of differentiated products which are linked through a notion of substitutability. The utilization dimension in the model of this book is analogous to the quantity dimension in monopolistic competition. The public goods dimension in the model of this book is a generalization of the number of firms or degree of product differentiation in monopolistic competition models. Notwithstanding these similarities, the approach to the problem through public goods considerations highlights several differences between traditional monopolistic competition and the model of this book. These differences suggest areas in which the standard monopolistic competition model can be generalized, improved, or otherwise changed. Pursuing such changes is important not only because the model becomes more realistic but also because in some cases the qualitative nature of the results of the analysis is affected.

The first difference involves the relaxation of restrictive assumptions regarding the firm's decision with respect to the quality level of the product. In monopolistic competition models, each firm can produce only one product. Additionally, in the Chamberlinian version of monopolistic competition, the single products of each firm are assumed to be symmetrically or uniformly differentiated. In terms of the general model developed in this book, such a restriction would mean that the public good amount of each firm would be exogenously constrained to equal some constant, that is, $Y_k = Y_{k'} = \hat{Y}$. In this case, expansion in the public goods dimension can come only from the addition of new firms to the monopolistically competitive group. In the generalized model presented here, each firm is allowed to vary the amount of the public good they produce.

Second, as a result of allowing an endogenous treatment of the quality level of each firm's good, a facilitating improvement can be made in the analysis. In monopolistic competition the measure of the amount of product diversity is simply the number of firms. But this means that the diversity question can only be answered after the entry question is answered. This requires the addition of a zero profit constraint so that the industry equilibrium can be calculated through the examination of the total, or boundary, conditions in each firm's maximization. This approach is messy at its best, owing to the restriction of the equilibrium number of firms to the set of integers.[12] In the approach taken in this book, the equilibrium level of production in the public good dimension is determined with respect to the internal profit maximization of each firm. There is no restriction to integers, and standard calculus can be used to describe the outcome.

With respect to the results of the analysis of the public good dimension, there are similarities between the general model and the traditional monopolistic competition models. Most analyses of the monopolistic competition setting conclude that nothing in general can be said about the ultimate level of product diversity. While it is sometimes thought that the excess capacity result reached in monopolistic competition implies that too many firms exist, it is more generally understood that the product differentiation disallows two different firms from merging to take advantage of the excess capacity. Therefore, the number of firms, or degree of diversity, may be above or below the optimal amount. The same is true for the public good level of each firm in the general model. Equation (10.10) lists several terms which illustrate the difference between the conditions for profit maximization and the conditions for optimality, and these terms can take on any sign.

The example of the amusement park providing different rides or attractions may once again be called on to help develop the intuitive side of the analysis. The public goods are the rides or attractions. The parks set the admission price and thereby affect the total utilization of the rides, but let us concentrate first on the number of rides itself. In the monopolistic competition models, each park, or firm, is constrained to supply the same number, N, of rides. This is the implication of the symmetry or uniformity assumption. The total number of rides, then, must be some multiple of N. To be precise, it will be N times the number of parks. In the general model developed in this book, each park is not constrained to provide exactly N rides. Rather, this decision is left up to the park. The monopolistic competition models can address the total number of rides issue only by calculating the equilibrium number of parks. As has been shown in a variety of models, the number of firms can be above or below the optimum. Therefore, the number of rides can be above or below the optimum. The outcome depends on the nature of the demand or utility functions.[13] and on the nature of the expected reactions of the other firms.[14] The model in this book addresses the issue of total number of rides by examining each park's decision with respect to the number of rides it will provide. Again the outcome can be above or below the optimum, depending on the nature of the utility function, the expected reactions from the other parks, and the nature of the park's price discrimination.

The third difference between the model in this chapter and monopolistic competition involves the utilization dimension. Traditional monopolistic competition models generally conclude that there are underproduction incentives for the output of each firm. There are two separate approaches to this result. There is the familiar excess capacity result that firms do not produce enough output to reach the minimum point on their average cost curves. There is also the usual monopoly distortion problem through which profit maximization, uniform pricing, and downward-sloped demand curves yield underproduction. Without contesting the validity of these arguments, suffice it to point out that both arguments require uniform pricing. The uniform pricing assumption definitely simplifies the model but at the expense of greater generality and, arguably, at the expense of a better descriptive characterization of the markets involved. Additionally, when the uniform pricing assumption is relaxed, the results of the model change. Indeed, as this chapter shows, when price discrimination and nonlinear pricing are allowed, the underproduction incentive in the utilization dimension pales and offsetting and possibly dominating overproduction incentives arise.

In the above comparison between the model of this book and traditional monopolistic competition, we are led to seriously question the standard conclusion that firms in a monopolistic competition setting produce too little output. Likewise, we are also led to question the conventional wisdom with respect to public goods, for example, the conclusion that in a multiple firm setting private markets underproduce public goods. As long as the public good or, more precisely, the utilization of the public good is excludable, then markets can provide them. In such a setting there is no presupposition that markets will systematically underproduce in the public goods dimension. The underproduction or overproduction question turns on the interaction assumptions that are made between the firms and on the nature of the price discrimination. This chapter provides at least some reason to believe that for competitive or noncooperative interaction, overproduction incentives might prevail for each firm's output in the public goods dimension.

Finally, a short contrast between the multiple firm results and the monopolistic results of Chapter 8 concludes this chapter. The monopolist will underproduce the utilization units of the public good unless perfect price discrimination is possible. The competitive interaction effects in multiple producer markets, however, introduce overproduction incentives in the utilization dimension. In the public goods dimension, the nonperfectly discriminating monopolist has malincentives, the direction of which are not determined. The multiple firms have the same malincentives (equation [10.10a]), plus some extra overproduction incentives (equations [10.10b] and [10.10c]), in the public goods dimension.

Appendix to Chapter 10

Development of First Order Conditions for the Firm

The profits of the kth firm, π_k, are:

$$\pi_k = \sum_i \int_0^{y_{ik}} p_{ikj}\,dj - C_k(\sum_i y_{ik}, Y_k) \tag{10.5}$$

for all k, where C_k is the cost of the kth firm. The costs are measured in units of x; thus, there is a correspondence between these costs and the transformation function, F. Indeed,

$$\frac{\partial C_k}{\partial \sum_i y_{ik}} = - \left.\frac{d\sum_i x_i}{d\sum_i y_{ik}}\right|_F \tag{10A.1}$$

and

$$\frac{\partial C_k}{\partial Y_k} = - \left.\frac{d\sum_i x_i}{dY_k}\right|_F \tag{10A.2}$$

Equation (10A.2) can be rewritten to emphasize the utilization dimension:

$$\begin{aligned}\frac{\partial C_k}{\partial Y_k} &= \frac{\partial}{\partial Y_k}\int_0^{\sum_i y^o_{ik}} \frac{\partial C_k}{\partial \sum_i y_{ik}}\,d\sum_i y_{ik} + \left.\frac{\partial C_k}{\partial Y_k}\right|_{\sum_i y_{ik} = 0} \\ &= \frac{\partial}{\partial Y_k}\int_0^{\sum_i y^o_{ik}} - \left.\frac{d\sum_i x_i}{d\sum_i y_{ik}}\right|_F d\sum_i y_{ik} - \left.\frac{d\sum_i x_i}{dY_k}\right|_{F,\sum_i y_{ik} = 0}\end{aligned} \tag{10A.2$'$}$$

Consider the profit maximization of the k'th firm. The k'th firm will maximize (10.5) for k' over the choices of $y_{i'k'}$ for all i' and $Y_{k'}$. This formulation is potentially misleading in the case of price-taking individuals (and price-setting firms). If individuals are price takers, then the firm actually sets utilization prices, $p_{i'k'j}$, and public good quantity, $Y_{k'}$, while the consumer sets the utilization level, $y_{i'k'}$. Of course, since there is a relationship between the pricing function and the quantity of utilization for any level of public good quantity, the profit maximization can be represented as stated. Whether or not individuals are price takers, the firms surely are not and must take into account the effect that changes in $y_{i'k'}$ or $Y_{k'}$ will have on inframarginal prices. Additionally, extreme care must be exercised in the discussion of the interaction among the K firms lest we be misled by the formulation that has firms setting quantities rather than prices.

Since the utilization and the amount of the public good produced by the k'th firm will affect the demand for the products of the other firms, there will be some reaction on the part of the competitor firms. These reactions must be taken into account in the maximization of (10.5). The kth firm may react by changing its public good amount, Y_k, its total utilization, $\sum_i y_{ik}$, or its prices, p_{ikj}. Since the prices charged by the k'th firm depend on the utilization and public good output of all the other firms, the rival's expected reactions in both these quantity dimensions will be considered by the k'th firm. Therefore, these reactions are explicitly considered below. Accordingly, the first order conditions for the k'th firm's maximization of (10.5) are:

$$(10.6)\quad p_{i'k'j}\Big|_{j\,=\,y_{i'k'}} + \sum_i \int_0^{y_{ik'}} \frac{dp_{ik'j}}{dy_{i'k'}}\,dj + \sum_{k\neq k'} \sum_i \left(\sum_{i^*} \int_0^{y_{i^*k'}} \frac{dp_{i^*k'j}}{dy_{ik}}\,dj\,\frac{dy_{ik}}{dy_{i'k'}}\right) + \sum_{k\neq k'} \left(\sum_{i^*} \int_0^{y_{i^*k'}} \frac{dp_{i^*k'j}}{dY_k}\,dj\,\frac{dY_k}{dy_{i'k'}}\right) = \frac{dC_{k'}}{d\sum_i y_{ik'}}$$

for all i', and:

$$(10.7)\quad \sum_i \frac{d}{dY_{k'}} \int_0^{y_{ik'}} p_{ik'j}\,dj + \sum_{k\neq k'} \sum_i \left(\sum_{i^*} \int_0^{y_{i^*k'}} \frac{dp_{i^*k'j}}{dy_{ik}}\,dj\,\frac{dy_{ik}}{dY_{k'}}\right) + \sum_{k\neq k'} \left(\sum_{i^*} \int_0^{y_{i^*k'}} \frac{dp_{i^*k'j}}{dY_k}\,dj\,\frac{dY_k}{dY_{k'}}\right) = \frac{dC_{k'}}{dY_{k'}}$$

These conditions are discussed in the text of Chapter 10.

Discussion of Alternative Reaction Conditions

In the discussion of the terms in (10.8c) and (10.8d) the text of Chapter 10 covers the case where each firm expects its rivals to hold prices and qualities constant and thereby let utilization output level adjust. Let us here briefly consider other possibilities. Suppose that the firms make commitments to certain utilization levels and that these commitments were observable and believable by the rivals.[15] If such commitment-making is simultaneous, the Cournot assumption in the utilization dimension is relevent. In such a case, $dy_{ik}/dy_{i'k'} = 0$ and (10.8c) vanishes. If the timing of commitment-making is endogenous, however, the rational interaction would consist of a competition to establish a hierarchy of commitment-making firms in von Stackelberg fashion. Once this ordering is established, $dy_{ik}/dy_{i'k'} = 0$ for k above k' in the hierarchy and $dy_{ik}/dy_{i'k'} < 0$ for k below k' in the hierarchy. This resulting interaction has overutilization incentives (i.e., $dy_{ik}/dy_{i'k'} < 0$ for at least some k) for all firms, k', except the lowest in the hierarchy.[16]

In contrast to the expectation that the rivals will be passive, $dy_{ik}/dy_{i'k'} = 0$, as in the output constancy interaction, or accommodating, $dy_{ik}/dy_{i'k'} < 0$, as in the case of price constancy, the rivals may adopt a punishing reaction, $dy_{ik}/dy_{i'k'} > 0$, as a collusive or cartel enforcement mechanism or as a predatory device. If the k'th firm expects this sort of reaction from its rival, it is less likely to go ahead with its expansion plans. The result is an underproduction incentive in the utilization dimension.

Finally, we briefly consider alternatives to the reactions discussed in Chapter 10 for the interactions involved in (10.10b) and (10.10c). The text treats the case where the k'th firm's output in the public goods dimension is unobservable by the rivals. Now suppose that firms can directly observe each other's public good amount. If so, the Cournot interaction in the public good dimension is no longer a plausible one. Rather, firms can influence each other's decisions by making commitments to certain public good amounts. The competition to make commitments would lead to the establishment of a hierarchy of commitment makers in von Stackelberg fashion. In this scenario, $dY_k/dY_{k'} = 0$ when the kth firm is above the k'th in the hierarchy, and $dY_k/dY_{k'} < 0$ when the kth firm is below the k'th. This latter derivative being less than zero establishes an overproduction incentive according to (10.10c) in the public goods dimension for all but the lowest firm in the hierarchy. Intuitively, when the k'th firm makes a commitment to expand its amount in the public goods dimension, the kth firm, if it can observe and believe the commitment, takes the change as given and optimizes accordingly. This means that the kth firm acts as if it has suffered a decrease in demand for the utilization of its public good amount, and it will contract its controlled variables, price and public good amount, yielding $dY_k/dY_{k'} < 0$, which is the overproduction condition highlighted in (10.10c). Meanwhile, the overproduction condition in (10.10b) is still likely to exist because the decrease in demand for the utilization units of the kth firm leads to lower levels of utilization as long as the new lower demand curves are not dramatically more elastic than the original ones.

If cooperative or predatory reactions are expected in the public goods dimension, the above results are modified. Predatory action would include $dY_k/dY_{k'} > 0$, for example, matching the public good increase of your competitor. In this case the term in (10.10c) represents an underproduction incentive.

CHAPTER ELEVEN:
Conclusions

This book calls on two great traditions in price theory: the monopolistic competition revolution fostered by Chamberlin in the 1930s, and the public goods models formalized by Samuelson in the 1950s and put into perspective by Buchanan (and others) in the 1960s. Each of these traditions started when it was noticed that something was missing in the received formulations of prices and markets. Each of these traditions attempted to merge polar opposite cases to find a middle ground that was more descriptively realistic. And each of these traditions spawned a multitude of extensions that led to lively debates in the literature. To a large degree, the extensions are still being pursued and the debates carry on to the present.

For Chamberlin, the split of all markets into competitive on the one hand and monopolistic on the other just did not describe the reality around him. A middle ground was needed. And while theories of imperfect competition, especially oligopoly theory, had already developed quite far, these left Chamberlin wanting. It was the product differentiation aspect, which made each firm a monopolist (sort of) yet still allowed interfirm competition, that caught Chamberlin's eye. Even today analysis of the interaction among sellers of differentiated products is still a common theme of research in the industrial organization literature.

Buchanan was disappointed in the way a dichotomy was developing between private markets and private goods on the one hand and public goods and public finance on the other. Samuelson and others had recognized that the world did not consist of pure private goods at one pole and pure public goods at the other pole, but no one had made much progress in analyzing the middle ground. Buchanan's insight, one that is echoed in most of his work and contributed to his selection for a Nobel Prize, was that individual decisionmaking should be stressed regardless of the setting, be it private goods, collective goods, or some hybrid. Needless to say, combinations of public goods and private goods, which lead to models of mixed goods, and combinations of public and private provisions, which lead to models of public choice, are currently important areas of research.

In at least one respect, then, Chamberlin and Buchanan do the same thing. They both take the best parts of two polar opposite paradigms and try to forge a synthesis. Chamberlin combines the rivalry and competition for profits leading to a zero profit equilibrium from models of competition, with the price-searching and downward-sloping demand curves from models of monopoly. Buchanan combines the individual rationality, maximization, and market behavior from standard private goods models with the necessarily collective nature of decisionmaking in the face of public goods.

However, each of these syntheses is only a start; each can be extended or improved upon. For example, Chamberlin and most modern theorists of monopolistic competition or product differentiation have ignored the possible influence of price discrimination or other complex pricing schemes in their analyses. Yet because of the monopoly power implied by the product differentiation, the relaxation of the uniform pricing assumption seems a fruitful way to proceed. Of course, in the public goods arena, price discrimination and other complex pricing arrangements have always been central to the analysis. Meanwhile, in public goods models, most of the attention has been paid to the public goods dimension while analysis of the utilization dimension has been simplified, assumed away, or overlooked altogether. It is, of course, the analysis of the utilization dimension that has always been the central focus in monopolistic competition.

I attempt a further synthesis in this book. By taking the best parts of received public goods and mixed goods paradigms, and the best parts of the analysis of private goods in the monopolistic competition tradition, we have arrived at a general model from which these antecedents fall out as special cases. Using the insights of Chamberlin, Samuelson, and Buchanan as a springboard, the approach that is set out in this book makes several important advances that will be summarized in this chapter. First, the approach set out here advances the frontiers of price theory. Second, the approach adopted in this book is descriptively more accurate of real-life problems and institutions than the received theory and therefore supplies a stronger base for empirical analysis. Third, the approach intuitively helps to consolidate many of the alternative formulations of public goods, thereby clearing up some of the confusion associated with public goods analysis. Finally, and no doubt of tantamount interest to some readers of this book, my analysis points out areas in the public goods and industrial organization literature where mistakes in normative analysis have led to inappropriate policy conclusions. Each of these points will be addressed in turn.

Advancing Price Theory

While an unrepentant instrumentalist might have trouble with effort expended on the advancement of price theory solely for the sake of such advancement, most economists will approve of such an endeavor. After all, it is not the case that everything that is possible to know about price theory is already known. Nor is it the case that everything that is thought to be known about price theory is completely understood or even completely correct. There are many areas of price theory, some of which are addressed in this book, that are ripe for generalization, extension, modification, or otherwise being improved. In any case, this book does not have to justify itself on pure theory alone. The following sections will further treat pure theoretical issues but also will open the discussion of the policy implications embedded in this analysis and will pave the way for empirical examination of the issues analyzed herein. For now, however, a discussion of the theoretical advances made in the book seems an appropriate way to proceed in this summary chapter.

How one views the theoretical impact of the book depends on one's perspective. On a very general level, the book claims to merge public goods theory with monopolistic competition. But let us unpack that statement by considering a few different perspectives from which to view the merging of the two models.

First, from the public goods perspective, the advancement made involves adding a degree of sophistication to the impure public goods or mixed goods case. The standard theory of private goods and the Samuelsonian theory of pure public goods are fairly well accepted parts of orthodox price theory. There remains the issue of the impure public goods, the case in which neither the pure private goods paradigm nor the pure public goods model seem to capture reality. Certainly, impure public goods have been discussed before. Indeed, Chapter 4 discusses thirteen different possibilities for the combination of private goods and public goods. For the most part, however, the received theories of mixed goods involve attempts to ferret out the characteristics of the midrange along some linear continuum with pure public goods on one pole and pure private goods on the other. The feeling one often gets while meandering along any of these continua is that some curious, special case is being analyzed, while the useful analysis attaches to the pure polar cases. My analysis introduces the mixed goods case as a multidimensional problem. Mixed goods are not so much "between" public goods and private goods as they are goods for which both private consumption and nonrival consumption are important. This makes mixed goods the general case rather than some curious special case. And it is from the general mixed goods case that the pure cases are derived as the special cases which lack a certain dimensionality.

Second, from the excludable public goods perspective, or the competitive provision of public goods perspective, the advance made is to treat these topics within the framework of the general mixed goods case just highlighted. Previously, private market provision of public goods had been analyzed by several different authors, with several different conclusions. But the analysis was couched in terms of pure public goods. These models are reviewed in chapters 5 and 6. So while mixed goods had been discussed, and while competitive provision had been discussed, no one had combined the two topics. My analysis does precisely that. Interestingly, the subsequent analysis takes on the flavor of monopolistic competition as highlighted in Chapter 9.

Third, from the public finance perspective, the analysis advances the sophistication of the pricing or valuation scheme that the public sector may use to evaluate the benefits of a public good. In the typical, pure public good case, individuals may bluff or hide their preferences, attempt to free-ride, and so on. Since each individual may have a different valuation of the public good, the problem of properly estimating the value of the public good becomes severe. However, if the public good consumption can also be measured in some dimension for which consumption is rival, this provides an alternative way of evaluating and pricing the public good. In the simplest sense, the distinction is between funding a publicly provided good out of the general tax revenues or funding it, partially or in full, out of user fees. For example, a national park could be provided for out of general tax revenues and supplied free to all users. Alternatively, user fees could be charged each time the national park is entered or utilized by a person or group. Bear in mind that there is no reason to constrain the user fees to a uniform price schedule. Depending on how the user fees are set, the user fee system may be able to collect from a given individual total payments that are more closely in line with that individual's valuation of the good in the first place.

Charging user fees on each entrance to the park does not turn the national park into a pure private good. Indeed, there is still the decision in the public goods dimension of how much of society's scarce resources to devote to the park. Charging user fees does, however, highlight and illuminate the utilization dimension. Politicians and public finance practitioners would do well to seriously consider funding more public projects at least partially by user fees. Immediately coming to mind are roads, bridges, parks, Coast Guard services, the court system, and so on. In many of these cases a second benefit is that of better distribution of the good that is produced. Since many of the goods named above are subject to overcrowding, pricing in the utilization dimension in order to control that dimension of consumption is called for. Employing user fees to control for overcrowding is by no means a new result. However, even if overcrowding is not a factor, the first benefit of getting more information about demand may be, by itself, sufficient cause to employ user fees.

The opposition to user fees is sometimes based on an oversimplified view of the allocation decision. Suppose, for example, that the public good must be provided, if at all, in one lump with no possible variation in amount. Also suppose that there is no possible problem with overcrowding. The decision to supply such a good turns on whether the sum, taken over all individuals, of the total valuation of the lumpy quantity of public good is greater or less than the total cost of the public good. Now assume also that it is clear that summed benefits exceed costs. In this situation the user fee would provide no extra information, would not affect the nonexistent crowding, but would exclude some people from enjoying the use of the good. In this situation the user fee is clearly not efficacious.

However, the above characterization almost never realistically captures the actual decision that must be made. The problem with this scenario is that it ignores the full complexity of the public goods dimension. There is always the possibility of marginal tinkerings with the level of the public good that is to be provided. By examining only the all-or-none decision with respect to a given amount of the public good, the marginal adjustments to the level of the public good are ignored. Meanwhile, without user fees, no information is being generated about these marginal adjustments in the public goods dimension. Too often these adjustments are left to the political manipulations of legislatures, budget committees, commissions, or administrative bureaus that have no real incentive to attempt to measure the demand accurately. The implementation of user fees in such a situation supplies more information about the demand for the public good and gives the users of the public good more of a stake (since they have to pay) in bringing about the proper level of the public good.

Fourth, and finally, from the industrial organization perspective, the analysis advances the study of differentiated oligopoly models and monopolistic competition models by focusing on the need to consider price discrimination in such competitive settings. Price discrimination and other complex pricing schemes cannot be analyzed fully in pure monopoly settings because that setting ignores the impact of price discrimination on a firm's competitive position. Surely the pure theories of price discrimination, two-part pricing, declining (or increasing) block pricing, delivered pricing, and other forms of complex pricing were originally introduced and analyzed in pure monopoly settings. It is all right to first examine price discrimination in the pure monopoly setting, provided we know why we are doing so. The proper reason is because the monopoly setting provides the simplest setting in which to illustrate how systems other than uniform pricing work. Unfortunately, the illustration of price discrimination in monopoly misleads some into the view that price discrimination applies only in the pure monopoly model while everything else—monopolistic competition, oligopoly, differentiated oligopoly, public utility regulation, contestable markets, and pure competition—only use uniform pricing. The truth is the other way around. Uniform pricing only makes sense in the pure competition paradigm, while in every other situation the possibility of complex pricing should be considered. To my mind the emphasis on uniform pricing has always been the unfortunate consequence of models of pure or atomistic competition where "the market" sets the price. With the price set parametrically, the firm can concentrate on the profit-maximizing output by using the familiar and intuitive marginal-cost-equals-marginal-revenue criterion. Realistically, however, the market never sets the price; the firms do. And there is no natural constraint requiring the firm to charge the same price for all units. The sad truth is that it just happens to be easier to model it that way.

The competitive provision of public goods models stumbled upon the consideration of price discrimination in competitive settings. Even in this literature, there were theorists who wanted to deny the possibility of price discrimination in a competitive setting. Without any guidance from models of price discrimination in competitive private goods settings, it is not surprising that several different notions of price discrimination developed in the public goods setting. The various notions differed on what price discrimination means, how it would be instituted, and what the consequences would be, both for equilibrium and for welfare economics.

These early models give us a base from which to consider price discrimination in competitive private, or mixed, goods settings. There is much work to be done. This book has only started the task. Coming from a mixed goods setting, which comes from public goods models where price discrimination is natural, this book considers complex pricing even in the face of competition. The analysis is kept on a general level for the most part, and in the analysis of equilibrium it is apparent that many possibilities present themselves. Indeed, Chapter 10 details several underproduction and overproduction incentives that exist depending on the nature of the pricing and the conjectural variation. In light of these results we must surely suspect any results derived in duopoly settings of any kind if pricing is constrained to be uniform. Unfortunately, this fact makes the vast majority of existing analyses obsolete. In this instance, advances in price theory of the type initiated in this book are sorely needed.

Toward Empirical Applicability

Notwithstanding the discussion of several theoretical advances made herein, the instrumentalist will still want to know whether any testable implications are forthcoming from the theoretical analysis. Although I readily admit that this is not the motivation for my research, perhaps I can supply an inkling of how one might proceed to apply the theory in this book. First of all, note that on a casual empirical level, the model in this book beats all competition hands down. By this I mean that the model is descriptively more accurate than the received formulations. Casual empirical testing indicates that sellers rarely use uniform pricing schedules. Thus, any model yielding the result of uniform pricing is already falsified. A model must at least allow the possibility of nonlinear pricing to have a chance at an accurate description of market outcomes with respect to the form of the pricing function.[1]

There are testable implications embedded in the general models of chapters 8 and 10, but they are difficult to draw out. For one example, consider the discussion of the conjectural variations in chapter 10 and its appendix. The nature of the equilibrium compared to the Pareto optimum depends on these conjectural variations. Normative conclusions involving underproduction or overproduction aside, there are positive implications that can be derived if changes in the conjectural variation can be isolated. If, for example, the model shows that the expectation of (quantity) matching behavior from one's rivals leads to Pareto relevant underproduction, while conciliatory price constancy (and output-decreasing) behavior leads to overproduction, then the change from one regime to another would lead to a change in production. A change in the conjectural variation could be isolated if it were somehow correlated with an observable signal, for example a change in the regulatory environment, an administration's change in antitrust enforcement, a judicial change in the interpretation of antitrust law or, perhaps, entry that upsets a preexisting cartel type arrangement.

The instrumentalist will no doubt point out that some of the same implications are also derivable from simpler oligopoly and cartel models. However, the institutional background in the general model of this book is richer because it covers two dimensions of consumption instead of one and therefore, in a sense, doubles the possibilities in order to isolate changes in conjectures. For example, the empirical examination of price wars and preemptive quantity or capacity expansion usually involve only uniform pricing and a single quantity dimension (the utilization dimension) but do not consider the interaction in a public goods or quality dimension. Adding such considerations to the received analysis can allow for additional implications to be derived and tested or can help to explain what might otherwise be paradoxical results.

Interpreting the Analysis of Public Goods

Arguably, economists have overdone it with respect to the analysis of public goods. Some say public goods lead to a pure theory of public expenditure, some say public goods are like joint supply, some say public goods are like externalities, some say externalities are like public goods, some say crowded public goods are mixed goods. Some economists focus on rival and nonrival consumption, some focus on the costs of excluding nonpayers, some focus on demand revelation, some focus on private versus public provision—this list could go on and on. Indeed, witness the thirteen different formulations of mixed goods that were documented in Chapter 4. Economists have a problem here because if someone starts talking about public goods and each economist conjures up a different image and a different issue, then it is unlikely that any progress will be made.

It may seem that my purpose is to add one more paradigm—to this plethora of paradigms—that public goods and monopolistic competition have something in common. While at one level this is true, I believe that my analysis does more than simply expand the number of competing paradigms. My analysis is not another special or narrow case to be logged separately from the various other models. I would hope that my analysis is broad enough to capture the other models as special cases and to highlight the extra restrictions that show up the received models as special cases. To this end the major insight of my analysis is that the general, mixed goods case involves two dimensions of consumption, one which is like a pure public good and one which is like a private good. All of the received models make different special assumptions with respect to one or both of these dimensions. In some models the public goods dimension will be an all-or-nothing decision; in other models the utilization dimension will be constrained to equal unity, and so on. By realizing that the mixed goods problem is a two-dimensional problem, as opposed to some one-dimensional combination of the polar cases, a better understanding of mixed goods and of the pure private and pure public goods is achieved.

For example, consider the connection between public goods and externalities. It seems appropriate to draw some parallel because both models include a type of summation of marginal benefits (or costs) set equal to marginal costs (or benefits). What, however, is the correct parallel? At first, perhaps since the analysis of externalities came first, it seemed appropriate to consider the pure public good as a type of limit case of positive externality, and therefore to borrow from the analysis of externalities in the discussion of public goods. This was tidy for the followers of Pigou/Samuelson orthodoxy, because both positive externalities and pure public goods were associated with underproduction. However, the argument was not airtight. Externalities had to have something to do with transactions costs, nonexcludability, or incompletely specified property rights, whereas public goods focused on nonrival consumption and did not necessarily have to evidence the other traits.

Nevertheless, the similarity between the equations illustrating Pareto optimality still begged for some type of connection. If public goods were not a special case of positive externality, then maybe it was the other way around. The transactions costs or nonexcludability in the externality case led to the nonrival consumption. Therefore, externalities were a special case of the more general public good model. That is, externalities provided just one of many reasons for the nonrival characteristic of public goods. Compared to the first view that public goods were a subset of externalities, no change had to be made in the normative analysis because both public goods and positive externalities still evidenced underproduction. Coase, Demsetz, and Thompson, however, upset this cozy connection, especially with regard to the conclusion of underproduction. Coase, for externalities, and Demsetz and Thompson, for public goods, agreed in arguing against the orthodox underproduction result, but interestingly, they did not ultimately reach the same conclusions as each other.

There are still other possibilities. No doubt some economists view the similarity between the optimal conditions for externalities and public goods as nothing more than a curious coincidence. Still others consider the case of externalities as some sort of mixed good. The problem, however, is apparent. Mention public goods and externalities in the same sentence and at least four different views will be taken—either public goods as externalities, externalities as public goods, externalities as mixed goods, or that there is no connection between the two.

My analysis makes sense out of this muddle. Pure public goods and externalities are both simplifications of the same general model that has two dimensions of consumption. Each model has a public goods dimension, the existence of which explains the similarity in the optimality conditions. However, the utilization dimension is treated differently. The simplification made in pure public goods models is to completely drop consideration of the utilization dimension. The simplification often made in models of externalities is to somehow combine the public goods dimension and the utilization dimension into one dimension. Indeed, in models of externalities it is typically the consumption (or production) in a private good dimension that is the production, and therefore the consumption, in the public goods dimension. This is most clearly seen in the models of congestion reviewed in Chapter 3. In the congestion models, consumption of travel and production and consumption of congestion are simultaneously undertaken in one dimension—the number of people crossing a crowded bridge. My claim is that it takes careful consideration of the utilization dimension to fully grasp the relationship between public goods and externalities in particular, or, in general, between public goods and any of the other paradigms mentioned above.

In addition to achieving a synthesis of the received formulations of public and mixed goods, as well as product quality determination and monopolistic competition, this book helps with the categorization of new examples of public goods. How many times have you read or heard the expression, "It is like a public good"? Usually this is stated with emphasis or flair near the end of an argument. When the rest of the analysis is just getting to the stage where our intuition is starting to be strained, the coup de grace, "It is like a public good," is meant to have us nod in agreement with the argument being proffered. Often, but not always, the normative conclusion that public goods are associated with underproduction is expressly intended.

What do we do when confronted with this phrase? If our understanding of public goods happens to be the same as that of the person to whom we are listening, then we might completely understand the argument. Alternatively, however, if we are comfortable with a public goods paradigm different from the one espoused by the person to whom we are listening, we will probably be thrown off track unless we stop to ask in what sense it is like a public good. Unfortunately, this latter course of action usually seems to end all progress in that conversation.

With an understanding of the general public goods model presented in this book, we should be able to make an immediate assessment of what is meant by the phrase, "like a public good." We probably will be able to pick out the dimension in which the nonrival consumption is occurring. Once we have done this, there are several questions we should ask ourselves immediately. Is this consumption in the public good dimension excludable or nonexcludable? Does pricing occur in this dimension? Is there more than one seller in this dimension? Can the amount in the public goods dimension be varied? Are such variations in public good amount continuous or lumpy? Is there also a utilization dimension? Are there special simplifications in the utilization dimension that must be considered? Does pricing or exclusion occur in the utilization dimension? Are there multiple firms in the utilization dimension? In the course of answering these questions we will often be led to consider several different institutional settings through which the "public good" could be supplied. By the time we have considered all the various institutions that might possibly surround the example, our understanding of the issue is likely to be on a par with, or even above, the understanding of the person who originated the phrase.

Policy Implications

There are several policy implications that are only thinly veiled in the above sections. This final section completely unveils them.

First, the discussion above concerning user fees indicates that perhaps more emphasis might be given to the use of user fees in public finance. When a publicly provided good has two dimensions of consumption, a public goods dimension and a utilization dimension, the public sector may fruitfully employ user fees in the utilization dimension not only to limit congestion in that dimension but also to gain information about demand intensity and to more closely price-discriminate in the public good dimension. This, of course, is not a startlingly new result, but it is worthy of mention here because it follows so nicely from the general model with two dimensions of consumption. Furthermore, I wish to highlight the two dimensions because sometimes, even when user fees are used, the connection between the two dimensions is lost.

My favorite example is the congested toll bridge. Casual empiricism indicates that low tolls and overcrowded facilities are fairly common occurrences with respect to toll bridges. Yet even with all of the collective time wasted sitting in traffic jams, people seem unable to make the connection between the utilization dimension and the public goods dimension. At least one commonly made argument is that tolls should be removed when the total collections (through time) completely pay for the indebtedness undertaken on the historical cost of the bridge. After all, why should the public have to keep paying for the facility after it has already been paid for? This no-(or low-) toll policy is invariably associated with congestion and the usual array of window-dressing nonsolutions. Witness the generally ineffective carpool lanes and the nightmarishly expensive mass transit subsidization as two of the more common piecemeal attempts to combat the bridge congestion.

A clearer understanding of the relationship between the utilization dimension and the public goods dimension indicates that higher tolls are the proper response to the bridge crowding for two different reasons. First, and simplest, higher tolls in the utilization dimension will reduce the crowding through the reduction in the quantity demanded. Bear in mind that I envision not minor tinkering, such as the increase from seventy-five cents to a dollar, recently implemented in California, but rather a quantum leap in the tolls to five or ten dollars. Most beginning students of economics would come up with this solution. It is also likely that the private sector owner of a publicly used toll bridge would reach the same solution. The argument that an unfair and expensive burden would be placed on drivers I find particularly disingenuous in light of the eight or ten dollars that are typically already being paid for parking, and in light of the probably much greater value of the time being wasted in traffic jams.

The second reason that high tolls in the utilization dimension are efficacious has to do with the connection to the public goods dimension. Even if demand is so inelastic that the significantly higher tolls do little to alleviate the crowding, the high tolls are revealing a vital piece of information about the collective value placed on the bridge. The response in this case is clear. The high revenues collected in tolls are an indication that the public goods dimension is very valuable and should be augmented. Either the construction of more lanes, the addition of another level on the bridge, or even the construction of another bridge is the proper response in the public goods dimension. Such additional facilities in the public goods dimension could be financed out of the toll revenues in the utilization dimension. If the toll revenues were projected to be insufficient to cover the cost of additional construction, then perhaps the extra lanes, additional level, or new bridge should not be added. There is no way of obtaining this information, however, without first raising price in the utilization dimension to gauge demand in the public goods dimension.

The consideration of the user fees in the utilization dimension leads to the second area of policy considerations, namely the question of public or private provision in the first place. As has been argued convincingly in the literature, it is the nonexclusion property of some public goods, rather than their nonrival nature, that leads to the inability of the private sector to provide them. If user fees are a possibility in the utilization dimension, however, then there may be the possibility of exclusion in that dimension. Once nonpayers can be excluded from consumption, private markets can handle the provision of the good as easily, or perhaps more easily, than the public sector. Certainly, the private supplier would have access to all the same information about demand (revealed by the pricing in the utilization dimension) that the public supplier would. And in the private supplier case, the usual Public Choice style incentive problems associated with public provision could be avoided.

Note, however, that the good cannot be considered a private good just because pricing and exclusion can take place in the utilization dimension. Indeed, there is still the public goods dimension to be concerned about. What we really have is a mixed good, with two dimensions of consumption. If one of the dimensions can be set up so that exclusion is possible, the private sector has a role to play in the provision of the good. The policy implication is clear. Pure public goods that lead to a pure theory of public expenditure because of nonexclusion in the only possible dimension of consumption (the public good dimension) are extremely rare, if not nonexistent. Seemingly, there is a much greater role for private markets to play in the provision of goods that have some public good characteristics or are somehow "like a public good."

In fact, perhaps all goods have some public goods characteristics. If quality is not set exogenously, and indeed it is not, then the pure private good case with no public goods dimension seems irrelevant. Public goods dimensions, embodied in mixed goods that also have utilization dimensions, are all around us, being supplied quite effectively by the private sector. Policymakers would be well advised to investigate the efficiency with which many mixed goods are produced in the private sector, with an eye toward determining if many of the mixed goods supplied in the public sector should be transferred to decentralized markets. It is not the case that the private sector supplies only pure private goods and that every good with a public good dimension, whether it is a pure public good or a mixed good, leads to a market failure unless supplied in the public sector. Rather, it is the case that the private sector supplies mixed goods effectively, that almost all goods are mixed goods, and that the private sector should be more heavily relied upon in the production of many goods that are currently the sole responsibility of the public sector. This result is certainly contrary to the tone of Samuelson's pure theory of public expenditure.

The third area of policy implications involves the possible underproduction that might take place if the public good provision were left to the private sector. Notwithstanding the efficient production results reached by Demsetz and Borcherding, and the overproduction results reached by Thompson, the conventional wisdom is that private sector underproduction is the usual result when the market is confronted with public good type problems. Perhaps the underproduction is thought to have more to do with the nonexclusion property of some public goods rather than the nonrival property addressed in this book and in the mathematical analysis of public goods. Regardless of where the underproduction comes from, there are still the issues of which dimension is responsible for the problem and which dimension might be exploited for a solution.

For example, suppose we wanted to leave production of the public good in the private sector for obvious Public Choice reasons. Suppose also that we thought the private sector equilibrium entailed a Pareto relevant underproduction. Suppose also that we thought that a subsidy was called for to combat this underproduction. Which dimension should be subsidized? Consider a park. Should the government subsidize parks based on their production in the public goods dimension, that is, subsidy payments based on acreage of the park, or number of rides or attractions in a park, or miles of maintained hiking trails? Or should the government subsidize parks in the utilization dimension by basing subsidy payments on the number of visitors to the park? Indeed, once the decision to subsidize the park has been made, there is still the question of the correct dimensional form for the subsidy. A clear understanding of the relationship between the public goods dimension and the utilization dimension is necessary for this decision to be made systematically. There is no apparent general solution to this question. A case-by-case approach may have to be taken to determine the dimension most appropriate for the subsidy.

This brings us to the fourth area of policy implications, an area that might also be considered a subset of the immediately preceding argument. Above, a case-by-case approach was indicated with respect to the dimension for a subsidy, *assuming* that a subsidy was required to combat an underproduction problem in the first place. However, the analysis of the private sector equilibrium presented in Chapter 8 for monopoly and Chapter 10 for multiple firms indicates that this assumption must also be critically examined on a case-by-case basis. Indeed, in some instances, depending on the nature of the pricing and the nature of the interaction between the firms, overproduction incentives might dominate in equilibrium. In this case, any subsidy from the public sector is likely to make things worse rather than better. Even the least cynical reader can no doubt conjure up examples where public sector subsidization leads to an obviously inefficient overproduction of the subsidized activity. In light of this argument, it is no longer clear that the market systematically underproduces public goods. Therefore, it no longer follows that public sector provision or public sector subsidization is automatically called for in the face of public goods. The extent of any case-by-case analysis must now encompass not only which dimension to subsidize but also the more basic question of whether or not to subsidize in the first place.

I must close this book and this section on policy implications with two warnings. The first warning is to those who wish to pursue the case-by-case analysis called for above. Unfortunately, it is wishful thinking that such a case-by-case approach will lead to a workable policy, because it is nearly impossible to do what is required. In order for the public sector to determine whether or not and in which dimension a subsidy is required, the public sector must know the exact extent of each person's demand for the good. Such information is not free, so the public sector must expend effort and resources in trying to elicit demand revelation. Since Public Choice considerations indicate in a straightforward manner that the public sector does not have the correct incentives to arrive at an efficient amount of demand revelation, the public sector is likely to err in its efforts to measure demand. A laissez-faire approach is probably the best policy. Indeed, regardless of whether or not the public sector tries to measure demand, the private sector producer is trying to do the same thing. In order to effectively price-discriminate, the private seller will undertake expense to bring about demand revelation. At least the private sector incurs the direct incidence of the costs and benefits of this exercise, giving some assurances to the rest of society that such efforts will be undertaken economically. The interventionist position that the public sector can fix any private market failures and should attempt to do so relies on an information assumption that has costly information facing the private sector but costless information available to the policymakers. Such a position is untenable.

The other warning is that we must critically examine most of the existing, policy-guiding implications derived from oligopoly models in particular or industrial organization in general. The list of areas that are affected includes antitrust policy, contestable market theory, utility regulation, oligopoly models, and quality regulation, among others. The warning is apparent. Any policy that is guided by a theoretical model that has constrained the behavior of the private sector firms to allow only uniform pricing for pure private goods is based on an insecure footing. This means that most policies are suspect. Performance-based policies that focus on zero profits or average-cost pricing are suspect. Structural policies aimed at securing low concentration ratios, favorable Herfindahl indices, or low entry barriers are suspect. Particularly suspect are Robinson-Patman type behavioral policies prohibiting price discrimination. Indeed, we should recognize the folly in trying to force markets to be perfectly competitive by mandating uniform pricing and/or zero profits, thereby trying to mimic the assumptions or results of perfect competition models.

Realistically, most goods are mixed, having both rival and nonrival dimensions of consumption. Most goods will not be sold with uniform price schedules. Both the multidimensional nature of the mixed good product and the complex pricing practices of the sellers interact to yield results that have little precedent in the received theory because the received theory focuses almost exclusively on uniform pricing. To recall just one important implication, consider the discussion in Chapter 10 of overproduction incentives. This possibility is completely overlooked in uniform price models. Because the implications of the complex model differ substantially from the implications of simple models, and because the complex model is a descriptively more accurate characterization of the world, we must rethink at best and scrap at worst any policies based on the simple models.

The policy implications detailed here indicate that the goal of policymakers should not be to make markets look like the overly simplified and overly constrained perfectly competitive or perfectly contestable models of our textbooks. Meanwhile, the goal of economists should be to understand more about the workings of competitive markets in mixed goods with multiple dimensions of consumption and complex pricing. One of my goals in this book is to point policymakers and economists in these potentially more fruitful directions.

Notes

CHAPTER ONE

1. Samuelson, "The Pure Theory of Public Expenditure," *Review of Economics and Statistics* 36 (Nov. 1954): 387–89.

2. See Richard D. Auster, "Private Markets in Public Goods (or Qualities)," *Quarterly Journal of Economics* 91, no. 3 (Aug. 1977): 419–30; Thomas E. Borcherding, "Competition, Exclusion and the Optimal Supply of Public Goods," *Journal of Law and Economics* 21, no. 2 (Apr. 1978): 111–32; Geoffrey Brennan and Cliff Walsh, "A Monopoly Model of Public Goods Provision: The Uniform Pricing Case," *American Economic Review* 71, no. 1 (Mar. 1981): 196–206, and "Private Markets in (Excludable) Public Goods: A Reexamination," *Quarterly Journal of Economics* 100, no. 3 (Aug. 1985): 811–19; Dagobert L. Brito and William H. Oakland, "On the Monopolistic Provision of Excludable Public Goods," *American Economic Review* 70, no. 4 (Sept. 1980): 691–704; Michael E. Burns and Cliff Walsh, "Market Provision of Price-Excludable Public Goods: A General Analysis," *Journal of Political Economy* 89, no. 1 (Feb. 1981): 166–91; Harold Demsetz, "Joint Supply and Price Discrimination," *Journal of Law and Economics* 16, no. 2 (Oct. 1973): 389–405, and "The Private Production of Public Goods," *Journal of Law and Economics* 13, no. 2 (Oct. 1970): 293–306; and "Reply to Professor Thompson," *Journal of Law and Economics* 16, no. 2 (Oct. 1973): 413–15; Robert B. Ekelund, "The Fragile Nature of Public Goods Equilibria," *Review of Social Economy* 35, no. 3 (Oct. 1977): 204–11; William H. Oakland, "Public Goods, Perfect Competition, and Underproduction," *Journal of Political Economy* 82, no. 5 (Sept. 1974): 927–39; Earl A. Thompson, "A Note on Consumer-Producer Collusion in the Private Marketing of Collective-Type Goods," Discussion Paper No. 142, Department of Economics, University of California, Los Angeles (Jan. 1979); and "The Perfectly Competitive Production of Collective Goods," *Review of Economics and Statistics* 50, no. 1 (Feb. 1968): 1–12; and "The Private Production of Public Goods: A Comment," *Journal of Law and Economics* 16, no. 2 (Oct. 1973): 407–12; Cliff Walsh, "A

Reconsideration of Some Aspects of the Private Production of Public Goods," *Review of Social Economy* 39, no. 1 (Apr. 1981): 19–35. While this is by no means an exhaustive list, it represents a substantial portion of articles of this type. Even an exhaustive list of private provision articles would be but a small portion of all articles on public goods. In this sense, at least, these papers represent the views of a minority of writers on public goods.

3. Brito and Oakland, "Excludable Public Goods," p. 691.

4. See the list of references for works by Samuelson.

5. See Auster, "Private Markets"; and Stephen Shmanske, "Public Goods, Product Quality Determination, and Dimensionality of Consumption," *Public Finance* 37, no. 3 (Fall 1982): 387–403.

6. See Peter K. Else, "Further Thoughts on Public Goods, Private Goods and Mixed Goods," *Scottish Journal of Political Economy* 35, no. 2 (May 1988): 115–28; and Stephen Shmanske, "A Note on Else's Treatment of Quality and Public Goods," *Scottish Journal of Political Economy* 37, no. 2 (May 1990): 193–96.

7. See John G. Head, "Public Goods and Public Policy," *Public Finance* 17, no. 3 (1962): 197–219.

8. See R. A. Collinge, "Toward 'Privatization' of Public Sector Output: Decentralized Contracting for Public and Private Goods," *Journal of Public Economics* 27, no. 3 (Aug. 1985): 371–87; Tyler Cowen, "Public Goods Definitions and Their Institutional Context: A Critique of Public Goods Theory," *Review of Social Economy* 43, no. 1 (Apr. 1985): 53–63; Otto A. Davis and Andrew B. Whinston, "On the Distinction between Public and Private Goods," *American Economic Review* 57, no. 2 (May 1967): 360–73; John G. Head and Carl S. Shoup, "Public Goods, Private Goods and Ambiguous Goods," *Economic Journal* 79, no. 315 (Sept. 1969): 567–72; Robert J. Staaf, "Privatization of Public Goods," *Public Choice* 41, no. 3 (1983): 435–40; and to a lesser extent, James M. Buchanan, *The Demand and Supply of Public Goods* (Chicago: Rand McNally, 1968).

9. See, for example, Buchanan, *Public Goods;* A. Breton, "A Theory of Demand for Public Goods," *Canadian Journal of Economics and Political Science* 32 (Nov. 1966): 455–67; R. Dorfman, "General Equilibrium with Public Goods," in *Public Economics,* ed. J. Margolis and H. Guitton (London: Macmillan, 1969), pp. 245–75; and D. M. Winch, "Pareto, Public Goods and Politics," *Canadian Journal of Economics* 35 (Nov. 1969): 492–508. Buchanan, especially, can be credited for the birth of the Public Choice view and its introduction to the public goods literature.

10. See, for example, Edward H. Clarke, "Multipart Pricing of Public

Goods," *Public Choice* 11 (Fall 1971): 17–33; David Conn, "The Scope of Satisfactory Mechanisms for the Provision of Public Goods," *Journal of Public Economics* 20, no. 2 (Mar. 1983): 249–63; Jerry Green and Jean-Jacques Laffont, "On the Revelation of Preferences for Public Goods," *Journal of Public Economics* 8, no. 1 (Aug. 1977): 79–93; Theodore Groves and John O. Ledyard, "Some Limitations of Demand Revealing Processes," *Public Choice* 29 (1975): 107–24; and Thomas Muench and Mark Walker, "Are Groves-Ledyard Equilibria Attainable?" *Review of Economic Studies* 50, no. 2 (Apr. 1983): 393–96.

11. See, for example, Bruce R. Bolnick, "Lindahl, Bowen, and the Cost of Public Goods," *Public Finance* 33, no. 1–2 (1978): 23–32; Tran Huu Dung, "Externalities, Public Goods and Counternormal Effect," *Public Finance Quarterly* 10, no. 3 (July 1982): 393–99; Mervyn A. King, "A Pigovian Rule for the Optimum Provision of Public Goods," *Journal of Public Economics* 30, no. 3 (Aug. 1986): 273–91; and Gordon Winston, "Taxes, Leisure and Public Goods," *Economica* 32, no. 125 (Feb. 1965): 65–69.

12. See, for example, Timothy R. Muzondo, "Mixed and Pure Public Goods, User Charges, and Welfare," *Public Finance* 33, no. 3 (1978): 314–30.

13. See, for example, Eitan Berglas and David Pines, "Clubs, Local Public Goods, and Transportation Models: A Synthesis," *Journal of Public Economics* 15, no. 2 (1981): 141–62; Estelle James, "Optimal Pollution Control and Trade in Collective Goods," *Journal of Public Economics* 3, no. 3 (Aug. 1974): 203–16; Scott McKinney, "Public Good Producers and Spillovers: An Analysis of Duopoly Behavior," *Public Finance Quarterly* 12, no. 1 (Jan. 1984): 97–116; Todd Sandler, "Pareto Optimality, Pure Public Goods, Impure Public Goods, and Multiregional Spillovers," *Scottish Journal of Political Economy* 22, no. 1 (Feb. 1975): 25–38; and Todd Sandler and Jon Cauley, "Multiregional Public Goods, Spillovers, and the New Theory of Consumption," *Public Finance* 31, no. 3 (1976): 376–95.

14. See, for example, T. C. Bergstrom and R. C. Cornes, "Independence of Allocative Efficiency from Distribution in the Theory of Public Goods," *Econometrica* 51, no. 6 (Nov. 1983): 1753–65; Duncan K. Foley, "Lindahl's Solution and the Core of an Economy with Collective Goods," *Econometrica* 38, no. 1 (Jan. 1970): 66–72; and M. McGuire and H. Aaron, "Efficiency and Equity in the Optimal Supply of a Public Good," *Review of Economics and Statistics* 51, no. 1 (Feb. 1969): 31–39.

15. See, for example, Brennan and Walsh, "(Excludable) Public Goods"; Brito and Oakland, "Excludable Public Goods"; and Burns and Walsh, "Price-Excludable Public Goods."

16. There are numerous examples and variations of models of voluntary pro-

vision of nonexcludable public goods. See Theodore Bergstrom, Lawrence Blume, and Hal Varian, "On the Private Provision of Public Goods," *Journal of Public Economics* 29, no. 1 (Feb. 1986): 25–49; Christopher Bliss and Barry Nalebuff, "Dragon-Slaying and Ballroom Dancing: The Private Supply of a Public Good," *Journal of Public Economics* 25, 1 (Nov. 1984): 1–12; Gregory B. Christainsen, "Evidence for Determining the Optimal Mechanism for Providing Collective Goods," *American Economist* 26, no. 1 (Spring 1982): 57–61; and by Richard Cornes and Todd Sandler, "Easy Riders, Joint Production, and Public Goods," *Economic Journal* 94, 375 (Sept. 1984): 580–98, "On the Consistency of Conjectures with Public Goods," *Journal of Public Economics* 27, no. 1 (June 1985): 125–29, "The Simple Analytics of Pure Public Good Provision," *Economica* 52, no. 105 (Feb. 1985): 103–16, and "The Theory of Public Goods: Non-Nash Behavior," *Journal of Public Economics* 23, no. 3 (Apr. 1984): 367–79; Hirshleifer, Jack, "Form Weakest-Link to Best-Shot: The Voluntary Provision of Public Goods," *Public Choice* 41, no. 1 (1983): 371–86; Martin C. McGuire and Carl H. Groth, Jr., "A Method for Identifying the Public Good Allocation Process within a Group," *Quarterly Journal of Economics* 100, no. 5 (Supp. 1985): 915–34; Allen J. Scafuri, "On Consistency of Conjectures in the Private Provision of Public Goods," *Journal of Public Economics* 37, no. 3 (Dec. 1988): 395–98; and R. Sugden, "Reciprocity: The Supply of Public Goods through Voluntary Contributions," *Economic Journal* 94, no. 376 (Dec. 1984): 772–87.

17. See, for example, S. Borenstein, "Price Discrimination in Free Entry Markets," *Rand Journal of Economics* 16, no. 3 (Autumn 1985): 380–97; H. Hotelling, "Stability in Competition," *Economic Journal* 39 (Mar. 1929): 41–57; E. C. Prescott and M. Visscher, "Sequential Location among Firms with Foresight," *Bell Journal of Economics* 8, no. 2 (Autumn 1977): 378–93; and S. C. Salop, "Monopolistic Competition with Outside Goods," *Bell Journal of Economics* 10, no. 1 (Spring 1979): 141–56. Salop claims that his model "easily generalizes to elastic demands" (p. 142), and it probably does for uniform pricing schemes. However, incorporating complex pricing would not be accomplished easily. Two attempts that consider elastic demands and price discrimination are John G. Greenhut and M. L. Greenhut, "Spatial Price Discrimination and Locational Effects," *Economica* 42, no. 168 (Nov. 1975): 401–19, and George Norman, "Spatial Competition and Spatial Price Discrimination," *Review of Economic Studies* 48, no. 151 (Jan. 1981): 97–111.

18. Not all spatial models have this assumption. For example, see Martin J. Beckmann, "Spatial Price Policies Revisited," *Bell Journal of Economics* 7, no. 2 (Autumn 1976): 619–29; and Dennis R. Cappoza and Robert Van Order, "A Generalized Model of Spatial Competition," *American Economic Review* 68, no. 5 (Dec. 1978): 896–908. Even though Cappoza and Van Order consider elastic demands, they still constrain the firms

to uniform pricing policies. The real strides are made with the consideration of nonlinear pricing and price discrimination. Beckmann considers mill pricing, delivered pricing, and distance-dependent uniform pricing, but no forms of nonlinear pricing. But see Greenhut and Greenhut, "Spatial Price Distrimination," and Norman, "Spatial Competition."

19. Thompson, "Competitive Production of Collective Goods."

20. See, for example, James Buchanan, "Joint Supply, Externality and Optimality," *Economica* 33, no. 132 (Nov. 1966): 404–15; Demsetz, "Joint Supply"; Bryan Ellickson, "Public Goods and Joint Supply," *Journal of Public Economics* 9, no. 3 (June 1978): 373–82; Head, "Public Goods and Public Policy"; E. J. Mishan, "The Relationship between Joint Products, Collective Goods, and External Effects," *Journal of Political Economy* 77, no. 3 (May 1969): 329–49; William Oakland, "Joint Goods," *Economica* 36, no. 143 (Aug. 1969): 253–68; and Carl S. Shoup, "Public Goods and Joint Production," *Rivista Internazionale de Scienze Economiche e Commerciali* 12, no. 3 (Mar. 1965): 254–64.

21. See, for example, Alan W. Evans, "Private Good, Externality, Public Good," *Scottish Journal of Political Economy* 22, no. 1 (Feb. 1970): 79–89; S. E. Holtermann, "Externalities and Public Goods," *Economica* 39, no. 153 (Feb. 1972): 78–87; and R. A. Musgrave, "Provision for Social Goods," in *Public Economics*, ed. J. Margolis and H. Guitton, (London: Macmillan, 1969), pp. 124–44.

22. See H. Demsetz, "The Inconsistencies of Monopolistic Competition," *Journal of Political Economy* 80, no. 3 (June 1972): 592–97.

23. Only a handful of authors have addressed price discrimination and nonlinear pricing in multiple firm settings. See R. Chiang and C. S. Spatt, "Imperfect Price Discrimination and Welfare," *Review of Economic Studies* 49, no. 156 (Apr. 1982): 155–81; M. L. Katz, "Price Discrimination and Monopolistic Competition," *Econometrica* 56, no. 6 (Nov. 1984): 1453–71; Kevin W. S. Roberts, "Welfare Considerations of Nonlinear Pricing," *Economic Journal* 89, no. 353 (Mar. 1979): 66–83; Stephen Shmanske, "Contestable Two-Part Pricing in Differentiated Duopoly," California State University, Hayward, School of Business and Economics Faculty Working Paper No. 33 (Jan. 1988), and also "Price Discrimination and Monopolistic Competition," California State University, Hayward, School of Business and Economics Faculty Working Paper No. 20 (Feb. 1985); Michael Spence, "Multi-Product Quantity-Dependent Prices and Profitability Constraints," *Review of Economic Studies* 47, no. 150 (Oct. 1980): 821–41; Daniel F. Spulber, "Non-Cooperative Equilibrium with Price Discriminating Firms," *Economics Letters* 4 (1979): 221–27; and J. F. Wright, "Some Reflections on the Place of Discrimination in the Theory of Monopolistic Competition," *Oxford Economic Papers* 17, no. 2 (July 1965): 175–87.

24. See Michael Spence, "Product Selection, Fixed Costs and Monopolistic Competition," *Review of Economic Studies* 43, no. 133 (June 1976): 217–35.

CHAPTER TWO

1. Inspection of fourteen intermediate microeconomic theory textbooks yielded an interesting array of results. The books sampled are the following: Roger D. Blair and Lawrence W. Kenny, *Microeconomics with Business Applications* (New York: John Wiley and Sons, 1987); Edgar K. Browning and Jacquelene M. Browning, *Microeconomic Theory and Applications*, 2nd ed. (Boston: Little, Brown, 1986); Steven T. Call and William L. Holahan, *Microeconomics* (Belmont, Calif.: Wadsworth Publishing, 1980); Allan C. DeSerpa, *Microeconomic Theory: Issues and Applications* (Boston: Allyn and Bacon, 1985); B. Curtis Eaton and Diane F. Eaton, *Microeconomics* (New York: W. H. Freeman, 1988); David D. Friedman, *Price Theory: An Intermediate Text* (Livermore, Calif.: South-Western Publishing, 1986); David Hemenway, *Prices and Choices*, 2nd ed. (Cambridge, Mass.: Ballinger Publishing, 1988); Jack Hirshleifer, *Price Theory and Applications*, 4th ed. (Englewood Cliffs, N.J.: Prentice Hall, 1988); David N. Hyman, *Modern Microeconomics: Analysis and Applications* (Saint Louis: Times Mirror/Mosby College Publishing, 1986); Donald W. Katzner, *Walrasian Economics; An Introduction to the Economic Theory of Market Behavior* (Menlo Park, Calif.: Addison-Wesley, 1988); Heinz Kohler, *Intermediate Microeconomics: Theory and Applications*, 2nd ed. (Glenview, Ill.: Scott, Foresman, 1986); Edwin Mansfield, *Microeconomics: Theory and Applications*, 5th ed. (New York: W. W. Norton, 1985); Donald N. McCloskey, *The Applied Theory of Price*, 2nd ed. (New York: Macmillan, 1985); Hal R. Varian, *Intermediate Microeconomics: A Modern Approach* (New York: W. W. Norton, 1987)

Six of these texts (Blair and Kenny, Browning and Browning, Eaton and Eaton, Hemenway, Hyman, and Kohler) identify both the nonrivalry and nonexcludability characteristics as defining public goods. Four texts (Call and Holahan, Hirshleifer, Katzner, and Mansfield) identify only the nonrivalry aspect as the distinguished feature of public goods. The four remaining texts have still different views on what constitutes a public good. McCloskey mentions public goods but neither dwells on them nor defines them. Friedman highlights only the nonexcludability characteristic. DeSerpa defines public goods as having three characteristics: nonrivalry, nonexcludability, and indivisibility. Finally, Varian defines public goods as those for which all must consume the same amount.

2. See Auster, "Private Markets"; Borcherding, "Optimal Supply of Public Goods"; Brennan and Walsh, "Public Goods Provision," and "(Excluda-

ble) Public Goods"; Brito and Oakland, "Excludable Public Goods"; Burns and Walsh "Price-Excludable Public Goods"; Demsetz, "Joint Supply," "Private Production of Public Goods," and "Reply to Thompson"; Ekelund, "Public Goods Equilibria"; Jora R. Minasian, "Television Pricing and the Theory of Public Goods," *Journal of Law and Economics* 7, no. 2 (Oct. 1964): 71–80; Oakland, "Public Goods and Underproduction"; Samuelson, "Public Goods and Subscription TV"; Shmanske, "Public Goods"; Thompson, "Collective-Type Goods"; and "Competitive Production of Collective Goods"; and "Private Production of Public Goods"; and Walsh, "Aspects of Public Goods."

3. The demand revelation problem is addressed fully in the next chapter.

4. See Earl R. Brubaker, "Free Ride, Free Revelation, or Golden Rule?" *Journal of Law and Economics* 18, no. 1 (Apr. 1975): 147–61; Christainsen, "Providing Collective Goods"; Demsetz, "Private Production of Public Goods"; Borcherdung, "Optimal Supply of Public Goods."

5. See Staaf, "Privatization of Public Goods." Staaf does address the exclusion question as an endogenous choice of the producer but does so only for otherwise nonexcludable public goods. That private goods are automatically excludable is an implicit assumption in Staaf's analysis. See also Cowen, "Public Goods Definitions"; Kenneth D. Goldin, "Equal Access vs. Selective Access: A Critique of Public Goods Theory," *Public Choice* 29 (Spring 1977): 53–71; and Wolfgang Laux-Meiselbach, "Impossibility of Exclusion and Characteristics of Public Goods," *Journal of Public Economics* 36, no. 1 (June 1988): 127–37. All of these papers highlight the notion that it is the institutions surrounding the use of any product rather than the characteristics of the product itself which determine the nature of excludability and also the nature of consumption vis-à-vis rivalry.

6. R. H. Coase, "The Lighthouse in Economics," *Journal of Law and Economics* 17 (1974): 357–76.

7. For the first use of this terminology of which I am aware, see Brubaker, "Free Ride."

8. See Laux-Meiselbach, "Characteristics of Public Goods."

9. There are numerous examples and variations of models of voluntary provision of nonexcludable public goods. See, Bergstrom, Blume, and Varian, "Private Provision of Public Goods"; Bliss and Nalebuff, "Private Supply of a Public Good"; Christainsen, "Providing Collective Goods"; Cornes and Sandler, "Joint Production and Public Goods," as well as "Consistency of Conjectures," "Pure Public Good Provision," and "Theory of Public Goods"; Hirshleifer, "Voluntary Provision of Public Goods"; McGuire and Groth, "Public Good Allocation"; Scafuri, "Private Provision of Public Goods"; and Sugden, "Supply of Public Goods."

10. This is certainly one of the views underlying private provision models that yield optimal provision. For the competitive case, see Demsetz, "Private Production of Public Goods"; and Borcherding, "Optimal Supply of Public Goods." For the monopoly case see Thompson, "Competitive Production of Collective Goods." While these models explicitly assume that exclusion is costless both marginally and inframarginally, it is basically the efficient incentives at the margin, brought about by the possibility of universal exclusion if the unit does not get produced, that leads to the Pareto efficiency of the equilibrium.

CHAPTER THREE

1. See James M. Buchanan, "An Economic Theory of Clubs," *Economica* 32, no. 125 (Feb. 1965): 1–14, for the original. A mathematical extension is offered in Bryan Ellickson, "A Generalization of the Pure Theory of Public Goods," *American Economic Review* 63, no. 3 (June 1973): 417–32.

2. See, for example, Berglas and Pines, "Local Public Goods"; and Sandler and Cauley, "Multiregional Public Goods."

3. See, for example, Robert Dorfman, "On Optimal Congestion," *Journal of Environmental Economics and Management* 11, no. 2 (June 1984): 91–106; and William Oakland, "Congestion, Public Goods, and Welfare," *Journal of Public Economics* 1 (1972): 339–57.

4. For example, see Berglas and Pines, "Local Public Goods"; Allan C. DeSerpa, "Congestion, Pollution and Impure Public Goods," *Public Finance* 33, no. 1–2 (1978): 68–83; Dorfman, "General Equilibrium with Public Goods"; Muzondo, "Mixed and Pure Public Goods"; Oakland, "Congestion"; Sandler, "Public Goods and Spillovers"; and Todd Sandler and John T. Tschirart, "Mixed Clubs: Further Observations," *Journal of Public Economics* 23 (1984): 381–89.

5. See Davis and Whinston, "Public and Private Goods"; Ekelund, "Public Goods Equilibria"; Head, "Public Goods and Public Policy"; Abba P. Lerner, "Conflicting Principles of Public Utility Price Regulation," *Journal of Law and Economics* 7, no. 2 (Oct. 1964): 61–70; Samuelson, "Aspects of Public Expenditure" as well as "Diagrammatic Theory of Public Expenditure" and "Public Expenditure and Taxation"; and Shmanske, "Public Goods." For a dissenting view, see Dorfman, "General Equilibrium with Public Goods."

6. The literature in this area is vast. See, for example, Clarke, "Multipart Pricing of Public Goods"; Conn, "Provision of Public Goods"; Green and Laffont, "Preferences for Public Goods"; Groves and Ledyard, "Demand Revealing Processes"; and Muench and Walker, "Groves-Ledyard Equilibria."

7. See David F. Bradford and Gregory G. Hildebrandt, "Observable Preferences for Public Goods," *Journal of Public Economics* 8, no. 2 (Oct. 1977): 111–31.

8. See Hajime Hori, "Revealed Preference for Public Goods," *American Economic Review* 65, no. 5 (Dec. 1975): 978–91.

9. See Mordecai Kurz, "Experimental Approach to the Determination of the Demand for Public Goods," *Journal of Public Economics* 3, no. 4 (Nov. 1974): 329–48.

10. For example, see Peter Bohm, "Estimating Demand for Public Goods: An Experiment," *European Economic Review* 3, no. 2 (1972): 111–30; Earl R. Brubaker, "Demand Disclosures and Conditions on Exclusion: An Experiment," *Economic Journal* 94, no. 375 (Sept. 1984): 536–53; Mark R. Isaac, James M. Walker, and Susan H. Thomas, "Divergent Evidence on Free Riding: An Experimental Examination of Possible Explanations," *Public Choice* 43, no. 2 (1984): 113–49; and Oliver Kim and Mark Walker, "The Free Rider Problem: Experimental Evidence," *Public Choice* 43, no. 1 (1984): 3–24.

11. See Edward H. Chamberlin, *The Theory of Monopolistic Competition* (Cambridge: Harvard University Press, 1933), p. 82.

12. See, for example, Avinash K. Dixit and Joseph E. Stiglitz, "Monopolistic Competition and Optimum Product Diversity," *American Economic Review* 67, no. 3 (June 1977): 297–308; and Spence, "Product Selection and Monopolistic Competition."

13. See, for example, Evans, "Private Good, Externality, Public Good." Many authors use externalities to arrive at mixed goods models. These will be discussed below in the extended treatment of mixed goods.

14. See Ronald Coase, "The Problem of Social Cost," *Journal of Law and Economics* 3, no. 2 (Oct. 1960): 1–44.

15. See Demsetz, "Private Production of Public Goods" and Borcherding, "Optimal Supply of Public Goods." These models will be discussed in depth in chapters 5 and 6.

16. See, for example, James M. Buchanan and Milton F. Kaflogis, "A Note on Public Goods Supply," *American Economic Review* 53, no. 3 (June 1963): 403–14. Once the interdependence between one agent's actions and another agent's utility (and, therefore, the other agent's actions or reactions) is recognized, a game theoretic approach is adopted. Buchanan and Kaflogis construct one such "game" in which dominant strategies lead to overproduction.

17. See Cornes and Sandler, "Theory of Public Goods." Kantian behavior is a type of golden rule behavior—do unto others as you would have them do unto you. Since Cornes and Sandler's model is couched in terms of

the voluntary provision of nonexcludable public goods, Kantian behavior essentially requires agents to recognize and internalize the benefits that others receive from the agent's own public goods production. If all agents do so, then optimal production may result.

18. See John McMillan, "The Free Rider Problem: A Survey," *Economic Record* 55, no. 149 (June 1974): 95–107.

19. See Mancur Olson, *The Logic of Collective Action: Public Goods and the Theory of Groups* (Cambridge, Mass.: Harvard University Press, 1965); Brubaker, "Demand Disclosures and Exclusion"; Christainsen, "Providing Collective Goods"; and Cornes and Sandler, "Theory of Public Goods."

20. See Buchanan's "Joint Supply and Optimality" and *Public Goods;* and Demsetz's "Private Production of Public Goods" and "Joint Supply."

21. See, for example, J. Hayden Boyd, "Joint Products, Collective Goods, and External Effects: Comment," *Journal of Political Economy* 79, no. 5 (Sept. 1971): 1138–40; David F. Bradford, "Joint Products, Collective Goods, and External Effects: Comment," *Journal of Political Economy* 79, no. 5 (Sept. 1971): 1119–28; Robert B. Ekelund and Joe R. Hulett, "Joint Supply, the Taussig-Pigou Controversy, and the Competitive Provision of Public Goods," *Journal of Law and Economics* 16, no. 2 (Oct. 1973): 369–87; Ellickson, "Public Goods and Joint Supply"; Head, "Public Goods and Public Policy"; Estelle James, "Joint Products, Collective Goods, and External Effects: Comment," *Journal of Political Economy* 79, no. 5 (Sept. 1971): 1127–35; E. J. Mishan, "Joint Products, Collective Goods, and External Effects: Reply," *Journal of Political Economy* 79, no. 5 (Sept. 1971): 1141–50; Mishan, "Collective Goods and External Effects"; Oakland, "Joint Goods"; Samuelson, "Welfare Conditions for Public Goods"; and Neil M. Singer, "Joint Products, Collective Goods, and External Effects: Comment," *Journal of Political Economy* 79, no. 5 (Sept. 1971): 1136–37.

22. For the original treatment see, Burton Weisbrod, "Collective Consumption Services of Individual Consumption Goods," *Quarterly Journal of Economics* 78, no. 3 (Aug. 1964): 471–77. Also see, Lawrence Leuzzi and Richard Pollock, "Option Demand: A Mixed Goods Case," *Public Finance* 31, no. 3 (1976): 396–405.

23. See Thompson, "Competitive Production of Collective Goods," for the original exposition. For comments on this overproduction possibility and the rejoinders see Demsetz, "Reply to Thompson"; Subrata K. Ganguly, "The Perfectly Competitive Production of Collective Goods: Comment," *Review of Economics and Statistics* 51, no. 4 (Nov. 1969): 478–79; Bruce M. Owen, "The Perfectly Competitive Production of Collective Goods: Comment," *Review of Economics and Statistics* 51, no. 4 (Nov. 1969): 475–76; James D. Rodgers, "The Perfectly Competitive

Production of Collective Goods: Comment," *Review of Economics and Statistics* 51, no. 4 (Nov. 1969): 476–78; Earl A. Thompson, "The Perfectly Competitive Production of Collective Goods: Reply," *Review of Economics and Statistics* 51, no. 4 (Nov. 1969): 479–82, and also "Private Production of Public Goods."

24. For general discussions of price discrimination see Louis Phlips, *The Economics of Price Discrimination* (Cambridge: Cambridge University Press, 1983); and Jean Tirole, *The Theory of Industrial Organization* (Cambridge, Mass.: MIT Press, 1988).

25. See Ekelund and Hulett, "Joint Supply and Public Goods."

26. See Demsetz, "Private Production of Public Goods."

27. See Samuelson, "Welfare Conditions for Public Goods" and "Public Expenditure and Taxation."

28. See King, "Optimum Provision of Public Goods," and Ulrich Kohli, "Technology and Public Goods," *Journal of Public Economics* 26, no. 2 (Apr. 1985): 379–400.

29. Thompson, "Competitive Production of Collective Goods," takes issue with the price-taking behavior on the part of the individual consumer. This issue will be addressed in chapters 5 and 6.

30. For theoretical treatments see Robin Boadway, "Similarities and Differences between Public Goods and Public Factors," *Public Finance* 28, no. 3–4 (1973): 245–57; K. Kaizuka, "Public Goods and Decentralization of Production," *Review of Economics and Statistics* 47, no. 1 (Feb. 1965): 118–20; Kohli, "Technology and Public Goods"; and Thompson, "Competitive Production of Collective Goods." For an application see, Stephen Shmanske, "News as a Public Good: Cooperative Ownership, Price Commitments, and the Success of the Associated Press," *Business History Review* 60 (Spring 1986): 55–80.

31. See Auster, "Private Markets"; Else, "Public Goods and Mixed Goods"; Shmanske, "Public Goods," and "Else's Treatment of Quality."

32. See Kelvin J. Lancaster, "A New Approach to Consumer Theory," *Journal of Political Economy* 74, no. 1 (Feb. 1966): 132–57.

33. For example, see Borenstein, "Price Discrimination"; Hotelling, "Stability in Competition"; Prescott and Visscher, "Sequential Location with Foresight"; and Salop, "Monopolistic Competition with Outside Goods."

34. See R. Schmalensee, "Monopolistic Two-Part Pricing Arrangements," *Bell Journal of Economics* 12, no. 2 (Autumn 1981): 445–66, for the monopoly treatment and Shmanske, "Contestable Two-Part Pricing," for the duopoly treatment.

35. Dixit and Stiglitz, "Monopolistic Competition and Product Diversity," and Spence, "Product Selection and Monopolistic Competition," briefly mention perfect price discrimination in multiple firm settings. Shmanske, "Price Discrimination and Monopolistic Competition," considers perfect price discrimination as one end of a continuum of pricing policies.

36. For the original treatment see Shmanske, "Public Goods."

CHAPTER FOUR

1. See Head and Shoup, "Public, Private, and Ambiguous Goods."

2. See Staaf, "Privatization of Public Goods." See also Meiselbach, "Characteristics of Public Goods" for closely related ideas.

3. Evans, "Private Good"; John G. Head, "Mixed Goods in Samuelson Geometry," *Public Finance* 31, no. 3 (1976): 313–39.

4. See Buchanan, "Theory of Clubs."

5. See Boyd, "Joint Products; Comment"; Buchanan, "Joint Supply and Optimality," *Public Goods*, and with Kaflogis, "Note on Public Goods Supply"; Evans, "Private Good, Externality, Public Good"; Head, "Mixed Goods"; Holtermann, "Externalities and Public Goods"; James "Joint Products: Comment"; Mishan's "Joint Products: Reply," "Collective Goods and External Effects," and "The Postwar Literature on Externalities: An Interpretive Essay," *Journal of Economic Literature* 9, no. 1 (Mar. 1971): 1–28; and Mancur Olson and Richard Zeckhauser, "The Efficient Production of External Economies," *American Economic Review* 60, no. 3 (June 1970): 512–17.

6. See Jan Tinbergen, "On Collective and Part-Collective Goods," *De Economist* 12, no. 2 (1984): 171–82.

7. Oakland, "Congestion, Public Goods."

8. Sometimes the term "fixed cost" is used carelessly when overhead cost is meant. This confusion should be avoided at all costs. An overhead cost does not vary with output except at the quantity zero. A fixed cost does not vary in the short run but is nonexistent in the long run. Some writers have been led to conclude that a good may be a private good in the short run because of the potentially rival (although not rival because of zero marginal cost) consumption and because of the marginal equalities that have each person's marginal rate of substitution equal to zero. Meanwhile, the good is a public good in the long run, as the "fixed" cost is varied to supply more of the nonrival good. See Mishan, "Literature on Externalities," and Singer, "Joint Products; Comment." There are, in

fact, two dimensions of consumption; one looks like a private good and one looks like a public good. However, what is called a fixed cost is actually an overhead cost. It exists in both the long and short run and can be varied in both the long and short run. Consequently, the length of the time horizon, be it short run, long run, or intermediate run, has nothing whatsoever to do with the analysis.

9. See Davis and Whinston, "Public and Private Goods"; Head, "Public Goods and Public Policy"; Lerner, "Public Utility Price Regulation"; Samuelson, "Aspects of Public Expenditure," "Diagrammatic Theory of Public Expenditure," and "Public Expenditure and Taxation"; and Shmanske, "Public Goods."

10. Samuelson, "Diagrammatic Theory of Public Expenditure," p. 356.

11. For example, see Harold Demsetz, "Why Regulate Utilities?" *Journal of Law and Economics* 11, no. 1 (Apr. 1968): 55–65.

12. See Shmanske, "Public Goods."

CHAPTER FIVE

1. Thompson, "Competitive Production of Public Goods"; Demsetz, "Private Production of Public Goods"; Oakland, "Public Goods and Underproduction.

2. See Borcherding, "Optimal Supply of Public Goods"; Brennan and Walsh, "(Excludable) Public Goods" and "Public Goods Provision"; Brito and Oakland, "Excludable Public Goods"; Burns and Walsh, "Price-Excludable Public Goods"; Demsetz, "Joint Supply" and "Reply to Thompson"; Ekelund, "Public Goods Equilibria"; Ekelund and Hulett, "Joint Supply and Public Goods"; Ganguly, "Competitive Production: Comment"; Owen, "Competitive Production: Comment"; Rodgers, "Competitive Production: Comment"; Thompson, "Competitive Production: Reply," "Private Production of Public Goods," and "Collective-Type Goods"; and Walsh, "Aspects of Public Goods."

3. For example, see Borenstein, "Price Discrimination"; Dixit and Stiglitz, "Monopolistic Competition and Product Diversity"; Beth Hayes, "Competition and Two-Part Tariffs," *Journal of Business* 60, no. 1 (Jan. 1987): 41–54; Katz, "Price Discrimination and Monopolistic Competition"; S. Oren, S. A. Smith, and R. B. Wilson, "Competitive Nonlinear Tariffs," *Journal of Economic Theory* 29 (1983): 49–71; Motty Perry, "Sustainable Positive Profit Multiple-Price Strategies in Contestable Markets," *Journal of Economic Theory* 32 no. (1984): 246–65; Roberts, "Nonlinear Pricing"; Shmanske, "Price Discrimination and Monopolistic Competition," and "Contestable Two-Part Pricing"; Spence, "Product Selection

and Monopolistic Competition"; and Spulber, "Equilibrium with Price-Discriminating Firms."

4. For obvious reasons, firms cannot set both minimum prices and minimum quantities. However, for a given price a firm could set a maximum quantity. For example, setting a maximum quantity limit on a good offered at a low price while acting as a quantity taker at a higher second price that catches any excess demand existing at the low price might be one method that a monopolist would use to price-discriminate through market segmentation. It is in this sense that a firm might not be a price setter/quantity taker. This scheme will unravel in a multiple firm setting.

5. The scenario described in the text requires the additional assumption that the customers can enforce exclusive selling arrangements between themselves. If they cannot, then the first buyer will end up in competition with the second buyer in trying to sell to the third buyer. The limit in this case is that the original seller can use two-part pricing for, at most, two people, capturing only their own consumer surplus because both of these consumers recognize that they will earn no profit on sales to others. If exclusive selling arrangements are enforceable, then each seller pledges not to compete for any other business further down the line.

6. Actually the case of lighthouses may be ambiguous. A consumer of lighthouse services cannot retain the light in order to resell the warning to another ship. However, if the lighthouse services are made excludable, perhaps by requiring a coded signal to turn the lighthouse on, access to the coded signal could be resold.

7. Thompson, "Collective-Type Goods."

8. Shmanske, "News as a Public Good."

9. See Shmanske, "Price Discrimination and Monopolistic Competition."

10. See Thompson, "Collective-Type Goods," which discusses price discrimination that is imposed in a sequential framework in the marketing of innovations. See also Shmanske's "News as a Public Good" and "Price Commitments and the Private Supply of a Public Factor: The Case of the Associated Press," California State University, Hayward, School of Business and Economics Faculty Working Paper No. 19 (1985), which discuss price discrimination that uses a pricing formula in a cooperative setting for the sale of news items. See also, James M. Buchanan, "Public Goods in Theory and Practice," *Journal of Law and Economics* 10, no. 2 (Oct. 1967): 193–97; Minasian, "Television and Public Goods"; and Samuelson, "Public Goods and Subscription TV," who address price discrimination and the associated information requirements when the public good is a TV signal.

11. With respect to energy costs, most economists would probably call this a bizarre assumption rather than a simplifying one. Note, however, that many economists would also argue about the usefulness of a zero information cost assumption using the same two adjectives.

12. See William J. Baumol, John C. Panzar, and Robert D. Willig, *Contestable Markets and the Theory of Industry Structure* (New York: Harcourt Brace Jovanovich, 1982).

13. Of course, Oakland did not use the terminology of contestability, which was developed after his analysis. The same holds true for Demsetz. As will be explained below, the Oakland equilibrium is not impervious to hit-and-run entry by a price-discriminating firm, so it is not technically contestable. However, given the constraint of no price discrimination, the market is contestable. The discussion of contestability in private goods markets with nonuniform pricing is still in its infancy. See Borenstein, "Price Discrimination"; Oren, Smith, and Wilson, "Competitive Nonlinear Tariffs"; Perry, "Multiple-Price Strategies"; Shmanske, "Contestable Two-Part Pricing"; and Spulber, "Equilibrium with Price-Discriminating Firms."

CHAPTER SIX

1. Ekelund, "Public Goods Equilibrium."

2. This seems to be an excellent example of the division of knowledge and ability of the market process to reveal, develop and use the necessary information. See F. A. Hayek, "The Use of Knowledge in Society," *American Economic Review* 35, no. 5 (Dec. 1945): 519–30.

3. See Brennan and Walsh, "Public Goods Provision"; Brito and Oakland, "Excludable Public Goods"; and Burns and Walsh, "Price-Excludable Public Goods."

4. Ibid.

5. Demsetz, "Private Production of Public Goods," and Thompson, "Competitive Production of Collective Goods." Also of interest are the comments and rejoinders on these models and Borcherding's criticism of both models. See Borcherding, "Optimal Supply of Public Goods"; Demsetz, "Joint Supply," and "Reply to Thompson"; Ekelund and Hulett, "Joint Supply and Public Goods"; Ganguly, "Competitive Production: Comment"; Owen, "Competitive Production: Comment"; Rodgers, "Competitive Production: Comment"; and Thompson, "Competitive Production: Reply," and "Private Production of Public Goods," and "Collective-Type Goods."

6. See the section on demand revelation in Chapter 3 and the references cited there.
7. See Shmanske, "News as a Public Good," for analysis of a collective of newspapers that purchase jointly consumed news items from Associated Press, a zero profit producer of news items.
8. Demsetz, "Private Production of Public Goods"; Thompson, "Competitive Production of Collective Goods"; and Borcherding, "Optimal Supply of Public Goods."
9. In fact, Demsetz had already made his notion of potential competition, or competition for the market, explicit in his paper on public utilities (Demsetz, "Why Regulate Utilities?"). This paper is in many ways a forerunner to the model that we now call contestable markets.
10. See Thompson, "Collective-Type Goods."

CHAPTER SEVEN

1. In the case of a commercial ship passing the lighthouse, the lighthouse may more appropriately be called a public factor. See Boadway, "Public Goods and Public Factors"; Kaizuka, "Public Goods and Production"; and Thompson, "Competitive Production of Collective Goods."
2. See Buchanan, "Public Goods in Practice"; Minasian, "Television and Public Goods"; Samuelson, "Pitfalls of Public Goods"; and Samuelson, "Public Goods and Subscription TV."
3. See Buchanan, *Public Goods.*
4. The relevant portion of Buchanan's text is reproduced here. Equations (9) and (10) are Buchanan's two optimal conditions, and X_2 refers to the quantity of the public good. ". . . (9) and (10) will no longer be identical. Here either technological considerations will determine the precise location of X_2 or, more generally, the optimal mix will be determined by a consideration of both evaluation and cost factors. Before (9) or (10) is satisfied, these subsidiary conditions defining optimality in the component mix must be satisfied" (Buchanan, *Public Goods*, pp. 73–74).
5. See Demsetz, "Private Production of Public Goods," which leaves out the utilization dimension but does not confuse the two dimensions, and Ekelund and Hulett, "Joint Supply and Public Goods," which does confuse the two dimensions by trying to apply the welfare economics relevant in the utilization dimension to the marginal rates of substitution in the public goods dimension.
6. The literature is vast. For examples, see Buchanan, "Joint Supply";

DeSerpa, "Impure Public Goods"; Evans, "Private Good, Externality, Public Good"; Holterman, "Externalities and Public Goods"; Musgrave, "Provision for Social Goods"; Muzondo, "Mixed and Pure Public Goods"; Oakland, "Congestion"; Sandler, "Public Goods and Spillovers"; and Sandler and Cauley, "Multiregional Public Goods."

7. See Evans, "Private Good, Externality, Public Good."

8. See Brennan and Walsh, "Public Goods Provision"; Brito and Oakland, "Excludable Public Goods"; DeSerpa, "Impure Public Goods"; Muzondo, "Mixed and Pure Public Goods"; Oakland, "Congestion"; Sandler, "Public Goods and Spillovers"; and Sandler and Cauley, "Multiregional Public Goods."

9. Brito and Oakland, "Excludable Public Goods"; Brennan and Walsh, "Public Goods Provision."

10. See, for example, Weisbrod, "Collective Services of Individual Goods"; and Leuzzi and Pollock, "Option Demand." The option demand is meant to capture a value that the consumer gets by having the public good around even if the consumer does not use it. Several problems with this view were identified above in Chapter 3. Arguably, the best way to think of option demand is as a proxy for the value of expected future utilization. As such, option demand should probably be modeled this way.

11. I purposely write out the usual ratios of marginal utilities as slopes of implicit functions. Below, this will help us to keep track of the levels of certain variables when they are held constant.

12. The approximation is close for infinitesimal changes when the expenditure on y_i is a small part of the consumer's budget, or when the income elasticity of demand is close to zero. The correspondence is exact when the income elasticity is identically zero. See Robert D. Willig, "Consumer's Surplus without Apology," *American Economic Review* 66, no. 4 (Sept. 1976): 589–97.

13. Lerner, "Public Utility Price Regulation," eloquently compares the public good model with the familiar decreasing cost example. Davis and Whinston, "Public and Private Goods," attempt to integrate pure public goods with goods "characterized by extreme decreasing costs" (p. 368). Head, "Public Goods and Public Policy," notes the similarity between public goods and goods produced subject to "sharply decreasing costs" (p. 213). Ekelund, "Public Goods Equilibria," believes that the excludable public good case is a proper subset of familiar natural monopoly problems. For a dissenting opinion see Dorfman, "General Equilibrium with Public Goods," who denies that urban transit is a public good solely "by virtue of the strongly decreasing costs of producing their services" (p. 250).

CHAPTER EIGHT

1. However, if x is a composite good of which some components are substitutes or complements to either Y or y, and if the seller can perfectly price-discriminate, then the consumption of x may affect the pricing of y. Thompson, "Competitive Production of Collective Goods," discusses this possibility. The analysis of such a possibility is undertaken below with the introduction of multiple public good sellers. The analysis of the multiple producer case essentially takes the related goods out of the composite good numeraire and examines them explicitly on equal terms with all the other units of the public good. The numeraire, x, will then contain only goods which are unrelated to the public good. Salop, "Monopolistic Competition with Outside Goods," explores a similar effect in a monopolistic competition setting. He develops a distinction between outside goods and members of the Chamberlinian group but only considers simple pricing schemes.

2. See Shmanske, "Contestable Two-Part Pricing," for a model that specifically examines the total conditions in a duopoly market with two-part pricing. The total conditions put a constraint on the sellers' ability to price-discriminate.

3. There is another condition, an equilibrium condition, that must be met for the combination of (8.8′) and (8.4) to be possible. The quantities solved for in (8.4) are the optimum quantities for the consumer. The quantities solved for in (8.8′) are the optimum quantities for the firm. The equilibrium condition is that these quantities be equal. Prices are adjusted up or down to bring about this equilibrium.

4. Indeed, any quality choice decision is essentially a public goods decision where pricing takes place in a private goods dimension that I call the utilization dimension.

5. Rodgers, "Competitive Production: Comment," mistakenly applies the all-or-nothing pricing assumption to Thompson's "Competitive Production of Collective Goods" overproduction theorem, which involves competitive producers and does not assume all-or-none pricing. The overproduction developed in the text is for a monopoly producer, does involve a type of all-or-none pricing, and is therefore different from Thompson's.

6. Of course, in such an instance the utilization decisions of the customers may now be distorted.

7. For a considerable increase in notation we could allow the monopoly seller to offer utilization units of different quality levels or different amounts of the public good to different individuals. This would provide the seller with another avenue of price discrimination, which would probably be better labeled as quality discrimination. In this book the

ability of people to consume different amounts in the public goods dimension is explored in the multiple producer case but not in the monopoly case.

8. Brito and Oakland, "Excludable Public Goods"; Brennan and Walsh, "Public Goods Provision."

9. Although as noted above, if the pricing in the utilization dimension is of an all-or-none variety, then overproduction may still come about with imperfect price discrimination.

CHAPTER NINE

1. The models of location or spatial competition do allow a type of product quality choice.

2. In general, utilization costs will be positive. The temporary consideration of the zero utilization cost case facilitates the comparison of the model in this book with the received public goods models.

3. For examples see Dixit and Stiglitz, "Monopolistic Competition and Product Diversity"; Shmanske, "Price Discrimination and Monopolistic Competition"; and Michael Spence, "Product Differentiation and Welfare," *American Economic Review* 66, no. 2 (May 1976): 407–14.

4. This is equation (2) in Dixit and Stiglitz, "Monopolistic Competition and Product Diversity," p. 298. This utility function is not subscripted by consumer. Dixit and Stiglitz interpret it either as a social utility function or as the utility function of a representative individual.

5. The key assumption is that the firms are selling equal amounts in the public goods dimension. Once we have assumed that the public good amounts coming from each firm are identical, we can set that level equal to one with no loss in generality.

6. See Shmanske, "Contestable Two-Part Pricing," which addresses this issue for duopoly.

7. See, for example, Roger W. Koenker and Martin K. Perry, "Product Differentiation, Monopolistic Competition, and Public Policy," *Bell Journal of Economics* 12, no. 1 (Spring 1981): 217–31; Shmanske, "Price Discrimination and Monopolistic Competition"; Spence, "Product Differentiation and Welfare," and "Product Selection and Monopolistic Competition."

8. Demsetz, "Inconsistencies of Monopolistic Competition."

9. The difference in the approaches concerns whether attention is focused on the extensive margin or the intensive margin. The monopolistic competition models examine the public goods dimension by calculating the

number of firms in equilibrium. The quality of each firm is set exogenously, but the number of firms is endogenous. This is the extensive margin. The approach adopted in this book holds the number of firms constant but examines each firm's quality choice. Here, the number of firms is exogenous but the quality of each firm's product is endogenous. This is the intensive margin.

CHAPTER TEN

1. Nash reactions could be assumed for any two of the three possible reactions: price, utilization, and public good quantity. Care must be taken if Nash interactions are made for all three possible reactions simultaneously. It may not make sense for a rival to hold everything constant in the face of some change by another firm in the industry. For example if one producer expands production and lowers price, other producers will not be able to hold utilization quantity constant if they also hold price and quality constant. These issues are addressed verbally below.

2. See Koenker and Perry, "Product Differentiation and Public Policy."

3. Shmanske, "Contestable Two-Part Pricing," develops one such analysis for a trimmed-down, duopoly version of the general model considered in this chapter.

4. For sophisticated technical analyses of endogenous reaction conditions, see Eric Maskin and Jean Tirole, "A Theory of Dynamic Oligopoly, I: Overview and Quantity Competition with Large Fixed Costs," *Econometrica* 56, no. 3 (May 1988): 549–69, plus "A Theory of Dynamic Oligopoly, II: Price Competition, Kinked Demand Curves, and Edgeworth Cycles," *Econometrica* 56, no. 3 (May 1988): 571–99, and "A Theory of Dynamic Oligopoly, III: Cournot Competition," *European Economic Review* 31 (1987): 947–68; Daughety, Andrew F., "Reconsidering Cournot: The Cournot Equilibrium Is Consistent," *Rand Journal of Economics* 16, no. 3 (Autumn 1985): 368–79, and Michael H. Riordan, "Imperfect Information and Dynamic Conjectural Variations," *Rand Journal of Economics* 16, no. 1 (Spring 1985): 41–50.

5. Such is the case in the wire service industry as documented by Shmanske in "Private Supply of a Public Factor" and "News as a Public Good." The Associated Press (AP) established a pricing formula for the sale of the public good, news, to its newspaper-publishing customers. Notably, the AP's competition in the first half of the twentieth century, the United Press Association (UPA), did not make commitments to its prices. Because of this, the newspapers could use their purchases of the AP news to bargain for, and receive, lower prices from the UPA. Meanwhile, purchases of UPA news had no effect on the prices charged by the AP. This pricing practice gave the AP an advantage over the UPA

because the AP news was valuable as news and as a bargaining chip while the UPA news was valuable as news only.

6. Such a division of consumers is the case in Katz, "Price Discrimination and Monopolistic Competition." Katz considers interpersonal price discrimination but essentially only considers uniform pricing.

7. See Thompson, "Competitive Production of Collective Goods."

8. The interested reader should skip to the appendix at this point.

9. See also Koenker and Perry, "Product Differentiation and Public Policy."

10. See ibid.

11. It is possible that rivals will attempt a predatory, punishing reaction of raising quality in response to the k'th firm's increase in utilization. This supplies a disincentive to the k'th firm to expand and therefore leads to underutilization. Usually, however, the competitive, noncooperative interaction is as stated in the text.

12. See Shmanske, "Price Discrimination and Monopolistic Competition"; and Spence, "Product Differentiation and Welfare," for examples of a solution method involving numerical calculations. This numerical approach, although tedious, is actually the logically correct way to proceed. Other approaches used in such settings are wanting. One approach is to treat only the large-numbers case so that the number of firms can be approximated as a continuous variable. In this approach, standard calculus applies. However, by treating the large-numbers case, the oligopolistic nature of the problem pales in importance. This is unfortunate, since the small-numbers bargaining problem may be the most important institutional characteristic in the setting. In the small-numbers case sometimes the number of firms is treated as continuous so that calculus applies, with the added provision that the equilibrium is actually one of two integers that immediately bound the nonintegral solution that the calculus provides. To determine which of the two integers is the correct solution involves precisely the same numerical calculations that are carried out in the papers cited above.

13. For examples, see Spence, "Product Differentiation and Welfare" or "Product Selection and Monopolistic Competition."

14. For example, see Koenker and Perry, "Product Differentiation and Public Policy."

15. It may be better to think in terms of firms choosing a capacity level in the first stage of a two-stage game where the second stage competition will be in prices. See D. Kreps and J. Scheinkman, "Cournot Precommitment and Bertrand Competition Yield Cournot Outcomes," *Bell Journal of Economics* 4, no. 2 (Autumn 1983): 326–37; and C. Davidson and R. Denekere, "Long Run Competition in Capacity, Short Run Com-

petition in Price, and the Cournot Model," *Rand Journal of Economics* 17, no. 3 (Autumn 1986): 404–15. Also in this regard see, N. Singh and X. Vives, "Price and Quantity Competition in a Differentiated Duopoly," *Rand Journal of Economics* 15, no. 4 (Winter 1984): 546–54.

16. For a discussion of this rational competitive interaction see Earl A. Thompson and Roger L. Faith, "A Pure Theory of Strategic Behavior and Social Institutions," *American Economic Review* 71, no. 3 (June 1981): 366–80.

CHAPTER ELEVEN

1. In this regard Shmanske, "Contestable Two-Part Pricing," derives a model that allows noncooperative duopolists the option of uniform pricing or two-part pricing. Under a variety of conditions the sellers choose two-part pricing over uniform pricing. The implication that complex pricing dominates uniform pricing is borne out in the real world. For example, consider that one of the latest innovations in retail marketing has been the phenomenal success of the warehouse clubs. These clubs essentially employ a two-part pricing schedule with a lump sum membership fee and low per unit prices.

References

Auster, Richard D. "Private Markets in Public Goods (or Qualities)." *Quarterly Journal of Economics* 91, no. 3 (August 1977): 419–30.

Baumol, William J.; John C. Panzar; and Robert D. Willig. *Contestable Markets and the Theory of Industry Structure.* New York: Harcourt Brace Jovanovich, 1982.

Beckmann, Martin J. "Spatial Price Policies Revisited." *Bell Journal of Economics* 7, no. 2 (Autumn 1976): 619–29.

Berglas, Eitan, and David Pines. "Clubs, Local Public Goods and Transportation Models: A Synthesis." *Journal of Public Economics* 15, no. 2 (1981): 141–62.

Bergstrom, T. C., and R. C. Cornes. "Independence of Allocative Efficiency from Distribution in the Theory of Public Goods." *Econometrica* 51, no. 6 (November 1983): 1753–65.

Bergstrom, Theodore; Lawrence Blume; and Hal Varian. "On the Private Provision of Public Goods." *Journal of Public Economics* 29, no. 1 (February 1986): 25–49.

Blair, Roger D., and Lawrence W. Kenny. *Microeconomics with Business Applications.* New York: John Wiley and Sons, 1987.

Bliss, Christopher, and Barry Nalebuff. "Dragon-Slaying and Ballroom Dancing: The Private Supply of a Public Good." *Journal of Public Economics* 25, no. 1 (November 1984): 1–12.

Boadway, Robin. "Similarities and Differences between Public Goods and Public Factors." *Public Finance* 28, no. 3–4 (1973): 245–57.

Bohm, Peter. "Estimating Demand for Public Goods: An Experiment." *European Economic Review* 3, no. 2 (1972): 111–30.

Bolnick, Bruce R. "Lindahl, Bowen, and the Cost of Public Goods," *Public Finance* 33, no. 1–2 (1978): 23–32.

Borcherding, Thomas E. "Competition, Exclusion and the Optimal Supply of Public Goods." *Journal of Law and Economics* 21, no. 2 (April 1978): 111–32.

Borenstein, S. "Price Discrimination in Free Entry Markets." *Rand Journal of Economics* 16, no. 3 (Autumn 1985): 380–97.

Boyd, J. Hayden. "Joint Products, Collective Goods and External Effects:

Comment." *Journal of Political Economy* 79, no. 5 (September 1971): 1138–40.

Bradford, David F. "Joint Products, Collective Goods, and External Effects: Comment." *Journal of Political Economy* 79, no. 5 (September 1971): 1119–28.

Bradford, David F., and Gregory G. Hildebrandt. "Observable Preferences for Public Goods." *Journal of Public Economics* 8, no. 2 (October 1977): 111–31.

Brennan, Geoffrey, and Cliff Walsh. "A Monopoly Model of Public Goods Provision: The Uniform Pricing Case." *American Economic Review* 71, no. 1 (March 1981): 196–206.

———. "Private Markets in (Excludable) Public Goods: A Reexamination." *Quarterly Journal of Economics* 100, no. 3 (August 1985): 811–19.

Breton, A. "A Theory of Demand for Public Goods." *Canadian Journal of Economics and Political Science* 32 (November 1966): 455–67.

Brito, Dagobert L., and William Oakland. "On the Monopolistic Provision of Excludable Public Goods." *American Economic Review* 70, no. 4 (September 1980): 691–704.

Browning, Edgar K., and Jacquelene M. Browning. *Microeconomic Theory and Applications*. 2nd ed. Boston: Little, Brown, 1986.

Brubaker, Earl R. "Demand Disclosures and Conditions on Exclusion: An Experiment." *Economic Journal* 94, no. 375 (September 1984): 536–53.

———. "Free Ride, Free Revelation, or Golden Rule?" *Journal of Law and Economics* 18, no. 1 (April 1975): 147–61.

Buchanan, James M. *The Demand and Supply of Public Goods*. Chicago: Rand McNally, 1968.

———. "An Economic Theory of Clubs." *Economica* 32, no. 125 (February 1965): 1–14.

———. "Joint Supply, Externality, and Optimality." *Economica* 33, no. 132 (November 1966): 404–15.

———. "Public Goods in Theory and Practice." *Journal of Law and Economics* 10, no. 2 (October 1967): 193–97.

Buchanan, James M., and Milton F. Kaflogis. "A Note on Public Goods Supply." *American Economic Review* 53, no. 3 (June 1963): 403–14.

Burns, Michael E., and Cliff Walsh. "Market Provision of Price-Excludable Public Goods: A General Analysis." *Journal of Political Economy* 89, no. 1 (February 1981): 166–91.

Call, Steven T., and William L. Holahan. *Microeconomics*. Belmont, Calif.: Wadsworth Publishing, 1980.

Cappoza, Dennis R., and Robert Van Order. "A Generalized Model of Spatial Competition." *American Economic Review* 68, no. 5 (December 1978): 896–908.

Chamberlin, Edward H. *The Theory of Monopolistic Competition*. Cambridge, Mass.: Harvard University Press, 1933.

Chiang, R., and C. S. Spatt. "Imperfect Price Discrimination and Welfare." *Review of Economic Studies* 49, no. 156 (April 1982): 155–81.

Christainsen, Gregory B. "Evidence for Determining the Optimal Mechanism for Providing Collective Goods." *American Economist* 26, no. 1 (Spring 1982): 57–61.

Clarke, Edward H. "Multipart Pricing of Public Goods." *Public Choice* 11 (Fall 1971): 17–33.

Coase, Ronald H. "The Lighthouse in Economics." *Journal of Law and Economics* 17 (1974): 357–76.

———. "The Problem of Social Cost." *Journal of Law and Economics* 3, no. 2 (October 1960): 1–44.

Collinge, R. A. "Toward 'Privatization' of Public Sector Output: Decentralized Contracting for Public and Private Goods." *Journal of Public Economics* 27, no. 3 (August 1985): 371–87.

Conn, David. "The Scope of Satisfactory Mechanisms for the Provision of Public Goods." *Journal of Public Economics* 20, no. 2 (March 1983): 249–63.

Cornes, Richard, and Todd Sandler. "Easy Riders, Joint Production, and Public Goods." *Economic Journal* 94, no. 375 (September 1984): 580–98.

———. "On the Consistency of Conjectures with Public Goods." *Journal of Public Economics* 27, no. 1 (June 1985): 125–29.

———. "The Simple Analytics of Pure Public Good Provision." *Economica* 52, no. 105 (February 1985): 103–16.

———. "The Theory of Public Goods: Non-Nash Behavior." *Journal of Public Economics* 23, no. 3 (April 1984): 367–79.

Cowen, Tyler. "Public Goods Definitions and Their Institutional Context: A Critique of Public Goods Theory." *Review of Social Economy* 43, no. 1 (April 1985): 53–63.

Daughety, Andrew F. "Reconsidering Cournot: The Cournot Equilibrium Is Consistent." *Rand Journal of Economics* 16, no. 3 (Autumn 1985): 368–79.

Davidson, C., and R. Denekere. "Long Run Competition in Capacity, Short Run Competition in Price, and the Cournot Model." *Rand Journal of Economics* 17, no. 3 (Autumn 1986): 404–15.

Davis, Otto A., and Andrew B. Whinston. "On the Distinction between Public and Private Goods." *American Economic Review* 57, no. 2 (May 1967): 360–73.

Demsetz, Harold "The Inconsistencies of Monopolistic Competition." *Journal of Political Economy* 80, no. 3 (June 1972): 592–57.

———. "Joint Supply and Price Discrimination." *Journal of Law and Economics* 16, no. 2 (October 1973): 389–405.

———. "The Private Production of Public Goods." *Journal of Law and Economics* 13, no. 2 (October 1970): 293–306.

———. "Reply to Professor Thompson." *Journal of Law and Economics* 16, no. 2 (October 1973): 413–15.

———. "Why Regulate Utilities?" *Journal of Law and Economics* 11, no. 1 (April 1968): 55–65.

DeSerpa, Allan C. "Congestion, Pollution, and Impure Public Goods." *Public Finance* 33, no. 1–2 (1978): 68–83.

———. *Microeconomic Theory: Issues and Applications*. Boston: Allyn and Bacon, 1985.

Dixit, Avinash K., and Joseph E. Stiglitz. "Monopolistic Competition and Optimum Product Diversity." *American Economic Review* 67, no. 3 (June 1977): 297–308.

Dorfman, Robert. "General Equilibrium with Public Goods." In *Public Economics*, ed. J. Margolis and H. Guitton, pp. 245–75. London: Macmillan, 1969.

———. "On Optimal Congestion." *Journal of Environmental Economics and Management* 11, no. 2 (June 1984): 91–106.

Dung, Tran Huu. "Externalities, Public Goods and Counternormal Effect." *Public Finance Quarterly* 10, no. 3 (July 1982): 393–99.

Eaton, B. Curtis, and Diane F. Eaton. *Microeconomics*. New York: W. H. Freeman and Company, 1988.

Ekelund, Robert B. "The Fragile Nature of Public Goods Equilibria." *Review of Social Economy* 35, no. 3 (October 1977): 204–11.

Ekelund, Robert B., and Joe R. Hulett. "Joint Supply, the Taussig-Pigou Controversy, and the Competitive Provision of Public Goods." *Journal of Law and Economics* 16, no. 2 (October 1973): 369–87.

Ellickson, Bryan. "A Generalization of the Pure Theory of Public Goods." *American Economic Review* 63, no. 3 (June 1973): 417–32.

———. "Public Goods and Joint Supply." *Journal of Public Economics* 9, no. 3 (June 1978): 373–82.

Else, Peter K. "Further Thoughts on Public Goods, Private Goods, and Mixed Goods." *Scottish Journal of Political Economy* 35, no. 2 (May 1988): 115–28.

Evans, Alan W. "Private Good, Externality, Public Good." *Scottish Journal of Political Economy* 22, no. 1 (February 1970): 79–89.

Foley, Duncan K. "Lindahl's Solution and the Core of an Economy with Collective Goods." *Econometrica* 38, no. 1 (January 1970): 66–72.

Friedman, David D. *Price Theory: An Intermediate Text*. Livermore, Calif.: South-Western Publishing, 1986.

Ganguly, Subrata K. "The Perfectly Competitive Production of Collective Goods: Comment." *Review of Economics and Statistics* 51, no. 4 (November 1969): 478–79.

Goldin, Kenneth D. "Equal Access vs. Selective Access: A Critique of Public Goods Theory." *Public Choice* 29 (Spring 1977): 53–71.

Green, Jerry, and Jean-Jacques Laffont. "On the Revelation of Preferences for Public Goods." *Journal of Public Economics* 8, no. 1 (August 1977): 79–93.

Greenhut, John G., and M. L. Greenhut. "Spatial Price Discrimination and Locational Effects." *Economica* 42, no. 168 (November 1975): 401–19.

Groves, Theodore, and John O. Ledyard. "Some Limitations of Demand Revealing Processes." *Public Choice* 29 (1975): 107–24.

Hayek, F. A. "The Use of Knowledge in Society." *American Economic Review* 35, no. 5 (December 1945): 519–30.

Hayes, Beth. "Competition and Two-Part Tariffs." *Journal of Business* 60, no. 1 (January 1987): 41–54.

Head, John G. "Mixed Goods in Samuelson Geometry." *Public Finance* 31, no. 3 (1976): 313–39.

———. "Public Goods and Public Policy." *Public Finance* 17, no. 3 (1962): 197–219.

Head, John G., and Carl S. Shoup. "Public Goods, Private Goods, and Ambiguous Goods." *Economic Journal* 79, no. 315 (September 1969): 567–72.

Hemenway, David. *Prices and Choices*. 2nd ed. Cambridge, Mass.: Ballinger Publishing, 1988.

Hirshleifer, Jack. "From Weakest-Link to Best-Shot: The Voluntary Provision of Public Goods." *Public Choice* 41, no. 1 (1983): 371–86.

———. *Price Theory and Applications*. 4th ed. Englewood Cliffs, N.J.: Prentice Hall, 1988.

Holtermann, S. E. "Externalities and Public Goods." *Economica* 39, no. 153 (February 1972): 78–87.

Hori, Hajime. "Revealed Preference for Public Goods." *American Economic Review* 65, no. 5 (December 1975): 978–91.

Hotelling, H. "Stability in Competition." *Economic Journal* 39 (March 1929): 41–57.

Hyman, David N. *Modern Microeconomics: Analysis and Applications*. Saint Louis: Times Mirror/Mosby College Publishing, 1986.

Isaac, R. Mark; James M. Walker; and Susan H. Thomas. "Divergent Evidence on Free Riding: An Experimental Examination of Possible Explanations." *Public Choice* 43, no. 2 (1984): 113–49.

James, Estelle. "Joint Products, Collective Goods, and External Effects: Comment." *Journal of Political Economy* 79, no. 5 (September 1971): 1127–35.

———. "Optimal Pollution Control and Trade in Collective Goods." *Journal of Public Economics* 3, no. 3 (August 1974): 203–16.

Kaizuka, K. "Public Goods and Decentralization of Production." *Review of Economics and Statistics* 47, no. 1 (February 1965): 118–20.

Katz, M. L. "Price Discrimination and Monopolistic Competition." *Econometrica* 56, no. 6 (November 1984): 1453–71.

Katzner, Donald W. *Walrasian Economics: An Introduction to the Economic Theory of Market Behavior*. Menlo Park, Calif.: Addison-Wesley, 1988.

Kim, Oliver, and Mark Walker. "The Free Rider Problem: Experimental Evidence." *Public Choice* 43, no. 1 (1984): 3–24.

King, Mervyn A. "A Pigovian Rule for the Optimum Provision of Public Goods." *Journal of Public Economics* 30, no. 3 (August 1986): 273–91.

Koenker, Roger W., and Martin K. Perry. "Product Differentiation, Monopolistic Competition, and Public Policy." *Bell Journal of Economics* 12, no. 1 (Spring 1981): 217–31.

Kohler, Heinz. *Intermediate Microeconomics: Theory and Applications*. 2nd ed. Glenview, Ill.: Scott, Foresman, 1986.

Kohli, Ulrich. "Technology and Public Goods." *Journal of Public Economics* 26, no. 2 (April 1985): 379–400.

Kreps, D., and J. Scheinkman. "Cournot Precommitment and Bertrand Competition Yield Cournot Outcomes." *Bell Journal of Economics* 4, no. 2 (Autumn 1983): 326–37.

Kurz, Mordecai. "Experimental Approach to the Determination of the Demand for Public Goods." *Journal of Public Economics* 3, no. 4 (November 1974): 329–48.

Lancaster, Kelvin J. "A New Approach to Consumer Theory." *Journal of Political Economy* 74, no. 1 (February 1966): 132–57.

Laux-Meiselbach, Wolfgang. "Impossibility of Exclusion and Characteristics of Public Goods." *Journal of Public Economics* 36, no. 1 (June 1988): 127–37.

Lerner, Abba P. "Conflicting Principles of Public Utility Price Regulation." *Journal of Law and Economics* 7, no. 2 (October 1964): 61–70.

Leuzzi, Lawrence, and Richard Pollock. "Option Demand: A Mixed Goods Case." *Public Finance* 31, no. 3 (1976): 396–405.

McCloskey, Donald N. *The Applied Theory of Price*. 2nd ed. New York: Macmillan, 1985.

McGuire, M., and H. Aaron. "Efficiency and Equity in the Optimal Supply of a Public Good." *Review of Economics and Statistics* 51, no. 1 (February 1969): 31–39.

McGuire, Martin C., and Carl H. Groth, Jr. "A Method for Identifying the Public Good Allocation Process within a Group." *Quarterly Journal of Economics* 100, no. 5 (Supplement 1985): 915–34.

McKinney, Scott. "Public Good Producers and Spillovers: An Analysis of Duopoly Behavior." *Public Finance Quarterly* 12, no. 1 (January 1984): 97–116.

McMillan, John. "The Free Rider Problem: A Survey." *Economic Record* 55, no. 149 (June 1974): 95–107.

Mansfield, Edwin. *Microeconomics: Theory and Applications*. 5th ed. New York: W. W. Norton, 1985.

Maskin, Eric, and Jean Tirole. "A Theory of Dynamic Oligopoly, I: Overview and Quantity Competition with Large Fixed Costs." *Econometrica* 56, no. 3 (May 1988): 549–69.

———. "A Theory of Dynamic Oligopoly, II: Price Competition, Kinked Demand Curves, and Edgeworth Cycles." *Econometrica* 56, no. 3 (May 1988): 571–99.

———. "A Theory of Dynamic Oligopoly, III: Cournot Competition." *European Economic Review* 31 (1987): 947–68.

Minasian, Jora R. "Television Pricing and the Theory of Public Goods." *Journal of Law and Economics* 7, no. 2 (October 1964): 71–80.

Mishan, E. J. "Joint Products, Collective Goods, and External Effects: Reply." *Journal of Political Economy* 79, no. 5 (September 1971): 1141–50.

———. "The Postwar Literature on Externalities: An Interpretive Essay." *Journal of Economic Literature* 9, no. 1 (March 1971): 1–28.

———. "The Relationship between Joint Products, Collective Goods, and External Effects." *Journal of Political Economy* 77, no. 3 (May 1969): 329–49.

Muench, Thomas, and Mark Walker. "Are Groves-Ledyard Equilibria Attainable?" *Review of Economic Studies* 50, no. 2 (April 1983): 393–96.

Musgrave, R. A. "Provision for Social Goods." In *Public Economics,* ed. J. Margolis and H. Guitton, pp. 124–44. London: Macmillan, 1969.

Muzondo, Timothy R. "Mixed and Pure Public Goods, User Charges, and Welfare." *Public Finance* 33, no. 3 (1978): 314–30.

Norman, George. "Spatial Competition and Spatial Price Discrimination." *Review of Economic Studies* 48, no. 151 (January 1981): 97–111.

Oakland, William. "Congestion, Public Goods, and Welfare." *Journal of Public Economics* 1 (1972): 339–57.

———. "Joint Goods." *Economica* 36, no. 143 (August 1969): 253–68.

———. "Public Goods, Perfect Competition, and Underproduction." *Journal of Political Economy* 82, no. 5 (September 1974): 927–39.

Olson, Mancur. *The Logic of Collective Action: Public Goods and the Theory of Groups.* Cambridge, Mass.: Harvard University Press, 1965.

Olson, Mancur, and Richard Zeckhauser. "The Efficient Production of External Economies." *American Economic Review* 60, no. 3 (June 1970): 512–17.

Oren, S.; S. A. Smith; and R. B. Wilson. "Competitive Nonlinear Tariffs." *Journal of Economic Theory* 29 (1983): 49–71.

Owen, Bruce M. "The Perfectly Competitive Production of Collective Goods: Comment." *Review of Economics and Statistics* 51, no 4 (November 1969): 475–76.

Perry, Motty. "Sustainable Positive Profit Multiple-Price Strategies in Contestable Markets." *Journal of Economic Theory* 32 (1984): 246–65.

Phlips, Louis. *The Economics of Price Discrimination.* Cambridge: Cambridge University Press, 1983.

Prescott, E. C. and M. Visscher. "Sequential Location among Firms with Foresight." *Bell Journal of Economics* 8, no. 2 (Autumn 1977): 378–93.

Riordan, Michael H. "Imperfect Information and Dynamic Conjectural Variations." *Rand Journal of Economics* 16, no. 1 (Spring 1985): 41–50.

Roberts, Kevin W. S. "Welfare Considerations of Nonlinear Pricing." *Economic Journal* 89, no. 353 (March 1979): 66–83.

Rodgers, James D. "The Perfectly Competitive Production of Collective Goods: Comment." *Review of Economics and Statistics* 51, no. 4 (November 1969): 476–78.

Salop, S. C. "Monopolistic Competition with Outside Goods." *Bell Journal of Economics* 10, no. 1 (Spring 1979): 141–56.

Samuelson, Paul A. "Aspects of Public Expenditure Theories." *Review of Economics and Statistics* 40, no. 4 (November 1958): 332–38.

———. "Contrast between Welfare Conditions for Joint Supply and for Public

Goods." *Review of Economics and Statistics* 51, no. 1 (February 1969): 26–30.

———. "Diagrammatic Exposition of a Theory of Public Expenditure." *Review of Economics and Statistics* 37, no. 4 (November 1955): 350–56.

———. "Pitfalls in the Analysis of Public Goods." *Journal of Law and Economics* 10, no. 2 (October 1967): 199–204.

———. "Public Goods and Subscription TV: A Correction of the Record." *Journal of Law and Economics* 7, no. 2 (October 1964): 81–83.

———. "The Pure Theory of Public Expenditure." *Review of Economics and Statistics* 36 (November 1954): 387–89.

———. "Pure Theory of Public Expenditure and Taxation." In *Public Economics*, ed. J. Margolis and H. Guitton, pp. 98–123. London: Macmillan, 1969.

Sandler, Todd. "Pareto Optimality, Pure Public Goods, Impure Public Goods, and Multiregional Spillovers." *Scottish Journal of Political Economy* 22, no. 1 (February 1975): 25–38.

Sandler, Todd, and Jon Cauley. "Multiregional Public Goods, Spillovers, and the New Theory of Consumption." *Public Finance* 31, no. 3 (1976): 376–95.

Sandler, Todd, and John T. Tschirart. "Mixed Clubs: Further Observations." *Journal of Public Economics* 23 (1984): 381–89.

Scafuri, Allen J. "On Consistency of Conjectures in the Private Provision of Public Goods." *Journal of Public Economics* 37, no. 3 (December 1988): 395–98.

Schmalensee, R. "Monopolistic Two-Part Pricing Arrangements." *Bell Journal of Economics* 12, no. 2 (Autumn 1981): 445–66.

Shmanske, Stephen. "Contestable Two-Part Pricing in Differentiated Duopoly." California State University, Hayward, School of Business and Economics Faculty Working Paper No. 33, January 1988.

———. "News as a Public Good: Cooperative Ownership, Price Commitments, and the Success of the Associated Press." *Business History Review* 60 (Spring 1986): 55–80.

———. "A Note on Else's Treatment of Quality and Public Goods." *Scottish Journal of Political Economy* 37, no. 2 (May 1990): 193–96.

———. "Price Commitments and the Private Supply of a Public Factor: The Case of the Associated Press." California State University, Hayward, School of Business and Economics Faculty Working Paper No. 19, 1985.

———. "Price Discrimination and Monopolistic Competition." California State University, Hayward, School of Business and Economics Faculty Working Paper 20, February 1985.

———. "Public Goods, Product Quality Determination and Dimensionality of Consumption." *Public Finance* 37, no. 3 (Fall 1982): 387–403.

Shoup, Carl S. "Public Goods and Joint Production." *Rivista Internazionale de Scienze Economische e Commerciali* 12, no. 3 (March 1965): 254–64.

Singer, Neil M. "Joint Products, Collective Goods, and External Effects: Comment." *Journal of Political Economy* 79, no. 5 (September 1971): 1136–37.

Singh, N., and X. Vives. "Price and Quantity Competition in a Differentiated Duopoly." *Rand Journal of Economics* 15, no. 4 (Winter 1984): 546–54.

Spence, Michael. "Multi-Product Quantity-Dependent Prices and Profitability Constraints." *Review of Economic Studies* 47, no. 150 (October 1980): 821–41.

———. "Product Differentiation and Welfare." *American Economic Review* 66, no. 2 (May 1976): 407–14.

———. "Product Selection, Fixed Costs and Monopolistic Competition." *Review of Economic Studies* 43, no. 133 (June 1976): 217–35.

Spulber, Daniel F. "Non-Cooperative Equilibrium with Price Discriminating Firms." *Economics Letters* 4 (1979): 221–27.

Staaf, Robert J. "Privatization of Public Goods." *Public Choice* 41, no. 3 (1983): 435–40.

Sugden, R. "Reciprocity: The Supply of Public Goods through Voluntary Contributions." *Economic Journal* 94, no. 376 (December 1984): 772–87.

Thompson, Earl A. "A Note on Consumer-Producer Collusion in the Private Marketing of Collective-Type Goods." Discussion Paper No. 142, Department of Economics, University of California, Los Angeles, January 1979.

———. "The Perfectly Competitive Production of Collective Goods." *Review of Economics and Statistics* 50, no. 1 (February 1968): 1–12.

———. "The Perfectly Competitive Production of Collective Goods: Reply" *Review of Economics and Statistics* 51, no. 4 (November 1969): 479–82.

———. "The Private Production of Public Goods: A Comment." *Journal of Law and Economics* 16, no. 2 (October 1973): 407–12.

Thompson, Earl A., and Roger L. Faith. "A Pure Theory of Strategic Behavior and Social Institutions." *American Economic Review* 71, no. 3 (June 1981): 366–80.

Tinbergen, Jan. "On Collective and Part-Collective Goods." *De Economist* 12, no. 2 (1984): 171–82.

Tirole, Jean. *The Theory of Industrial Organization.* Cambridge, Mass.: MIT Press, 1988.

Varian, Hal R. *Intermediate Microeconomics: A Modern Approach.* New York: W. W. Norton, 1987.

Walsh, Cliff. "A Reconsideration of Some Aspects of the Private Production of Public Goods." *Review of Social Economy* 39, no. 1 (April 1981): 19–35.

Weisbrod, Burton. "Collective Consumption Services of Individual Consumption Goods." *Quarterly Journal of Economics* 78, no. 3 (August 1964): 471–77.

Willig, Robert D. "Consumer's Surplus without Apology." *American Economic Review* 66, no. 4 (September 1976): 589–97.

Winch, D. M. "Pareto, Public Goods, and Politics." *Canadian Journal of Economics* 35 (November 1969): 492–508.

Winston, Gordon, "Taxes, Leisure and Public Goods." *Economica* 31, no. 125 (February 1965): 65–69.

Wright, J. F. "Some Reflections on the Place of Discrimination in the Theory of Monopolistic Competition." *Oxford Economic Papers* 17, no. 2 (July 1965): 175–87.

Index

Public Goods, Mixed Goods, and Monopolistic Competition was composed into type on a Linotron 202 phototypesetter in ten point Caledonia with three points of spacing between the lines. Caledonia was also selected for display. The book was designed by Cameron Poulter, typeset by Graphic Composition, Inc., printed by Thomson-Shore, Inc., and bound by John H. Dekker & Sons, Inc. The paper on which this book is printed carries acid-free characteristics for an effective life of at least three hundred years.

TEXAS A&M UNIVERSITY PRESS : COLLEGE STATION